On the control

of

complex industrial organizations

On the control
of
complex industrial organizations

J. E. VAN AKEN

Martinus Nijhoff Social Sciences Division
Leiden\Boston\London 1978

658.4
A 313

ISBN 90 207 0791 4

Printed in the Netherlands by Intercontinental Graphics.

for Marja

PREFACE

This book is concerned with control issues in complex industrial organizations. The word *control* is used here in a rather wide sense, including decision-making, coordination and planning as well as activities such as the design and implementation of organizational structures or computerized information systems.

There are various ways of defining *complexity;* here we use this term to indicate that the organizations in question consist of many suborganizations which are operationally interdependent but at the same time have a fair degree of independence of control. The control of the interactions between these suborganizations through *coordination* will be a key issue in this book.

The discussion will be confined to *industrial* organizations; our results are only applicable to a limited extent to other types of organizations such as universities, hospitals or government offices.

The main contribution we intend to make in this book is the development of a *system of concepts on control and coordination* in industrial organizations which can be used in the design of organizational control structures such as planning systems, information systems or relations between positions or departments. Rather eclectic use has been made of various scientific disciplines in the development of this conceptual system with some bias towards the use of system theory and cybernetics.

The book is intended for professional workers in the field of 'organizational control technology', such as automation and organization specialists in complex organizations and workers in the related disciplines at University. However, I have tried to write it in such a way that it is also accessible to non-specialists with a professional interest in the subject matter – in particular the users of organizational control structures: managers and 'managees'.

The book consists of five parts: part I gives some background information, after which part II introduces some basic concepts concerning organization structures. Part III presents an analysis of the dynamics of complex industrial organizations. In part IV the basic features of organizational control systems are discussed, with special reference to the coordination mechanisms embedded in them. Finally, part V summarizes the whole book and gives some suggestions for further research.

For a quick introduction to this book one could read the summary in section 17.1, followed by the chapter summaries preceding parts II, III and IV.

The material presented here is based on eight years' work on operations research, informatics and organization design in the research group of the Corporate automation department of Philips Industries. This work included assignments to various Product Divisions of the company.

Three projects were of particular importance for this book, viz. BIC-I, BIC-II and PROSPECT. After the termination of those projects my next assignment was the elaboration of their theoretical basis. It was the manager of the above-mentioned research group, Dr. H.J. Heyn, who suggested that the results of this work should also be used for a thesis. For this, for his encouragement and for his support of the project, especially at a critical moment, I owe him a great deal of thanks.

Many of the ideas in this thesis originated during work with others. I would like to acknowledge my debt to them here. While it would be impossible to name them all, I would like to single out for special mention those who worked with me in the BIC- and PROSPECT-projects: A.G. Abels, J.F. De Rijk, H. Grünwald, R.L. Krooshof, G.L. Polderman, C. Van der Enden, J.W.D. Van Overhagen, F.A. Van der Velden, A.M.E. Weegels and P. F. Westenend in BIC-I; J.M.S. Bedet, P.J. De Graaf, J.F. De Rijk, B.J. Koppelman, G. Peeters, A.A. Vlaardingerbroek and A.M.E. Weegels in BIC-II and B. Day, J.J. Frima, J.C. Geevers, G. Peeters, G.L. Polderman, P. Quinton, G. Romeyn, P. Van Beek A.J. Van den Heuvel and C. Versteeg in PROSPECT.

It is difficult to recast the results of applied work in industry in the more academic form required for a thesis. I owe many thanks to Prof. W. Monhemius, Dr. A.C.J. De Leeuw and Prof. P.M.E.M. Van der Grinten of Eindhoven University of Technology and to Prof. S.E. Elmaghraby, Prof. G. Hofstede and Prof. A.G. Hopwood of the European Institute for Advanced Studies in Management in Brussels; without their invaluable advice this task would have been insurmountable.

I would also like to thank Dr. R. Bathgate for improving my use of English, Miss T. D'Silva for fast and very accurate typing (and correction of residual errors in my English) and for making the lay-out of the book, and M.G.M.L. Van den Hurk, C. Favie and Mrs. D. Snijders for drawing the figures.

Finally I owe more thanks than I can say to the four women on the home-front, especially one to whom this book is dedicated.

J.E. Van Aken

Eindhoven
December 1977

CONTENTS

PART I

BACKGROUND

1. INTRODUCTION

1.1 Organization and control

This book discusses some issues in the field of organization and control, with special reference to complex industrial organizations. However, our treatment of this subject proceeds from a general interest in the organization of human activity.

Large organizations are not confined to the age of industrialization. Some four to five thousand years ago the Egyptians developed a very large organization to exploit the annual flooding of the Nile, which was so successful that they could afford the 'luxury' of the pyramids. The Chinese and Persian Empires, the Roman Empire and its army and the Roman Catholic Church are further examples of large and successful organizations.

We may even claim that the phenomenon or organization, i.e. *the willingness of two or more human beings to combine their efforts through a relatively stable network of social relations,* is next only to the phenomenon of language as a driving force of human progress: it is doubtful whether humanity could have left − or even entered − the Stone Age without organization. As organizational problems, such as leadership and division of labour, arise as soon as a few human beings combine their efforts, we can safely state that an organizer practises an older profession than 'the oldest profession in the world'.

Our interest in organizations in general has had some consequences for this book. One of them is a tendency to use generalizable concepts. For instance, control and controllability are defined in such a way that these concepts are also applicable to organizations other than complex industrial ones.

An important class of such generalizable concepts are *level independent concepts* i.e. concepts applicable to all levels of human cooperation: family, grocery store, retail chain, multinational enterprise, a national state and various forms of cooperation between sovereign states. Examples of level independent concepts in this book are compound position, demand servo, conversion system and Ablauf-level[1]. The use of level independent concepts is especially

[1]Examples of the use of level *de*pendent concepts, where this book uses level *in*dependent concepts, are Blumenthal's (1969) 'activity centre', 'decision centre', 'management control centre', Anthony's (1965) levels of 'operational control', 'management control', 'strategic planning' and Chandlers (1962) 'field unit', 'department headquarters', 'divisional central office', 'general office'. These concepts have a *fixed* empirical content, so they can only be used on one specific level of human co-operation.

powerful, when we are dealing with large scale organizations as is the case here: the same concept can be used at a corporate, divisional and departmental level. Further, it makes it possible to integrate the analysis of the organization as a whole with that of parts of the organization.

However interesting the applicability of such general concepts to other fields may be, the centre of interest here nevertheless remains the control of complex industrial organizations.

The restriction to industrial organizations is made, because the control problems to be discussed here differ in several respects from those in other types of organizations. The core of an industrial organization consists of one or more 'conversion systems', i.e. systems converting physical inputs to physical outputs (such as a factory or a production department). A possible difference in control situation is the nature of the inertia of such a system, which has physical aspects as well as social ones. Another possible difference is the evaluation of present and desired states. For conversion systems the preferences of the participants are strongly influenced by the need for maintaining an equilibrium between the output and the demand for that output and for maintaining an equilibrium between the resources consumed in producing the output and the resources obtained in exchange for it. Such control problems are relatively well-structured compared to the ambiguity of the control situation of e.g. government agencies or universities (see for the latter case Cohen and March, 1974).

The discussions presented here are based on experience gained in various Product Divisions of Philips Industries. This company offers a broad spectrum of different technologies and markets (see chapter 3). However, this does not mean that it covers the whole field of 'complex industrial organizations'. Therefore it is possible that the contributions of this book are not immediately applicable to other industrial organizations, e.g. those with a different technology (such as steel or bulk chemicals), with a different set of environments (e.g. more homogeneous like a non-multinational or differently organized like non-profit industrial organizations or industrial companies in the USSR or China) or operating on a smaller scale (having e.g. less than 10,000 employees).

The contribution we intend to give is a system of concepts on control and coordination in industrial organizations. Some of these concepts may themselves be original. However, the main claim for originality is that they form a coherent set, i.e. a *system*. Such a system of concepts should provide the parties involved in the creation of organizational control structures (managers, 'managees' and specialists) with a language, which they can use to describe and to handle their designs.

4

The development of this conceptual system is among other things based on an analysis of dynamic phenomena in complex industrial organizations. This analysis is performed from a technical and economic point of view as well as from a social point of view. In the first case the organization is described as a *network of production systems* each trying to adapt its output to the demand for that output. In the second case the organization is described as a *network of social groups,* each trying to accomplish its own mission as well as possible, protecting its interests against outside interferences (the 'outside' being both other groups within the organization and other groups outside the organization). The 'integration' of the control activities in the various units in the network (among other things through coordination) in such a way that the organization as a whole responds well to threats and opportunities, is the focus of interest in the subsequent discussion on control system design.

The ultimate interest of this book is in design, not in analysis. Design is contrasted with analysis by Simon (1969): *design,* i.e. how to make artificial things with desired properties, is the essence of the *professions* (like engineering, medicine, law, music); *analysis,* i.e. how natural things are and how they work, is the essence of the *sciences* (like physics, chemistry and psychology).

'Artefacts have no dispensation to ignore or violate natural laws' (Simon, 1969, p.3), so a great deal of analysis is needed for a successful design of an organizational control structure: the analysis of the properties of the components of an organization, human beings and social relations, of the tools used for control such as accounting systems and computerized information systems and of existing organizations, like March and Simon (1958), Woodward (1965), Perrow (1967), Pugh (1976) and many other publications, where the organization is seen as a natural thing.

In this book, however, the organization is seen as an artefact, which can purposefully be designed to serve human needs (for the moment we will not consider *whose* needs will be served). Design and development can be supported by professionals in the field of 'organizational control technology' (a term, taken from Banbury, 1975, p.449). This book tries to contribute some ideas to this profession.

The purposeful design and development of organizational control structures is subject to severe limitations and cannot be compared directly with the design and construction of e.g. a bridge or a car (neither can the *role* of the above mentioned professionals be compared directly with that of civil or mechanical engineers). One reason for this is that the properties of human beings as components of an organization and the properties of social relations in an organization are only partially known (see e.g. Banbury, 1975), another is that

5

it is not possible to construct social relations like nut-and-bolt connections in steel structures. This means that it is often preferable to change an organization in small steps (Banbury, 1975; this is called 'evolutionary design' by Gregory, 1966). Furthermore, the process of implementation, and preferably also of design, is one in which all parties concerned need to participate in order to make it successful.

The process of organizational change (often called 'organizational development') falls outside the scope of this book: we are interested in the shape of the structures to be seen ahead of us along the road, less in what happens along the road itself.

Organizations often perform a dual function: on the one hand the supply of goods and services to society, and on the other the satisfaction of physical and social needs of their own members. Full exploitation of the first function may harm the second (and consequently the first: people will work below their best or leave the organization); full exploitation of the second function may harm the first (and consequently the second: the organization does not survive). This book concentrates on the first function: as long as the performance of this function is desirable, control structures should serve the viability and controllability of the organization.

However, as Barnard (1938) puts it: 'the individual is always the basic strategic factor in organization'. Human individuals, as components of the organization, bring in their own individual tendencies and preferences; their actions may serve the organization as such, but surely will also serve their own goals (to the extent that they are free to do so). So the second function constrains the first: the optimum co-alignment of institutional and individual goals is always a major issue in control.

There are many concepts of organizations. In this book the organization is seen as a *set of people in a relatively stable network of social relations*. This network is studied, using a control paradigm (see section 11.1) and a design approach. This means that the network will be evaluated in terms of its capacity to survive and its controllability and that the ultimate interest is in the design and construction of the network (while bearing in mind that — as discussed above — human beings and social relations require 'technologies' which differ greatly from the traditional engineering disciplines).

1.2 The approach followed in this study

The background of this book is eight years' work on operations research, informatics and organization design issues in Philips Industries. It is particularly influenced by the author being project manager of the projects BIC-I, BIC-II and 'PROSPECT'. The objective of the BIC-projects was the analysis of the sources of the amplification of fluctuations in production and inventory levels in practically every Product Division of Philips (Van Aken et al. 1971, Van Aken 1973, Van Aken et al. 1975); the objective of the PROSPECT-project was the design of a control system which would provide a smoother mutual adaptation of production and sales levels − i.e. without amplification of fluctuations − for one of Philips' divisions (Van Aken et al., 1974a and 1974b).

The work involved was engineering-type work: analysing problem situations and drawing up proposals for improvement. The ultimate interest was improvement, not knowledge, hence the design orientation in this book.

The previous section stated as contributions of this book an analysis of dynamic phenomena in industrial organizations (part III) and a system of control and coordination concepts (part II and IV). The analysis can be seen as a kind of empirical theory based on numerous (unstructured) interviews and discussions all over Philips, participative observation of ongoing (planning) operations, analysis of production, inventory and sales figures and analysis with the help of simulation models, all carried out within the framework of the BIC-projects.

The conceptual system, on the other hand, is not an empirical theory, but rather a verbal model of control activities in industrial organizations, derived partly from our work in the PROSPECT-project (see chapter 16). The test of such a model is not true *versus* false, but whether or not it is advantageous to use them in designing organizational control structures.

In part IV we intend to show that this system is indeed usable, but it must be left to future research to test it further.

A design is 'a structure within a situation' (Gregory, 1966, p.4). A design handbook can contain statements of the format:

if (situation i) *then* (choose control structure j)

The book deals mainly with the way control structures and situations can be described. However, it is oriented towards such an *if* (...) *then* (...) approach (often called a 'contingency approach'). We will sometimes draw relations between certain situations and certain elements of control structures. Such statements, however, will be no more than (untested) hypotheses.

The model developed here is a verbal model, not a mathematical one, which implies that the degree of formalization and quantification is rather low: in our opinion social reality is so complex that it does not permit a description with the present-day mathematical tools. The procedure followed is: introduce an intuitively known concept, develop a formal definition and give (not always) some proposals for operationalization. The operationalization itself is not performed here.

This procedure is well-known in the natural sciences. The Dutch physicist Kamerlingh Onnes had a motto: 'weten door meten' (knowledge through measurement), which was rightly attacked by Casimir (1962). Supposing that Kamerlingh Onnes must have been somewhat spellbound by the rhyme of his motto, Casimir strongly advocates what I would call 'meten *na* weten' (measurement after knowledge has been obtained): first one probes the unknown, searches for new physical phenomena and only after one has enough physical insight into the phenomenon one starts to measure. Casimir gives many examples of discoveries in physics without measurement and of the dangers of too much emphasis on measurement[1]. Premature measurement may also be dangerous in the social sciences.

---

[1]Casimir mentions as a striking example Professor Lenard, who performed an enormous number of measurements on cathode-ray tubes for many years, with many assistants, but failed to discover the X-rays which were present during his experiments and which were discovered a few years later by Röntgen, who used the same type of tube.

2. THEORETICAL BACKGROUND

2.1 Introduction

It is often good to start a discussion in a specific scientific discipline or part of a discipline, with a survey of the 'state of the art'. This serves to introduce the subject, to acknowledge the debt to those 'on whose shoulders one stands', as Newton says, and to delineate the boundaries of the new contribution.

However, this book is not concerned with one specific scientific discipline, but with one specific problem area, viz. the design of organizational control structures. In dealing with such problems, eclectic use is made of various disciplines. To give an introduction to the state of the art of all these disciplines would either require a book in itself or be so general that it would add little to the reader's understanding. Thus, rather than to discuss the state of the art for all disciplines involved together, we will briefly discuss the relevant literature in each chapter separately.

Nevertheless, in the next two sections we will give a short survey of the main disciplines that form the background of this book: section 2.2 deals with some disciplines without direct empirical content, that influenced the methodological 'tools' used here (system theory, cybernetics and control theory), while section 2.3 is concerned with disciplines that deal with the empirical object of this book, the organization (organization theory and the theory of organizations). These sections are meant to place this book within the realm of science and to introduce a few of the basic concepts to be used later; they do not pretend to give a state of the art of each discipline.

2.2 System theory, cybernetics and control theory

This book deals with the design of control structures for large, complex organizations (like Philips Industries: some 400,000 people, using many different technologies, operating on many different markets, in many countries). In doing so, it will try to give a coherent model of the various parts and aspects of such structures. To this end the study of coherence, or 'the system approach', is essential.

Although the study of 'wholes' is almost as old as science itself, one can say that the modern system theory stream of thought originated in the 1930's from the biologist Von Bertalanffy (Laszlo, 1975, Von Bertalanffy, 1951). System theory, or using the somewhat more pretentious name General System Theory[1], has a two-fold objective (see e.g. De Leeuw, 1974):

(i) the promotion of the unity of science

(ii) the study of 'wholes'

In pursuit of the first objective, one can try to exchange methods between various disciplines for greater mutual understanding and to avoid duplication of work; or one can try to develop methods, system theories, which are applicable in various disciplines.

The second objective was a reaction to the reductionistic, mechanistic methods of nineteenth century science. System theory wanted to study 'wholes' with their coherence and complexity, rather than collections of disjoint components.

It is this second endeavour — or rather its tributary, system engineering — that has strongly influenced this study.

System engineering (see e.g. Jenkins, 1969, and Checkland, 1972) combines the study of the components of a system and their properties with a careful analysis of the interfaces, mutual relations and influences among the components. A system is a *set of interrelated elements,* (see further chapter 4), nothing less — the relations being a defining characteristic of the system — but also nothing more. So a system is not necessarily complex or organized, or probabilistic, nor does it need to have a goal. 'The whole is more than the sum of the parts', has nothing magical for the system engineer: of course the whole is more, there are also relations between the parts.

System theory is particularly important for part II and part IV of this book, where the structure of respectively industrial organizations and control systems is discussed. Although there is nowadays some convergence in system concepts, unanimity has not yet been reached so we had to choose which concepts to use (see chapter 4).

A key concept with respect to organization structures is that of *hierarchy*. In this book the ideas of Simon (1962) on this issue will be followed[2]: a hierarchic system is a system with a 'parts-within-parts' structure, i.e. a system with elements, which are themselves systems on the next level of the hierarchy.

---

[1]Some speak of General Systems Theory. Following Laszlo (1975), we prefer General System Theory to indicate that a system-theory can be general and to avoid the impression that there might exist in the real world some general systems.

[2]No use is made of the ideas of Mesarovic on this subject here, among other things because he does not use a clear definition of this concept (Mesarovic et al., 1970, p.34).

Chapter 4 will combine this concept with that of a *stratified system* (a system with subsystems, ordered according to a dominance criterion), to get the two defining properties of the classical line organization.

De Leeuw (1974) classified studies of organizations with the aid of system theory into two 'schools'. The *'organistic'* school tries to explain organizational phenomena in terms of biological analogies and paradigms. The *'axiomatic'* school on the other hand tries to develop methods, general system theories, that can be used in various disciplines, including organization theory. This book uses ideas from the axiomatic school. De Leeuw himself belongs to this school; another good example is the book by Mesarovic and Takahara: General Systems Theory (1975). It is striking, that both books discuss in fact the issue of control, which brings us to (technical) control theory and cybernetics.

The basis for control theory (see e.g. Elgerd, 1967), a discipline concerned with the analysis and design of dynamic systems, was laid about 1930 by Bode and Nyquist. The now well-known feedback loop played a central role in their studies; feedback was used as a very effective means to control the effects of disturbances on the behaviour of 'technical' systems (although it may endanger the stability of the controlled system).

Up to 1950 application remained restricted to simple systems, i.e. systems with one input and one output; the quantities controlled included temperature, flow, pressure, etc. From 1950 onwards control theory developed to comprise the analysis and design of dynamic systems, in which a predetermined criterion has to be optimized without restrictions on the complexity of the systems.

Control theory paved the way for cybernetics. The father of cybernetics was Wiener (1948), who studied the control of technical systems, such as radar antennae and anti-aircraft guns, during World War II. He found that the classical feedback loop had a much wider field of application than technical systems alone, that it is in fact used in nature on a large scale to control a wide variety of dynamic biological processes.

This 'discovery' has had a strong impact on science. The classical book in this field is Ashby's (1956) 'An Introduction to Cybernetics'; an example of subsequent developments is Beer's (1972) 'Brain of the Firm'. Some regard cybernetics as a part of General System Theory (either as a discipline developing one of the methodological tools of GST, or as a trend in the organistic school); others seem to equate cybernetics and GST (like Mesarovic and Takahara, 1975).

Control theory and cybernetics had their influence on the control of industrial organizations. One of the first to use control theory for this purpose was

Simon (1952), who proposed a simple feedback rule for inventory control. This rule was extended by Holt, Modigliani, Muth and again Simon (1960). Other representatives of this line of thought are Schneeweiss (1971) and Bensoussan et al. (1974).

One can see the work of Forrester (1961) and his co-workers on industrial dynamics as another example of the application of control theory and cybernetics, although they do not use the impressive set of mathematical tools of control theory, but use simulation instead (the main reason for this being their interest in non-linear processes, which are still difficult to analyse with control theory tools).

Control theory and cybernetics play an important role in part III of this book, which deals with control and the dynamics of complex industrial organizations.

2.3 Organization theory and theory of organizations

Rapoport and Horvath (1959) distinguish two kinds of theories about organizations, viz. organization theory and the theory of organizations. The first is of a *prescriptive* nature, dealing with the way one can — or should — organize human cooperation, while the second is of a *descriptive* nature: the organization is viewed as a natural thing that can be studied like other empirical objects such as atoms, galaxies and human beings. One studies what they are and how they work.

Of course there are interactions between these two fields: if organizations use the ideas of organization theory, the students of organizations as natural things will study how this works out. Their findings may in turn be used to change organization theory. It may be remarked that the work of some authors is difficult to classify, as description and prescription can lie close together.

The preceding sections may have made clear, that the design orientation of this book puts it in the domain of organization theory.

The early, often called 'classical', results of the study of organizations can be classified as organization theories:

(i)   scientific management (Taylor, 1911), concentrating on the organization of work on the shop floor, with the aid of e.g. time and motion studies

(ii) administrative management (e.g. Gulick and Urwick, 1937), dealing with the optimum grouping of jobs in administrative units (functional departmentalization) and the subsequent control of such units.

(iii) bureaucracy (Fayol, 1925), the analysis of ideal types of organizational structures, as tools for efficient disposition of 'cases'. (Weber, 1947, is often associated with the study of bureaucracies too, but his work is more descriptive than prescriptive).

As Thompson (1967) puts it, these schools use a 'closed system strategy': organizational structures are considered as being sealed off from their environment, insensible to outside phenomena and to the nature of the components of the organization, human beings. Their main criterion for organizational design is steady-state efficiency.

Of course people like Taylor, an experienced engineer, are not blind to reality: organizations do have environments. But the classics relied more on common sense than on scientific observations. Various schools developing theories of organizations have contributed to the filling in of the blind spots of common sense. To name a few:

(iv) the human relations school (Mayo, 1933; Roethlisberger and Dickson, 1939), who discovered some aspects of the human nature of organizations, such as motivation, and the informal organization.

(v) the decision-making model school (Simon, 1957, March and Simon, 1958, Cyert and March, 1963), who studied the cognitive limits of organizational decision-makers: the masterplan, needed for organizational design by the administrative management school, is found to be elusive, decision-makers have to decide in 'bounded rationality', use 'satisfycing' procedures rather than maximizing ones.

(vi) the open system approach, stressing the influence of the environment of the organization and the role of uncertainty (e.g. Thompson, 1967), leading to situational approaches or contingency theories (e.g. Kast and Rozenzweig, 1973).

Of course these findings had their impact on subsequent writers on organization theory, like Drucker (1974). This also applies to this book and in particular to part IV, which deals with the design of organizational control structures. Without rejecting the classical findings, we try to incorporate newer findings as well (situational approaches, the role of uncertainty, the role of control and decision-making and also phenomena such as conflict and power).

Some specific contributions to be used below are:
— the concept of *'position'* (Luhmann, 1964 and 1976), as the elementary unit of an organizational structure, leading to the definition of an organization as a system of occupied positions (see section 5.1).

13

- the distinction between the *creation* of a control structure and the actual *use* of it (to be called respectively *control in the large* and *control in the small*), due to Kosiol (1962)[1]
- the distinction between the two aspects of an organizational control structure, viz. the *'Aufbau'* (the system of positions) and the *'Ablauf structure'* (the decision-making procedures), also due to Kosiol (1962)
- the concepts *internal* and *external reduction of interference* and *transfer of interference* of De Sitter, 1973 (see chapter 10): the process of control can be described as one of reducing interferences; social systems can often choose between *absorption* of (part of) their interferences (internal reduction) and *transfer* of these interferences to connected social systems (external reduction)
- the *'futurity'* of a decision (Drucker, 1974a), the time over which the decision commits organizational resources (see section 14.2).

As mentioned in section 2.1, this is not a complete survey of the disciplines, which influenced this study. Some others, also dealing with organizational processes are
- *planning theory* (see e.g. Anthony (1965), Ansoff (1965), Emery (1969), Faludi (1973)), to be used in part IV
- *Informatics* (see e.g. Blumenthal, 1969; Langefors, 1974). Langefors distinguishes two problem fields in informatics: *infological problems* (what information should an information system — IS — provide to its users) and *datalogical problems* (how should the IS be constructed). Every IS is designed to serve a real world system (the 'object system'). He distinguishes 5 major areas of IS-designs:

1a	object-system analysis and design	(infological)
1b	information analysis	(infological)
2a	data-system architecture	(datalogical)
2b	data-system construction	(datalogical)
2c	data-system implementation and operation	(datalogical)

We will discuss area 1a and to some extent area 1b.
- *operations research* (see e.g. Ackoff and Sasieni, 1968; Elmaghraby, 1966; Van Hees and Monhemius, 1972). The above-mentioned study of organizational processes by means of simulation of the change in levels and flows of organizational resources of Forrester (1961) and his followers may also be regarded as belonging to this discipline[2]. Without using his

---

[1]Kosiol himself uses the terms 'Organisation' and 'Disposition'.

[2]Of course the analysis of the behaviour of an organization in terms of levels and flows of resources is not original in itself: accountants have been doing this for more than five centuries with their balance sheets and income statements.

14

specific methods, chapter 9 undertakes more or less the same task.

— *economics* (e.g. theory of the firm, accounting systems). A key question in economic theory is the equilibrium between demand and supply. This question is also tackled in chapters 8 and 9. However, economic theory is often only interested in subsequent equilibrium states; to study intermediate states too, chapter 8 will use control theory (the organization as a network of demand servo's) and simulation.

The ultimate interest of this book is in design issues. In this respect it may be seen as a return to the interests of the classics of organization theory (see e.g. Urwick, 1971, on these interests).

This area is attracting increasing attention again nowadays; examples are Ansoff and Brandenburg (1971) and Galbraith (1973, 1974, 1977). A very stimulating discussion on design itself is given by Simon (1969). Other studies in design methods, technically oriented but in my opinion also very useful in other design areas, have been made by Gregory (1966) and Nadler (1967).

3. THE FIELD OF THIS STUDY: PHILIPS INDUSTRIES

3.1 Introduction

This book is based on experience gained whilst working in Philips Industries. On the one hand this is a drawback, because it inevitably colours the argument to be given and hence possibly limits the general applicability of the ideas. On the other hand, experience gained in a very large organization can be an advantage, because large complex organizations often do show up the essentials of control structures better than smaller ones: increasing size leads to increasing internal differentiation and many of the informal and implicit (and hence often unrecognized) control loops of smaller organizations have to be explicitly and formally 'organized' in larger organizations, because the lower frequency of audio-visual contacts deteriorates many of these control loops.

In order to throw some light on the background of this book, this chapter will give some information on Philips Industries.

3.2 History

Philips Industries was founded in 1891 by the engineer Gerard Philips with the aid of some working capital from his father, a small town banker (see for the rest of this section also Bouman, 1956, Philips, 1976 and Teulings, 1976). The company was to produce and sell electric lamps. As this was a rather labour-intensive product, a rural low-wage setting, Eindhoven, was chosen as location.

In the last decennium of the nineteenth century the world electric-lamp market was already practically distributed among U.S. and German big capital: General Electric, Westinghouse, AEG and Siemens. So the new company ran into trouble almost immediately. As a result a younger brother of Gerard, Anton, who was to become a banker like his father, was taken into the company in 1895. It was he who was able (with great entrepreneurship and in particular with a sharp pricing policy, possible through his low-cost situation) to capture a large enough share of the world market to survive. Even at the very beginning Philips' home-market, the Netherlands, was much too small to guarantee survival: the company had immediately to operate on international markets, a situation which still exists today and which differs greatly from big competitors (still coming from the U.S.A. and Germany, but now also from Japan).

Hardly had Anton Philips established his position on the lamp market with his carbon-filament lamp when the advent of the tungsten-filament lamp in 1907 (General Electric) almost swept his company from the market. He succeeded in maintaining his position with great difficulty, but to avoid such a threat in the future, the company started its own research and development programme in 1914.

World War I came, and, although Holland's neutrality safeguarded Eindhoven from physical damage, it cut off the company from various strategic resources. Now Philips started a backward integration programme, for instance by founding its own glass factory.

After the war the radio (both radio valves and radio sets) became the second source of growth and this lasted until television (about 1950 black and white, colour round about 1970) took over (again components as well as sets). Already before World War II there were also other products, such as X-ray tubes, but the three pillars of lighting, radio and television remained the basis for growth and profitability (see figure 1 for the growth of Philips Industries).

The Great Depression dealt a severe blow to Philips Industries, but a rapid adaptation of costs to the lower sales volume kept the company out of the red and it survived (at the expense of a poor image on the labour market, which was long to be felt). The protectionism, i.e. the import restrictions, of the thirties enhanced Philips' internationality. In 1929 only one-third of its employees worked outside the Netherlands, while in 1939 only one-third worked inside the Netherlands.

World War II caused a lot of damage, but the recovery was rapid. The fast growth since the war was to a large extent based on the television business, but also on various acquisitions and a successful formula for international operations (see also section 3.4).

The organization concept Philips used after 1945 was a company as a 'federation of national organizations': all the company's activities in a country were brought into one organization, the 'National Organization' (N.O.) with its own management (such an organization was usually not incorporated). As Philips also established Product Divisions towards the end of the forties, the company created a matrix organization, long before such structures became popular in e.g. the U.S.A. and Germany (Knight, 1976). The Divisions got a dual management: each had a commercial and a technical manager.

Just as childhood events can influence a whole life, the effects of some experiences in the early days of Philips Industries can still be felt today.

17

The fact that two brothers, a technically minded and a commercially minded one, founded the company is responsible for the two-headed management of the Product Divisions (Philips, 1976, p.255), which has a great influence on the control of operations, see chapter 10[1]. The threat of the tungsten-filament lamp in 1907 may explain the strong emphasis on R & D in the company (its research laboratories, together with those of Bell and IBM, are among the best industrial research establishments in the world; see also table 3). The cut-off from resources in World War I led to the company's high degree of vertical ingration (which causes difficult control problems, see chapters 8 and 9). Finally, its birth in a small market forced the company right from the start to be international, to become a real multi-national.

3.3 Philips Industries in the seventies

At present Philips is operating in 68 countries, with National Organizations in various degrees of maturity: ranging from (small) importing organizations to N.O.'s with various sales organizations, factories, research laboratories and sometimes even a financing function (although in principle the financing of the company is performed at the corporate level).

Philips has 14 Product Divisions (see Table 1). The company has a two-dimensional matrix structure: every operation (except the corporate functions) is controlled by two managements: the National Organization management and the Divisional management (see further section 6.5). In the fifties the balance of power between those two was tipped towards the N.O., nowadays there is a tendency for it to shift more towards the Divisions.

The company has some 340 factories, using a wide variety of technologies, such as process technologies (e.g. glass factories and factories for magnetic materials), assembly lines for large series of consumer products (e.g. TV sets, refrigerators, mixers), factories for sophisticated professional equipment (medical X-ray equipment, electron microscopes) and machine works. This means also that the company, although far from being a conglomerate, has a rather heterogeneous mission (as compared with e.g. General Motors or IBM), which increases the complexity of control.

---

[1]Dual leadership is very rare; a famous example is of course the dual consulship of ancient Rome. This structure was explicitly used to restrict the power of leadership (and was therefore abandoned each time Rome ran into serious trouble).

1. Lighting (Eindhoven)
   electric lamps and luminaires

2. ELCOMA (Eindhoven)
   electronic components and materials

3. Audio (Eindhoven)
   radio, gramophone, audio recording

4. Video (Eindhoven)
   television

5. Major Domestic Appliances (Comerio, Italy)
   refrigerators, washing machines, dishwashers

6. Small Domestic Appliances (Groningen)
   shavers, mixers, coffeemakers, etc.

7. Telecommunication and Defence Systems (Hilversum/Hengelo)
   telephone exchanges, traffic control, radar systems, etc.

8. Medical Systems (Best)
   X-ray equipment, medical electronics, nuclear medicine, etc.

9. Science and Industry (Eindhoven)
   professional measuring systems

10. ELA (Eindhoven)
    professional video and audio equipment

11. Pharma (Amsterdam)
    pharmaceutical products

12. Allied Industries (Eindhoven)
    cardboard packings, plastics, miscellaneous

13. Glass (Eindhoven)
    glass for lamps and tubes

14. Data Systems (Apeldoorn)
    minicomputers, office computers, office equipment.

Table 1.   The Product Divisions of Philips Industries in 1977, with the site of the divisional headquarters and some of their products. Various activities, such as records, communication cables, machine works and basic research laboratories, fall outside these divisions.

We will now give some numerical data to fill in our picture of Philips Industries. These figures represent the 1976 situation. Most are representative for the company in the seventies (turnover has been showing a fairly steady exponential growth of about 10% per year over the past twenty years; profit, however, shows cyclical variations, a phenomenon which will be discussed in chapter 8.)

At the end of 1976 the number of employees was 391,500; 72% worked in Western Europe (including 23% in the Netherlands), 10% in the USA and Canada, and 18% in the rest of the world. Philips is still a thoroughly European company, but there is a trend towards more effort in the USA (see for example the recent take-overs of Magnavox and Signetics).

The turnover in 1976 was Dfl. 30.4 billion (some $12 billion); about 60% was made on consumer products, 40% on professional products. Profit after taxes was Dfl. 562 million; following U.S. accounting principles profit was about Dfl. 700 million or well over $300 million.

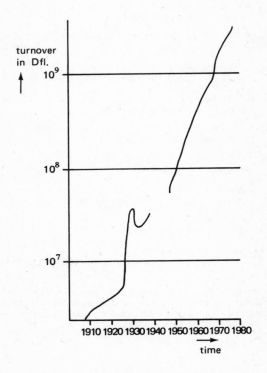

Fig. 1. Turnover of Philips Industries. The figures from before 1947 are estimates; to make them better comparable with post-war figures, they are corrected for the inflation during the war.

Assets	in 10^9 Dfl.	in %	Liabilities and Stockholders Equity	in 10^9 Dfl.	in %
Property and Equipment	10.4	35	Equity	10.2	34
Inventories	8.8	29	Long-term Liabilities	8.7	29
Accounts receivable	7.9	26	Short-term Liabilities	10.0	33
Sundries (incl. current assets)	3.0	10	Minority interests	1.2	4
TOTAL:	30.1	100	TOTAL:	30.1	100

Table 2   A condensed balance sheet for Philips Industries (31 December 1976)

Table 2 gives a summary of the 1976 balance sheet and table 3 some information on the income statement for 1976. They show that Philips is (still) a very labour-intensive company: the turnover per employeee is Dfl. 68,000 (some \$25,000), wages and social costs being 42% of turnover and 79% of added value. The costs of fixed assets are rather low compared with labour costs.

Further one may note that inventories amount to almost one-third of total assets. *Labour-intensiveness* and large *inventories* characterize, together with the rather high degree of *vertical integration*, the production control situation of Philips Industries as will be discussed in some depth in chapters 8 and 9.

	in 10^9 Dfl.	in %
Goods and services purchased	14.5	47.9
Wages and Social Costs	12.5	41.0
Depreciation	1.3	4.4
Interest paid	0.8	2.5
Tax on profit	0.6	2.0
Net profit	0.7	2.2
TURNOVER:	30.4	100.0

Table 3   Some information from the income statement of Philips Industries for 1976.
   Note: investment in R & D is about 7% of turnover, thus about 14% of added value.

3.4 Some notes on internal international relations

As Gloor (1972), General Manager of the Swiss Multinational Nestlé puts it: 'the most difficult, but also the most decisive decision any multinational has to make is the division of tasks, power and responsibilities between centre and subsidiaries'. For Philips Industries this refers to the relations between corporate and divisional headquarters on the one hand and the N.O.'s on the other.

It is by being a federation of national organizations that the company has been able to adapt itself harmoniously to local circumstances, it is French in France and Turkish in Turkey. Being a kind of chameleon is in our opinion the only acceptable way of being a multinational, as one should be very careful not to impose one's 'way of doing things' at home on other countries. Having a small home country is certainly a drawback commercially, but it can be an asset for running international operations, because this tends to give the centre some modesty in international affairs. To illustrate this: the official company language is English, not Dutch; correspondence between Eindhoven and subsidiaries in France and Germany is more often than not in French and German respectively.

The federative set-up is not always fully appreciated by outside parties, who may demand for instance that Eindhoven should settle a strike in Spain. Not only lack of detailed local knowledge but also the federative organizational structure would impede this (this is not to say that the Board of Management does not have any power over foreign operations, but that this power is very selectively used).

Philips Industries is a company with relatively few spelled out business policies or regulations. The most important exception to this is the accounting and budgeting system (introduced in 1928), which is standardized throughout the company to enable corporate and divisional headquarters to keep a clear view of all operations. For the rest there is little codification of tasks and responsibilities. The reason for this is clearly stated by Gloor (1972): 'newcomers to the field, such as the American multinationals, tend to write down rules and fix yardsticks, which is understandable because they lack the basic experience which one may call from an analogy the 'case law'. To a large extent such business principles must not be learned but inborn and absorbed by means of living long enough with an organization'.

PART II

THE STRUCTURE OF INDUSTRIAL ORGANIZATIONS

SUMMARY OF PART II

In the present part we discuss the structure of industrial organizations, largely by defining a system of concepts that can be used to describe organizational structures, in order to set the stage for the treatment of the control process in part III and of control system design in part IV.

Chapter 4 introduces various concepts from system theory, such as system, structure, open and closed system, subsystem, aspect system and *conversion system* (viz. a system which transforms physical inputs into physical outputs). It continues by discussing *hierarchic systems* and *stratified systems*. A hierarchic system is a system with a 'parts-within-parts' structure, while a stratified system is one with subsystems which are ordered according to a given priority criterion. These two concepts constitute the two defining characteristics of the structure of line management.

Chapter 5 defines an organization as a *system of occupied positions with their physical means of operation*. The *position* is the elementary unit of an organization: a task to be performed by one human actor and having a certain place in the organizational communication structure. A 'level-independent' concept is introduced: the *compound position,* a system of positions. For example, departments, divisions as well as the organization as a whole can be described as occupied compound positions with their physical means of operation. The organizational structure is the set of relations between (compound) positions; these relations can be of a physical or non-physical (i.e. informational) nature. The concepts of control and control system are discussed next. The execution of the task of a given (compound) position is controlled by a mix of control actions from the actors assigned to the (compound) position themselves (*selfcontrol*) and of control actions from actors in 'coordinating positions' (*coordination*). The 'levers' of coordination (influence and power) are discussed briefly. This chapter closes with a treatment of stratified hierarchies in organizations; the priority criterion for stratification used here is the official power distribution.

Chapter 6 discusses the technological structure of industrial organizations. Industrial organizations consist of a (hierarchic) network of conversion systems and non-conversion systems. The discussion focusses on the physical relations between the conversion systems. Several types of relations or connections are

25

distinguished and some influences of the type of relation on the control needs of the organization are mentioned. The chapter finishes by describing the technological structure of Philips Industries as a 6-level hierarchy of connected conversion and non-conversion systems.

4. SYSTEMS

4.1 Some concepts from system theory

This section will give some concepts from system theory which will be used below to describe the structure of industrial organizations.

As we have already mentioned, although there exists nowadays a certain degree of convergence in system theory, there is still no unanimity about the definition of various key concepts. Hence, the following definitions are not the only ones possible, nor are they always generally accepted. The main criteria for the selection of these definitions were their usefulness in the subsequent analysis and their fit in a coherent set, or system, of concepts. With a few exceptions, no attempt has been made to trace the origin of the definitions, and no credit will be claimed for the definitions given by us in this section.

Definition 1
An *element* is the smallest entity considered in an argument.

The element is the atom of analysis; it may be divisible, but in the analysis it is treated as an opaque unit.

Elements may have various properties or *attributes*. A special class of attributes comprises the *relations* between an element and other elements.

Definition 2
A *set* is a collection of elements.

A system will be defined as a special case of a set.

Definition 3
A *system* S is a set E of elements with a set R of relations between the elements, R having the property that all elements of E are directly or indirectly related.

Definition 3 implies that no subset of E is unrelated directly or indirectly to any other subset of E. *Coherence* is thus the first defining characteristic of a system, a property which distinguishes it from a set. The second defining property is the set E itself, defining which elements belong to S and which do not; in other words: the choice of the set E defines the *boundary* of S.

27

Definition 3 defines a system in terms of its internal structure, as a set of elements with mutual relations. Another definition, also frequently used (see e.g. Mesarovic and Takahara, 1975), is in terms of input and output and often a postulated internal state: the output of the system is a function (the transformation function) of input and state. In such a definition, a system is a 'black box' (see Ashby, 1956, p.86—117).

Definition 4
A *black box* is an entity the behaviour of which is not described in terms of its internal structure, but in terms of input, output and — if necessary — a postulated internal state.

Complexity and coherence are in this case studied in terms of input/output relations between black boxes.

Following Ackoff (1971) one can make a distinction between an *abstract* and a *concrete system*, the latter being a system with at least two elements, which are physical objects. A physical object has an unlimited number of properties. It depends on the problem a system researcher is interested in and on his discretion, which properties are considered as relevant and hence are included as attributes in the description of the system. A *social system* is a concrete system, at least two elements of which are human beings.

Definition 5
The *environment* of a system S consists of all elements outside S.

This definition states that in principle the environment of a system is the rest of the (concrete and abstract) Universe. In actual system research the environment of a system consists of the elements placed outside the system by the system researcher, but which are included in the argument, because he feels they are relevant for his research.

Definition 6
The *structure* of a system S is the set R of the relations of its elements with other elements. The *internal structure* R_i is the subset of R containing the relations between the elements of S. The *external structure* R_e is the subset of R containing relations of S with elements outside S.

Definition 7
A *closed system* is a system for which the set R_e of external relations is empty; an *open system* is a system for which R_e is non-empty.

Two powerful tools for study of the structure of systems are the concepts subsystem and aspect system[1].

Definition 8
A *subsystem* of a system S is a subset of E (the set of elements of S) with all the attributes of the elements in question. An *aspect system* of S is the set E with only a subset of the original attributes.

The concepts set, system, closed and open system, subsystem and aspect system are illustrated in Figure 2.

With the aid of the concepts given above, we are in a position to discuss the subjective aspects of system research on concrete systems. It depends on the problem a system researcher is interested in what section of reality he describes as a system, how the boundaries of his system are chosen and what properties (attributes) are included in his description. The system, as used in the discussion of a concrete system, is practically always an abstract system, an abstract image of that concrete system; it contains only the (subjectively) relevant properties of the concrete system and can hence be seen as an aspect system of the concrete system.

Definition 9
The *state* of a system S at a given moment of time is the set of values of the attributes of its elements at that time. An *event* is a change in the state of the system. A *process* is a sequence of related events over time.

It also depends on the judgement of the system researcher what sequence of events he will treat as a process. On the analogy of definition 6, we can define the *structure* of a process as the *relations between its elementary events*.

An open system can have various inputs and outputs. A class of inputs and outputs which is important for the discussion of industrial systems is that of the *physical* inputs and outputs. In the argument given below these physical inputs and outputs may be manpower, money and materials (raw materials, components, equipment, energy), crossing the boundary of the system. This brings us to the definition of an important class of systems, viz. conversion systems.

---

[1]See De Leeuw (1974, p.109) for the distinction between subsystem and aspect system. In definition 8 we use a somewhat wider interpretation of the concept of aspect system, as it can involve any subset of the original attributes of the elements of the system, while De Leeuw considers only subsets of a special class of attributes, viz. subsets of the original relations.

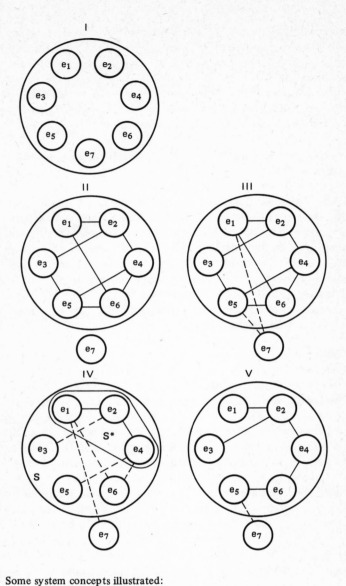

Fig. 2.   Some system concepts illustrated:
I: a *set* of seven element e_i
II: a *system* of six elements; the lines represent the relations between the elements. It is a *closed system*.
III: an *open system* of six elements; the full lines represent its *internal structure,* the dotted lines its *external structure*
IV: a system S with a *subsystem* S*; the full lines represent the internal structure of S*, the dotted lines its external structure.
V: an aspect system of S: some relations are omitted.

30

Definition 10

A *conversion system* is a system converting physical inputs into physical outputs; this conversion may involve changes in quality, quantity, place and/or time.

One can regard a conversion system as a system with metabolism. It is a very general concept. For instance, all living beings can be regarded as conversion systems. One can divide all systems into non-conversion and conversion systems. In Boulding's (1956) system hierarchy the first three levels (frameworks, clockworks and thermostats) contain non-conversion systems[1], while the higher, more complex levels (self-maintaining open systems, biological systems of increasing complexity and social systems) contain conversion systems (we will not consider Boulding's highest level, transcendental systems; inclusion of this level in a scientific argument involves some epistemological difficulties).

4.2 Hierarchic systems

Complex systems often have a special kind of internal structure, viz. a *hierarchic* one. With respect to the concept of hierarchy the ideas of Simon (1962, 1969, 1973) will be followed[2]. Since he does not use definitions, the definitions of this section are our own.

First, Simon's concept of *near-decomposability* must be introduced. In system theory it is often claimed — to advocate the study of coherence — that everything is related to everything. This may be true, but luckily some things are more related than others (otherwise the need to understand everything in order to understand anything would make it impossible to acquire any knowledge). In terms of Simon's concept we can say that concrete systems are usually nearly-decomposable.

---

[1]Of course clockworks and thermostats *as concrete systems* must be conversion systems, because they need energy to run. But systems *described* as clockworks or thermostats are non-conversion systems; the abstraction involved in the description has eliminated the conversion aspects of the concrete system.

[2]As we mentioned before, hierarchic systems are thoroughly studied by Mesarovic et al. (1970). However, their ideas are not followed here, because they do not use a clear definition and because their interpretation of this concept is wider than can be used in this study.

Definition 11

A *nearly-decomposable system* is a system which can be partitioned into subsystems with the property that the relations between the elements of each subsystem are stronger than those between elements from different subsystems.

This definition has the weakness of using the notion of the 'strength' of a relation, which is difficult to define without an empirical context. However, the meaning of this idea should become clearer in the course of the argument given below.

Now, concrete systems often have a special kind of near-decomposability, viz. *a hierarchic one*[1].

Definition 12

A *hierarchic system* is a system the elements of which are themselves systems and may in their turn also be hierarchic systems.

It is the 'parts-within-parts' structure (see Fig. 3 for an example), that is the defining characteristic of a hierarchic system in this book *and no other property*. Although this concept will frequently be used in the following discussion of organizational structures, the concept itself should be seen as 'totally divorced from its original denotation in human organizations of a vertical authority structure' (Simon, 1973, p.5).

Note that the levels of the hierarchy can be seen as a series of *aspect systems:* the whole system is described at each level, subsequent levels only give more detail.

Concrete hierarchic systems, i.e. concrete systems with a hierarchic near-composability, are very common. This is true both of natural things and of artefacts. An example from physics is the structure of matter: atomic nuclei, atoms, molecules, macro-molecules and so on, up to stars and galaxies. The 'strength' of the relations in this example can be defined in terms of the bond energy at each level (running from some 140 MeV at the nuclear level to about 0.5 eV at macro-molecular level).

An example from biology is the structure of striated muscle (see Fig. 3), which can be described as a 5-level hierarchy (if one uses the above-mentioned macromolecules as the lowest level). The highest level is the muscle itself,

---

[1]Simon does not discuss hierarchic near-decomposability explicitly, implying that near-decomposability itself is sufficient to get a hierarchic system. In our view it is not sufficient, because near-decomposability only implies that one can make subsystems and not necessarily subsystems-within-subsystems, as is needed for a hierarchic system (according to definition 12).

which consists at level 4 of bundles of muscle fibres, each bundle surrounded by connective tissue. Level 3 consists of muscle fibres, which are built at level 2 of fibrillae, the basic units of the contractile machinery of the muscle. Finally, each fibrilla is a bundle of (two kinds of) long macro molecules at level 1.

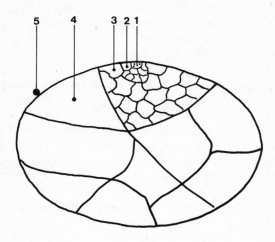

Fig. 3. An example of a hierarchic system: a striated muscle (shown in cross-section).
  level 1: macromolecules
  level 2: fibrillae
  level 3: muscle fibres
  level 4: bundles of muscle fibres
  level 5: the muscle itself

Artefacts often have a hierarchic structure too. Organizations such as the Roman Catholic Church or an army have a parts-within-parts structure. Simon (1973) gives an electronic computer as an example. Here the levels are: the physics of the hardware, the logic structure of operation of the registers of the central processing unit, the machine code and the programming languages (which themselves can have various levels of abstraction in the available commands).

Note that in this last example the elements of the system are not static units but elementary processes like the flow of electric currents, the shifting of a row of bits in a register and the execution of a command.

Simon gives an evolutionary explanation for the abundance of hierarchic structures: complexity cannot arise directly from simple units, but step by step from stable subsystems with an increasing complexity at each step. He illustrates this with the famous example of two watchmakers, each trying to assemble a watch with 10,000 parts, but being frequently disturbed. The first one never finished his job, as his assemblies fell apart each time he was disturbed; the second did finish, because he used a hierarchic structure for his watch: he built it from stable subassemblies of 100 parts each. Although the subassembly he was working on fell apart every time he was disturbed, the mean time between disturbances was long enough to enable him to finish a stable subassembly quite often; so he was able to make progress and to finish the job.

Note that such a discussion does not need to make a distinction between man-made things (like organizations or computers) and natural things (like the heavy elements, which are formed stepwise from lighter elements in stars, or the complex human being, evolved stepwise from ultimately unicellular organisms). In both cases it is easier to 'construct' complex concrete systems step by step from stable subassemblies with an increasing complexity at each step, than directly from non-compound units.

The previous paragraph gave a construction argument for the use of the concept of hierarchy. This concept is also very powerful in coping with complexity in analysis and design (not discussed explicitly by Simon). At any level of a hierarchic system, the subsystems can be treated as black boxes. This property of a hierarchic description greatly reduces the complexity of analysis: all the intricacies of the internal structure of the subsystem are covered under the veil of the black box, so one can concentrate on the interactions between the black boxes. If one wants to know more about an individual black box, one proceeds to the next level of detail and forgets about the internal structure of the other black boxes.

For instance, a civil engineer designing a bridge does not need to understand solid state physics to use steel. At his level of analysis, knowledge of the bending and tensile strength of his steel is sufficient; he uses a 'black-box approach' to steel. Only if one wants to develop steel with a higher strength one need 'open the black box' to study e.g. the structure of steel and the influence of lattice-deffects and carbon on strength. Another example is the electronic computer: you do not need to know much about physics or computer hardware to make a computer program: the hardware is a black box with certain input/output properties. A final example is hierarchic search. To choose a holiday destination, one can use a sequential search method by consulting the index of one's atlas. Hierarchic search will often be more efficient: first choose a country, then a region, then a city or village and finally choose a hotel or camping site there.

Whether a natural thing can be described as a hierarchic system depends on whether it has hierarchic near-decomposability (i.e. whether the clustering of elements according to the strength of their mutual relations produces a parts-within-parts structure). In constructing artefacts, like computer software, an army or an empire, one has more freedom. One can deliberately design the interdependencies among the parts in such a way that one gets a hierarchy: easy to analyse, to design, to construct and to control.

We conclude this section with one final definition:

Definition 13
The *span* of a level of a hierarchic system is the number of subsystems into which each subsystem is divided at the next level of the hierarchy.

4.3 Stratified hierarchic systems

The concept of hierarchic system will often be used below to discuss the internal structure of human organizations. Next to hierarchy, the parts-within-parts structure, organizational structures usually have a second property, viz. stratification[1].

Definition 14
A *stratified system* is a system the elements of which are ordered, individually or combined to subsets, according to a given priority criterion.

The above-mentioned priority criterion can be operationalized in many different ways. For instance, a platoon often marches as a stratified system, the soldiers being ordered according to their height. The pupils of a school can be described as a stratified system, using an ordering by classes. A PERT-planning gives a description of a project as a stratified system consisting of elementary activities, ordered according to the technically necessary precedence relations in time. Note, that stratification partitions a system into *subsystems,* while hierarchy partitions it in *aspect systems.*

Now, organizational structures usually involve a combination of stratification and hierarchy; in such cases the structure can be described as a stratified hierarchic system.

[1]The use of the term 'stratification' in this book should not be confused with the use Mesarovic et al. (1970) make of it in their book "Theory of Hierarchical Multilevel Systems".

Definition 15

A *stratified hierarchic system* is a hierarchic system having at each level one or more subsystems which have priority over the other subsystems at that level.

The following discussions of organizational structures as stratified systems will use the official power relations among the participants in the organization as priority criterion (see section 5.1 for the distinction official *versus* unofficial, and section 5.4 for a short discussion on power).

A stratified hierarchic system is a combination of a set of subsystems with a set of aspect systems. Such a system can be described starting from the hierarchic structure. Each level of the hierarchy consists of a number of subsystems (or elements). Now stratification means that at least one of these subsystems has priority over the other subsystems. Further, if we study the internal structure of these subsystems, we will find again at least one subsystem with priority over the other subsystems at that level.

To illustrate this, let us consider the structure of an infantry brigade (see Fig. 4). The highest level — in this case level 4 — is the brigade itself. Level 3 consists of a number of batallions and one dominant subsystem, the general with his staff. At level 2 each batallion consists of a number of companies and one dominant subsystem, the lieutenant-colonel with his staff. The whole system is mapped again at this level, so the general with his staff figure in it too. However, this subsystem will tend to deal predominantly with the batallions, leaving their internal structure usually out of consideration. The behaviour of the general with his staff can thus better be studied at level 3. Finally, at level 1 each company consists of several platoons and a captain. Of course this analysis can be continued down to the level of the individual soldier.

Stratified hierarchic systems are by no means restricted to organizational structures. A school can be described as such a system: the highest level is the school as a whole, consisting at the next level of a stratified set of forms. Each form can consist at the next level of an A, B and C stream, the pupils being stratified according to their learning capacities. At the lowest level, the pupils of each stream can be individually stratified. Another example is a project, which can be decomposed in a number of major tasks, stratified according to precedence in time. At lower levels each task can be further decomposed and again stratified according to precedence.

Organizational structures, as defined by the structure of line management, have two defining properties: hierarchy and stratification. They form two distinct design issues, which should not be confused. As we mentioned above, hierarchy can be used to cope with complexity (see also part IV). For instance,

36

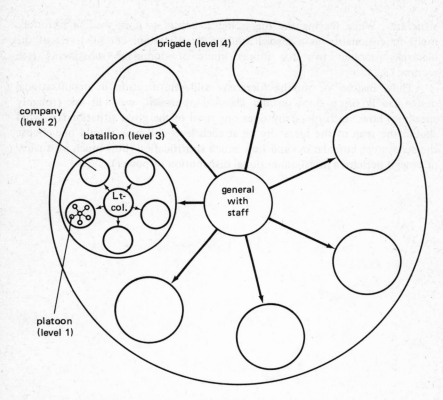

Fig. 4.   An infantry brigade as a 4-level stratified hierarchic system.
➡ : power relation.

one may cope with increasing complexity (e.g. due to increasing heterogeneity of interactions) by reducing the span of the hierarchy. On the other hand, as will be discussed below, stratification will be used to cope with conflicts between subsystem interests and the interests of the system as a whole (see e.g. the discussions on conflict in chapter 10 and on coordination in chapter 12).

To illustrate this distinction between hierarchy and stratification we may compare the structure of the Roman Catholic church with that of the Presbyterian churches: both use a hierarchic ordering of their members, but the Roman Catholic stratification uses a top-to-bottom approach, while the Presbyterian one uses a bottom-to-top approach (the parishes choose delegates, the delegates choose delegates for 'classes', the 'classes' choose the Provincial Assembly and these assemblies the National Assembly). Another point is that this separation permits a better analysis of multi-dimensional organization structures. While leaving the hierarchic structure as it is, we can introduce multi-dimensionality as a special kind of stratification: certain levels of the hierarchy contain two (or more) kinds of dominant subsystems (see section 13.2).

Thus, instead of mixing hierarchy and stratification in organizational design, as is often done in the classical approach, we will ask (roughly speaking) how much hierarchy does one need in the given situation (i.e. what should the span of the hierarchy be at each level and how should one choose the subsystem boundaries) and how much stratification (how much inequality of power, perhaps a multi-dimensional distribution of power).

5. ORGANIZATIONS

5.1 The structure of organizations

This chapter will discuss some structural aspects of organizations, while the next chapter will narrow the discussion down to industrial organizations.

Organizations can be conceptualized in many different ways; the one to be used below is chosen since it fits well into our subsequent treatment of control system design.

Section 1.1 described an organization as a combination of human effort in a relatively stable network of social relations. Now we are in the position to give a more accurate definition.

Luhmann's (1964, 1976) concept of 'position' will be used as the basic element of any organization.

> Definition 16
> A *position* is a set of addressable and relatively stable role expectations with the following three properties:
> (i) it is to be occupied by a person
> (ii) it is to carry out a programme
> (iii) it is to have limited communication possibilities with other positions.

The implications of the first and second property will be clear. With the third property Luhmann indicates that a position does not have an all-channel net of communication relations with the other positions in an organization, but that there are preferred relations with other positions. Due to this restriction every position gets a place (a position) in the communication structure of the organization. If an all-channel net of communications does exist (as is feasible for very small organizations), we will consider that as a limiting case of property three (which implies that such a case is included in definition 16).

An actor has to be assigned to a given position.[1] According to Luhmann the assignment of another actor to the position does not necessarily change its identity: it is a set of *impersonal* role expectations. Neither does a change in its

---

[1]Whenever we use the term 'actor', we mean an individual organizational participant.

programme or its communication relations necessarily change the identity of the position. Only if all three properties are changed simultaneously, the position changes inevitably. It should be noted that a 'position' is defined here as a set of role expectations. This implies that the characteristics of a position need not be explicitly defined in e.g. a task description. A position already exists, if there is some degree of consensus among the persons concerned (the occupant of the position and his social environment) about these role expectations.

Positions in organizations are often clustered in groups or departments, to permit their occupants to combine their efforts. Such departments have properties similar to those of positions, which permits us to define the following level-independent concept.

Definition 17
A *compound position* is a set of addressable role expectations with the following three properties:
(i) it has to be occupied by a number of persons
(ii) it has to carry out a programme or a set of programmes
(iii) it is to have limited communication possibilities with other compound positions.

The individual position can be seen as the limiting case of the compound position. This concept is applicable to all levels of aggregation: individual positions, departments, the divisions of a company, etc.
    Now, an organization can be defined with the aid of the concept of position.

Definition 18
An *organization* is a system of occupied positions with their physical means of operation.

An organization is thus conceptualized as a concrete system, consisting of human beings and e.g. buildings, machines and materials, but with the abstract system of roles as its defining characteristic. As the positions form a system, every position is directly or indirectly connected (by communication channels) with all the other positions of the organization.
    Definition 18 implies that an organization can also be seen as an occupied compound position. This may be helpful for discussion of the behaviour of the organization as a whole. It also means that the parts of an organization are defined in the same way as the organization itself. Although they generally differ in the way they are controlled, the way they acquire their resources,

etc., both the parts and the organization as a whole are conceptualized as systems of occupied positions.

Definition 18 is very general. It is not restricted to (large) bureaucracies, but includes every stable combination of human effort, ranging from a family and a grocery store to a large multinational or a National State.

Another property of definition 18 is that role consensus and role compliance define the organization and not for instance the attainment of a common goal (see e.g. Georgiou, 1974, on the problems arising if one conceptualizes the organization as a goal attainment device). Role compliance can be reached by various means, e.g. because the participants are self-motivated to comply or because other participants influence or force them to comply or by a combination of these causes.

The positions one includes in a description of a given organization define its boundaries as a social system. As in other areas of system research a system boundary is essentially arbitrary; although it depends on the near-decomposability of the objects to be studied, it also depends on judgement and the problem on hand. For instance, for some problems one may regard students as belonging to the university organization, for others they may be treated as belonging to its environment. Further, the participants only belong to the organization in their organizational role; which is another aspect of the organizational boundary.

Definition 6 defined the structure of a system as the set of relations between elements. Using definition 18 we can now define organizational structure as follows.

Definition 19
The *structure* of an organization is the set of relations between its occupied (compound) positions and other occupied (compound) positions.

As in definition 6 we can distinguish an *internal structure* and an *external structure*. The first refers to the relations between the positions of the organization, the second to relations with individual or compound positions outside the organization (like customers, competitors, suppliers and government agencies).

There are two kinds of relations between organizational programmes: *physical* and *non-physical* (usually informational). A production department of a factory, supplying other production departments with sub-assemblies, has a physical relation with these internal customers.

41

Information relations can exist to support the execution of the programmes of other positions (information support) or to support the control of the programmes of other positions (to be called coordination below). An example of the first kind is the relation of a research department with the departments using its know-how. Examples of the second kind are relations of managers with the departments they manage and of planning, coordination and accounting departments with the departments they service.

Now two kinds of organizational structure can be defined.

Definition 20
The *technological structure* of an organization consists of the physical relations and information support relations between its occupied (compound) positions, while the *control structure* consists of the information relations between the occupied (compound) positions, which are directly or indirectly used to control the execution of their programmes.

The discussion on control in section 5.2 and on technology in chapter 6 will further clarify this distinction between control structure and technological structure. The present discussion will be continued by introducing two other aspects of structure, viz. the *Aufbau* and the *Ablauf structure*. This distinction is due to Kosiol, 1962.[1]

Definition 21
The *Aufbau* of an organization is its system of positions. The *Ablauf structure* of an organization is the structure of the organizational processes.

According to this definition the Aufbau is the anatomy of the organization, the task and control structure. 'The Aufbau is a time-less structure of task units, stock-still waiting to be activated' (Van de Wouw, 1977). The organizational *processes* – both technological and control processes – *also show structure:* there are relations between the elementary events of these processes. That is the Ablauf structure. For instance, the set of instructions for the workers of an assembly line define a technological Ablauf structure, while the instructions for a decision or planning procedure define a control Ablauf structure.

Aufbau and Ablauf structure form a Janus-head: two aspects of the same entity, the organizational structure. They can be distinguished but not

---

[1]Kosiol does not give a precise definition of these two concepts. Neither does he distinguish between technological and control structure.

separated. The distinction is made because Aufbau and Ablauf structure constitute different (albeit related) design issues.

The control structure of an organization consists of information relations among its positions, which are usually only partly formalized. Formalization has two dimensions, viz. routine *versus* non-routine and official *versus* unofficial (Hopwood, 1977).

Information relations between positions are partly official, i.e. in principle known to all participants and approved by the dominant coalition, and partly unofficial. Unofficial does not necessarily mean obstructive or something like that, it only means that such relations are not officially approved. One can further distinguish routine relations, governing the repetitive actions in the organization, and non-routine relations, which develop from various incidents but can last for some time. These two dimensions determine what we may call the *formalization mix* (see Fig. 5).

routine	non-routine	
1 routine official	2 non-routine official	**official**
3 routine unofficial	4 non-routine unofficial	**unofficial**

Fig. 5.   The two aspects of the formalization mix for the relations between the positions in an organization.

Design activities usually concentrate on field 1 of the formalization mix, the routine-official control structure. However, as official structures (luckily) only specify a small — albeit important — part of the behaviour of the members of an organization, it is essential that the unofficial relations should sufficiently support the official ones. It is often the difficulty of 'constructing' effective unofficial relations, that makes (major) reorganizations so difficult.

The formalization mix itself is also a design issue: it depends on the situation how much of each of the four aspects is to be used. For instance, it may be sensible to use less official-routine relations for a research department than for an accounting department.

The definitions of organization and of structure given above may seem somewhat classical. However, this discussion of the formalization mix was meant to show that it is not the set of job descriptions with a list of employees' names and an organization chart that defines an organization and its structure. The organization is a social system involving very complex social relations. The official routine aspect of the organization is probably the most visible one, but the other three are just as real.

5.2 Control in organizations

The concept of control is a very important one in this book; we will use the following definition of it.

> Definition 22
> *Control* is the use of interventions by a controller to promote preferred behaviour of a system-being-controlled.

This definition applies both to technical systems, such as radar antennae, chemical plants and missiles, and to organizations. It makes a distinction between a controller and a system-being-controlled (see Fig. 6 which shows a controlled conversion system by way of example). For technical systems the controller can be a distinct *sub*system; for organizations the controller is always an *aspect* system, because every actor in the organization controls at least the execution of his own programme. The degree to which these actors are engaged in control may vary, however; to paraphrase George Orwell: *everyone controls, but some control more than others* (see e.g. the discussion on coordination in chapter 12).

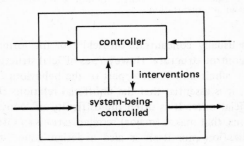

Fig. 6.   A controlled conversion system.
    ➡ : physical input and output
    → : information

The plural 'interventions' is used to indicate that control is considered as being a continuous process, not a single action. As for organizations, control does

44

not refer to a single decision (one choice between alternative interventions) but to a sequence of related decisions, with some relation between past and future performance. This also implies that the conditions for decision making should not change so swiftly that each decision becomes unique.

The controller has to promote certain behaviour, so it should be able to influence the behaviour of the system-being-controlled in one way or another. *This does not necessarily mean that it determines the behaviour of the system completely.*

Finally, as the controller has to promote preferred behaviour, this implies that it is able to *observe* this behaviour and to *evaluate* it in terms of a *set of preferences.*

Controllers almost always use the classical *feedback loop*,[1] which can be divided into three phases:

— the *sensor phase:* observation of the behaviour of the system-being-controlled and, if desired and possible, of its environment

— the *selector phase:* evaluation of systems behaviour using norms or preferences and selection of the appropriate intervention in case of a deviation from preferred behaviour

— the *effector phase:* application of the intervention.

The loop is closed by starting the observations again, i.e. by a new sensor phase.

This scheme applies both to technical systems and to organizations, provided one does not interpret the various concepts too narrowly in the latter case (see Hofstede, 1978, for the problems arising from too narrow an interpretation). In particular one should not try to assign control activities to only a subset of the actors of an organization (in search of a controller as a distinct *sub*system). Nor should one limit the evaluation of behaviour to quantitative aspects, as human actors are usually quite able to use qualitative data (too) for the assessment of organizational behaviour.

Further, the scheme should be seen as a conceptual one. Actual control is not exercised in a neat sequence of phases; in a turbulent environment a controller is continually busy processing the consequences of disturbances.

---

[1]Sometimes a distinction is made between *feedback* and *feedforward*. In the case of feedback the intervention is applied *after* the observation of non-preferred system behaviour; in the case of feedforward, the system behaviour is predicted and an intervention is applied, if possible, *before* the predicted non-preferred behaviour occurs. However, both cases are included in this scheme. The main difference between them is the evaluation of behaviour: feedback evaluates actual behaviour, feedforward predicted behaviour (of course the sensor phase also has to be organized differently).

The above definition of control referred to the actual control of the operations of a system. However, the construction or modification of the controller itself or of the system-being-controlled can also be seen as a mode of control. These modes will be called Control in the Small and Control in the Large respectively.[1]

Definition 23
Control in the Large (CL) is the construction or modification of a system, while *Control in the Small* (CS) is the subsequent control of the operations of that system.

This still fits in with our definition of control, if we regard CL as a higher-order control (see Fig. 7). Whenever there is a disturbance, one can choose between using CS or CS *and* CL: the former may be able to cope with this disturbance, but one might prefer to use CL as well, in order to be able to cope better with similar disturbances in the future.

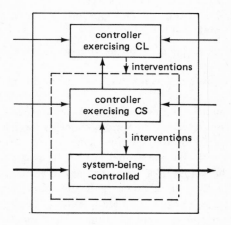

Fig. 7.   Control in the Large (CL) as a higher-order control, acting on the controller exercising Control in the Small (CS) on the system-being-controlled.

[1] The idea of distinguishing CL and CS is inspired on Kosiol's (1962) terms 'Organisation' and 'Disposition'.
        The terms CL and CS themselves are taken from Mesarovic et al. (1970, p.59), but their use of them is somewhat different from that used here. Control in the Large and Control in the Small are also used by Bonini (1964), but he uses these terms to contrast an overall approach to control with a partial approach, directed only to the smaller units of a firm.

In order to prepare the discussion of the design of control systems for organizations in Part IV we will give a definition of this concept. The definition conceptualizes an organizational controller as an entity consisting of actors and a control system (see Fig 8).

Definition 24
The *control system* of an organization is the system of formal and informal rules of behaviour, information systems and physical expedients used by the actors of an organization to control the technology of that organization.

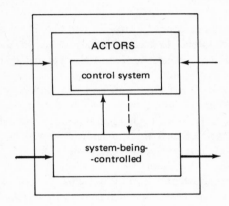

Fig. 8.   The controller of an organization, comprising actors and a control system.

5.3 Selfcontrol and coordination

The actors assigned to positions or to compound positions control the execution of their own programmes. This mode of control will be called *selfcontrol*.

There are usually technological relations between the programmes of different (compound) positions. These relations can cause interactions between actors or groups of actors. One could leave the control of these interactions to the selfcontrol of the actors concerned. However, the complexity of these interactions, conflicts between (groups of) actors, conflicts between the interests of (groups of) actors and the interests of the organiztion as a whole may lead to unsatisfactory behaviour of the organization as a whole. Therefore, in almost every organization various (compound) positions are charged with the task of controlling actors in other (compound) positions. This mode of control will be called *coordination*.

47

Definition 25
A *coordinating (compound) position* is a (compound) position, which has as a programme the control of the execution of programmes of other specified (compound) positions.

Definition 26
Selfcontrol is the control of the execution of the programmes of a (compound) position by the actors assigned to that (compound) position themselves. *Coordination* is the control of the execution of the programmes of a (compound) position by actors in coordinating (compound) positions.

It should be borne in mind that 'control' is used here in the sense of definition 21: control actions intend to change behaviour in the direction of certain preferences, but do not necessarily determine that behaviour completely. In general the execution of an organizational programme is controlled by a *mix* of selfcontrol and coordination (see section 12.5). Interactions between non-coordinating compound positions also influence the execution of programmes, but, as follows from definition 26, that will not be seen as coordination.

Definitions 25 and 26 also apply to individual positions, as an individual position is the limiting case of a compound position.

Coordination is the control of behaviour of human actors (in organizations) by other human actors. The 'levers' for such control are influence and power. The following section will give a short discussion of these topics; a complete discussion would take us outside the scope of this book.

5.4 The 'levers for coordination': influence and power

The phenomenon of power in organizations is receiving much attention in theory (see e.g. Etzioni, 1961, Blau, 1964, Crozier, 1964, Zald, 1970 and Hickson et al., 1971, 1974). In practice, however, it is still more or less taboo. As Dale (1963) says: 'the power process in management is like sex in the Victorian Age. Everyone knows about it, but nobody ever talks about it' (there are some signs, however, that this taboo is waning nowadays, just as has been the case with the sex-taboo).[1]

[1] Another comparison with sex is possible. In a series of studies Mulder (1972) stresses the pleasure-aspect of the wielding of power (neglected in the, mainly Anglo-Saxon, literature on power, which usually discusses only the utilitarian aspects). He develops an addiction theory, comparing the wielding of power with the use of hard drugs. In our opinion the comparison with sex is to be preferred; Mulder's comparison needlessly stigmatizes power, and there is little proof that the dependence of the user on his power is really that great.
  However important the pleasure aspect of the wielding of power may be, our further discussion will be restricted to the utilitarian aspects.

There are many definitions of power and influence, although the two concepts are not always distinguished. The following definitions are chosen because they are well suited for our discussion on the control of human behaviour and especially for the discussion on coordination in chapter 12.

Definition 27
Social system S_i has *influence* on social system S_j if it has the capacity to induce behaviour of S_j which deviates from its behaviour without intervention from S_i, but which is still in agreement with S_j's preferences.

In this definition S_i and S_j can be human individuals or groups of individuals.

Definition 28
Social system S_i has *power* over social system S_j if it has the capacity to induce behaviour of S_j which is in conflict with its preferences.

Power is thus seen as the capacity to make people do things they dislike. Influence and power are aspects of a relation between two social systems; influence and power of S_i are meaningless without an S_j. In general they are also reciprocal: a guard may be able to create conflict in the prisoners in his custody, but the prisoners can do the same to the guard. The degree of conflict may vary, however. The amount of power S_i has over S_j can be seen as proportional to the degree of conflict S_i is able to induce in S_j.

In general this degree is limited. If the degree of conflict in social system S_j lies outside its 'zone of acceptance'[1], the power of S_i ceases to control (in the sense of definition 21) the behaviour of S_j. So it is the behaviour of S_j that defines S_i's power over it: shooting someone is not wielding of power, but forcing someone to dig his own grave is.

The power of S_i is based on its capacity to create conflict in S_j. This, in its turn, is based on S_i's capacity to vary inputs to S_j which have value for its physical and/or social needs. The degree of the subsequent power of S_i over S_j depends on the *centrality* and *substitutability* of this input for S_j (see among others Hickson et al., 1974). The centrality of an input to a social system S_j is proportional to the conflict its absence would create in S_j (and hence is subjective, depending on S_j's preferences: a 100 guilder fine may create a greater conflict in a miser than in a rake). The substitutability of an input to a social system depends on its capacity to obtain a similar input elsewhere (this is the basis of the power of a monopoly: it can create conflict in its customers by asking a high price, because they are unable to find another supplier). The

[1] See Simon (1957, p.131).

49

power S_i has over S_j is thus based on the inputs to S_j he can vary and increases with increasing centrality and decreasing substitutability of these inputs.

The phenomenon of power is present in almost any social setting, it is not confined to large organizations. For instance, the creation of conflict in another may be used to control the behaviour of the other in husband-wife or parent-child relations too.

Actors in coordinating compound positions (*coordinators*) may use a mix of influence and power to control the behaviour of actors in the compound positions they are to coordinate (*coordinated groups*). As will be seen in chapter 12, some coordinators have no (official) power at all, so they have (in principle) to rely on influence.

A power difference can be defined as follows (see also Hofstede, 1976).

Definition 29
The *power ratio* of a system, consisting of coordinators and coordinated groups, is the ratio of the power of the coordinators over the coordinated groups to the power of the latter over the coordinators.

If the coordinated actors have no power at all (they are thus completely at the mercy of the coordinators) the value of the power ratio is infinite; usually its value is finite. If the power of the coordinators over the coordinated groups is less than in the reverse, the value of this ratio is less than unity and it is zero if the coordinator has no power at all. To survive, to obtain sufficient role compliance and sufficient controllability, organizations usually need a power ratio greater than unity. The power ratio one needs depends partly on the control situation, i.e. technology and environment. An army in time of war, for instance, may need a higher power ratio than a civilian organization. The desired value of the power ratio also depends on various properties of the coordinated groups. A very important property in this respect is motivation. A high motivation, 'automatically' present and/or stimulated by coordinators, may decrease the need for a high power ratio. Increasing motivation may shift the influence/power mix towards less use of power. The treatment of this very complex phenomenon, however, falls outside the scope of this book.

Another aspect influencing the power ratio in an organization is the 'zone of acceptance' of the participants. It is of course important for the survival of the organization that this 'zone of acceptance' is compatible with the power ratio needed (the 1917 mutinies in the French army are an example of a narrowing of the zone of acceptance of organizational participants to a point which threatened to fall below the zone needed for the survival of the organization).

50

Cultural factors also have a great influence on the actual power ratio used. See e.g. Hofstede (1976), who studied the power differences between superiors and subordinates in many countries. He found for instance, that the power ratio (the power-distance index in his terminology) in organizations in France and Italy is much higher than e.g. in Great Britain, The Netherlands and the U.S.A. See also Sasaki (1973) for cultural influences on the exercise of power in a comparison of Japan and the West.

5.5 Stratified hierarchies in organizations

One cannot distribute power like apples. The power distribution in an organization is only partly the result of deliberate design; it depends also on various factors, such as the properties of the participants and the technological structure (see for an example of the latter Crozier's (1964) study of the power of a group of maintenance engineers in an organization, providing inputs to the rest of the organization with a high centrality and a low substitutability).

However, deliberate design does also influence — even to a great extent — the power distribution in organizations. The Aufbau, i.e. the task and control structure, is in most cases constructed in such a way that for (some of) the coordinators and coordinated groups the power ratio is sufficiently greater than unity to ensure sufficient controllability. This power is usually vested in the official-routine relations and is based on the capacity of coordinators to dispose of organizational resources. These resources can be used to distribute *incentives* (both social and physical) in order to induce *contributions* from the coordinated participants.

As will be discussed in part 4, the Aufbau (the system of positions) is usually a special kind of system, viz. a stratified hierarchic system.

The priority criterion used for stratification is the power distribution as resulting from the official-routine relations.

The fact that the Aufbau is a *hierarchic* system of positions means that at every level of the hierarchy the subsystems (i.e. occupied compound positions) are again divided into subsystems down to the level of the individual occupied position. Every occupied compound position has selfcontrol, but this selfcontrol is split into selfcontrol and coordination at the next level of the hierarchy, etc. For example, in the infantry brigade of section 4.3, at level 3 one has a coordinator, the general with his staff, and coordinated groups (the batallions) with selfcontrol. But the selfcontrol of a batallion consists of coordination by the lieutenant-colonel and the selfcontrol of the companies. This goes right down to the ultimate selfcontrol: that of individual actors controlling their own programme (e.g. workers on an assembly line, researchers in their laboratory and also the manager of the financial department of a company negotiating a 250 million dollar loan with a consortium of banks).

The army brigade of section 4.3 is a classical example of a line organization. Similar stratified hierarchies can be found in other organizations. This simple structure may, however, be amplified by other coordinating mechanisms (as it is, by the way, in armies nowadays). For instance, planning departments and other staff departments may coordinate without having power, or one may use special kinds of stratification, such as a matrix structure (see section 13.2).

6. INDUSTRIAL ORGANIZATIONS

6.1 Technology

Definition 19 of section 5.1 distinguished between the technological structure and the control structure of an organization. We will use a rather wide conception of technology, similar to that of e.g. Thompson (1967). Not only industrial organizations but also e.g. hospitals, universities and armies have a technology.

> Definition 30
> The *technology* of an organization is the set of physical conversion functions and information support functions contained in the programmes of its (compound) positions, together with the physical expedients used to perform these functions.

This definition corresponds with Figure 6 of section 5.2: a system with control has a 'controller' and a 'system-being-controlled'; from now on the latter will be referred to as the 'technology' of the system.

Industrial organizations differ from other organizations in the fact that the core of their technology consists of the conversion in quality and/or quantity of physical objects. This fact has several consequences for control, which will be discussed in chapter 7.

As mentioned above, a design is a 'structure within a situation'. This chapter will discuss one aspect of the situation of the control system of an industrial organization, viz. its technological structure. The discussion will be focussed on the physical relations between (compound) positions, paying no attention to the information support relations (such as the relations of R & D departments with other departments). Furthermore, the discussion will be confined to the Aufbau of technology; its dynamical aspects (the technological Ablauf-structure) will be discussed in parts III and IV.

The technology of an industrial organization is 'artificial', i.e. designed by man and not by laws of nature (although by no means having dispensation from them). It is influenced both by the design of the actual conversion processes themselves and by the design of the control system. However, this chapter will consider the technological structure as given.

53

6.2 Conversion systems and non-conversion systems

An industrial organization can be seen as a system of occupied compound positions, such as departments, factories, warehouses and sales organizations. This system is usually a hierarchic one.

At any level of such a hierarchy one can divide the occupied compound positions into two kinds: *conversion systems* and *non-conversion systems*. The conversion systems convert material flows in quality, quantity, place and/or time. In this book the term material flows will cover flows of manpower, money and materials (raw materials, components, energy, equipment). The non-conversion systems are basically information-processing systems. Examples of conversion systems are factories, warehouses, sales organizations, purchasing departments, personnel departments and financial departments. Examples of non-conversion systems are the board of directors with staff, accounting departments, planning departments and also R & D departments (an engineering department with its own facilities for construction of equipment can be seen as a conversion system and without these facilities as a non-conversion system). Of course, non-conversion systems also have physical inputs and outputs, but one can abstract from these aspects in the following discussion. The distinction between these two kinds of organizational subsystems is made because their dynamic properties and hence also their control properties differ (as will be seen in part III).

Each conversion system can be described as a black box with physical inputs and outputs. The output differs from the input, so transformations must occur in the black box. To a certain extent, the system is able to cope with disturbances in input acquisition or output disposal, so it is not an automaton: it has a control function.

Figure 9 shows a conversion system with these four functions:

I: input function, the acquisition of resources (Manpower, Money, Materials) from inside or outside the organization
O: output function, the transfer of the output to other social systems inside or outside the organization
T: transformation function, the change in quality, quantity, place and/or time needed to transform the physical inputs into the outputs
C: control function, connected by flows of information to the environment of the system (which may consist of social systems both inside and outside the organization as a whole).

How these four functions are 'organized' inside the conversion system will be left out of consideration for the moment.

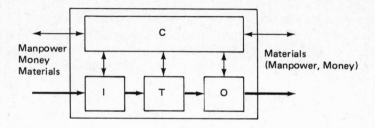

Fig. 9.   An industrial conversion system.
    I :   input function
    O :   output function   → physical flows
    T :   transformation function   → information
    C :   control function

Using the terms of Thompson (1967), one can call the T function the
'technical core' of the conversion system and the I and O functions its
'boundary spanning functions'. The technical core of a conversion system is
not necessarily its most important or most critical function. For a factory it
usually is, but for a sales organization or purchase department it may be
expected that the output or input functions respectively are the most critical.
This does not mean that the other functions are negligible in the latter systems.
For instance, the input function of a sales organization includes activities like
discussions with factories on delivery schedules, with development
departments on the specification of new products and with management on
budgets.

The following discussion on technological structure will be focussed on the
relations between the conversion systems of an industrial organization, because
these relations largely determine the control needs of such an organization.

6.3 Physical relations between conversion systems

The conversion systems of an industrial organization, as depicted in Fig. 9, are
connected by physical flows, flows of manpower, money and material.
Sometimes a connection is no more than an incidental exchange between two
conversion systems; however, it often has a more stable nature.
    There are various types of such stable connections. First one can make a
distinction between series and parallel connections (see Fig. 10).

55

Definition 31

Conversion system S_i has a *series connection* with conversion system S_j if (part of) the physical output of S_i is used as input for S_j. System S_i has a *parallel connection* with S_j if S_i and S_j draw (part of) their input from the same source or feed (part of) their output to the same drain.

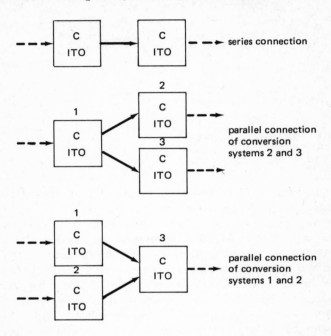

Fig. 10. The series connection and the parallel connection of industrial conversion systems.

A TV factory has series connections with several supplying factories and with many sales organizations. It can have parallel connections with other TV factories, e.g. if they all get their picture tubes from the same factory. Most conversion systems have a parallel connection with respect to the acquisition of money, as this is usually done by one corporate department. The Philips factories in Eindhoven have parallel connections with respect to manpower. Competitors on a given market are also connected in parallel.

One can also distinguish proportional and non-proportional connections.

Definition 32
Conversion system S_i, supplying conversion system S_j, has a *proportional connection* with S_j if the input from S_i needed by S_j, averaged over a certain period, is proportional to the output of S_j.[1]

Connections, for the supply of components or raw materials are usually proportional. On the other hand, a supplier of oil for the heating of a factory, or of other house-keeping materials is usually non-proportionally connected to the factory. A special case of a non-proportional connection is that involved in the supply of production equipment, because the input needed by the receiving system is in principle proportional to the increase in its output and not to the output itself. One could call this a *differential connection* (in reality such a connection is often of a mixed kind: a differential component for the increase of production and a proportional component for substitution of obsolete equipment).

A connection can be rigid or buffered.

Definition 33
Conversion system S_i, supplying conversion system S_j has a *rigid* connection with S_j if the input to S_j has to be continuously proportional to the output of S_i after a *fixed* interval of time. Such a connection is *buffered* if the time interval between the production of the output by S_i and the receipt of the input by S_j can vary.

Workers on a traditionally organized assembly line are rigidly connected. A packing department of a factory usually has a rigid connection with the production departments too; the connections between different production departments may also be rigid. Factories usually have buffered connections with one another.

Stocks are often used as the buffer between conversion systems. If production is not on stock but on order, the order portfolio performs the same function.

In many cases it is better to consider the connection between the technical cores of S_i and S_j in analysing the rigidity of a connection, because the boundary spanning functions usually perform the buffering (the buffer is thus inside S_i and/or S_j, not in an intermediate unit).

---

[1] The introduction of proportionality gives rise to a measurement problem. One can measure proportionality in terms of money, labour hours, machine hours, or simply in units (as for the connection between a personnel department and a factory).

The degree to which a connection is buffered may vary. For instance, the content of the buffer between a TV factory and a picture-tube factory (measured as the period over which the stock level involved covers the needs of the TV factory) usually varies between smaller margins than that between an IC factory and a TV factory.

So far we have only discussed connections between two 'adjacent' conversion systems. In studying systems of conversion systems one can distinguish various *configurations* of connected conversion systems. In a factory one may have several conversion systems with connections of material flows forming e.g. a production street, a flow shop or a job shop. However, a discussion of such configurations and their resulting coordination needs will not be given here.

Finally, we may discuss the various social processes available for the control of acquisition of the input and disposal of the output of social conversion systems. A very ancient method of obtaining physical inputs is simply using physical force (for example, the manpower required for many economic activities in the Roman Empire was often acquired in the form of slaves). A more modern, but not always very different, process for the control of physical flows between conversion systems is the market process, using a price mechanism[1]. A third kind may be called the budgetary process. This is used e.g. by government agencies, most Western-European utilities and Eastern-European companies. Input acquisition here is based on a negotiating process between government officials, political leaders and other interested parties. The social systems receiving the output provide the monetary resources by paying more or less the cost price of the output either directly (utilities) or indirectly (through taxes).

Organizations are to a large extent free to choose the social process they use to control their internal physical flows (this topic is widely discussed in economic literature as the transfer pricing problem, see e.g. Verlage, 1975). Some choose a kind of market process, using market prices as transfer price and permitting their conversion systems to buy elsewhere, if the internal conditions are not satisfactory. Others, like Philips Industries, choose a kind of

---

[1]The differences between the first and the second process diminish when there is a great difference in power between supplier and customer, as is for instance the case if there is a great difference in the capacity to use physical force. Merchants travelling through Attilla's empire, for instance, were never sure whether the Huns would choose the first or the second social process for the transfer of goods to themselves (Schreiber, 1976). Input acquisition for the slave trade in the eighteenth and the first half of the nineteenth century naturally started with the first process; input acquisition in colonial empires in the same period generally used the second, but the vast difference in the capacity to use physical force heavily influenced the pricing process. As the use of physical force is nowadays – with a few exceptions – monopolized by the National State, the market process is now more determined by *economic* power and influence.

budgetary process (Philips Industries use the full cost price as transfer price; delivery schedules are negotiated between internal customer and supplier; in principle the internal customer is not free to buy elsewhere, but the supplier should strive after a cost price well below the market price — if such a price exists).

The structure and nature of the connections between the conversion systems of an industrial organization have a great influence on the organization's coordination needs. Connections give rise to *dependences:* as a result of connections with other subsystems, the proper functioning of the technical core of a conversion system depends on the functioning of these other systems (this applies both to connections with conversion and with non-conversion systems).

A proportional series connection gives a *reciprocal* or a *sequential dependence* of the connected systems (Thompson, 1967)[1]. The conversion capacities of both systems must be matched, as must the quality, quantity and timing of the conversions. If this adaptation is mutual, we can speak of a *reciprocal* dependence. If on the average only one of the two conversion systems adapts its activities to the other one (as is feasible in case of a big difference in flexibility between the two systems), we can speak of a *sequential* dependence. For example, the glass factories of Philips Industries have a reciprocal dependence with the picture-tube factories, whereas a packing department of a factory usually has a sequential dependence on the production departments.

Differential connections give special control problems, because such connections tend to amplify disturbances (see section 8.3).

Parallel connections give *pooled dependences* (Thompson, 1967). If the capacity of the pooled source (or the pooled drain) is limited, the situation can often be described as a 'zero-sum game'[2] : profit for one means loss for the other (for example, if capital is scarce, the approval of one investment project means the rejection of others. Series connections, on the other hand, usually give non-zero-sum situations: expansion of TV factories leads to expansion of picture-tube factories).

It will be clear that rigid connections generally impose higher demands on the coordination of the activities in the connected systems than buffered

---

[1]The general idea of reciprocal and sequential dependence is taken from Thompson. However, a 'normal' series connection is viewed by Thompson as always giving a sequential dependence. We do not take this view, because if one system needs another for input acquisition, the other needs the first for output disposal. The concepts of sequential dependence is reserved in this book for situations where the dependence is really one-sided (see the examples given in the text).

[2]See e.g. Ackoff and Sasieni (1968) for a short introduction to game theory.

connections. In fact, the creation of buffered connections is one of the standard methods of reducing the need for coordination (Galbraith, 1973).

Finally, a market process for the control of internal physical flows may need less coordination than a budgetary process (however, this is certainly not always the case; big differences in power, or a high degree of internal interdependence may lead to unsatisfactory overall performance if the subsystems are free to pursue their own interests unrestrictedly).

6.4 A hierarchic system of conversion systems

The conversion system of Fig. 9 is the fundamental unit of an industrial organization. It is a level-independent concept: it can be used to describe the organization as a whole[1], but also to describe its parts.

Fig. 11 depicts the industrial organization as a whole for the case where the input/output relations with its environment are controlled by market processes.

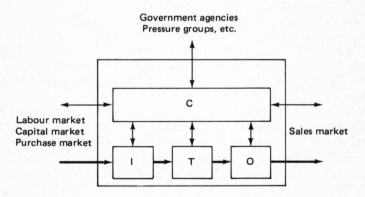

Fig. 11. The industrial organization as a whole and its environment.

The structure of the system of Fig. 11 can be studied at the next level of detail by decomposing it into subsystems. At this next level it consists of a network of conversion systems, connected with one another and with the organizational environment by physical flows. There are also non-conversion systems at this

[1]This concept can also be used at even higher levels. An input-output table of the sectors of a national economy essentially describes the economy as a network of conversion systems.

level. All subsystems are connected, directly or indirectly, by information flows. Fig. 12 shows an example of such a network.

As usual in system research, the boundaries of the subsystems at this level should follow the *near-decomposability* of the higher-level system. Definition 11 of section 4.2 used the criterion 'strength of relation' to determine whether a system is nearly-decomposable or not. Now a good measure of the 'strength of the relation' between the elements or subsystems of a conversion system is the rigidity of their physical connections (as discussed in the previous section). This does not remove all possible ambiguities inherent in subsystem design, but it can guide this process. Rigidly connected elementary conversion systems are thus described as being one subsystem, while ones with buffered connections are described as different subsystems.

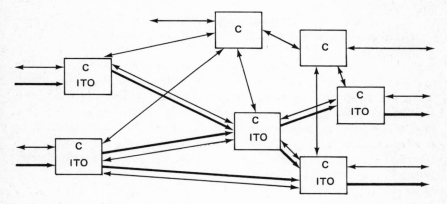

Fig. 12   A network of conversion systems, completed with non-conversion systems.
　　　　➡ physical connection
　　　　→ informational connection

As will be seen in the example given in the next section, the technological structure of an industrial organization closely resembles its control structure (having elements like divisions, departments, sub-departments). This is only to be expected: the control structure will usually be designed in such a way that departmental boundaries follow the lines of technological near-composability, and once a control structure is implemented the technological structure will follow the control near-decomposability (for instance, a department of a TV factory manufacturing sub-assemblies for the other departments may use a low level of intermediate stocks; once this activity is transferred to a specialized factory, servicing several other factories, the intermediate stocks will tend to be higher and will show more variations: the connection has been made less rigid). Control boundaries thus follow technological boundaries, and technological boundaries follow control boundaries.

The structure of the network of Fig. 12 can be studied in further detail at another level: each subsystem can again be partitioned into several conversion and non-conversion systems. At this lower level one may find, that the I and O functions of a higher-level conversion system are put into specialized subsystems (e.g. the T function of a division is put in several factories and its O function in several sales organizations). This does not mean that there can be conversion systems without a T or an I/O function; it means that the relative importance of the various functions has been changed (e.g. the O function of a factory does not need much manpower, if there are separate sales organizations).

This process can be continued, until we reach the level of the ultimate organizational conversion system: the individual human actor.

The structure of the physical connections among the conversion systems of an industrial organization, and between these systems and the environment, largely determine the control needs of the organization. This structure can be described as a hierarchic system of conversion systems, connected with one another and with the environment by physical flows. The connections may be series and parallel, proportional and non-proportional, rigid and buffered. The flows can be controlled by a variant of the market process or of the budgetary process.

6.5 An example: the technological structure of Philips Industries

As an example of the use of the concepts introduced in this chapter, we will give a rough description of the technological structure of Philips Industries.

As will be seen, this structure closely resembles the control structure, insofar as the latter is defined by departmental boundaries. In the case of Philips Industries, however, one aspect of the control structure is less clearly visible in the technological structure, viz. the matrix structure of control: as described in other terms in section 3.2, the activities of each internal conversion system (with the exception of corporate subsystems, see below) are coordinated by *two* (non-conversion) systems, viz. by the management of the National Organization of the country where it is located, and by the management of one of the Product Divisions. This is illustrated in Fig. 13.

The technological structure of Philips Industries can be described as a 6-level hierarchic system (see Fig. 14). At level 6 we have the company as a whole, which is decomposed at level 5 in 14 conversion systems: the Product Divisions listed in Table 1 (as we are interested in the internal technological structure, we choose the Product Divisions rather than the National Organizations for the decomposition of level 6 into level 5). There are various other conversion systems at level 5, such as internal manufacturers of metal and plastic parts, internal machine works and the corporate finance department.

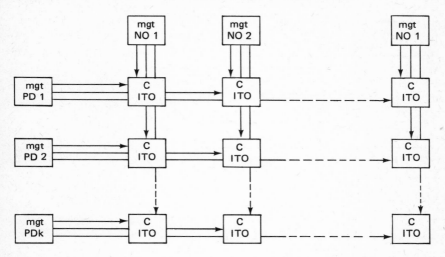

Fig. 13. The matrix structure of control in Philips Industries: the activities of each conversion system are coordinated by two managements, viz. Products Division management and National Organization management.

The glass division has a proportional series connection with the ELCOMA-division (electronic components), while ELCOMA and the corporate component factories have proportional series connections with almost all other divisions. Due to the latter connections, these other divisions are connected in parallel (see chapter 10 for some of the zero-sum games they play). The machine works have a differential connection with some divisions (see chapter 9 for the resulting control problems). Connections between divisions are usually buffered (with a few exceptions, for instance those between the glass factories and the TV tube factories, which are only slightly buffered). Finally, the connections between the finance department and the divisions also give rise to parallel connections between the divisions, respectively the National Organizations (manpower is usually acquired at a lower level).

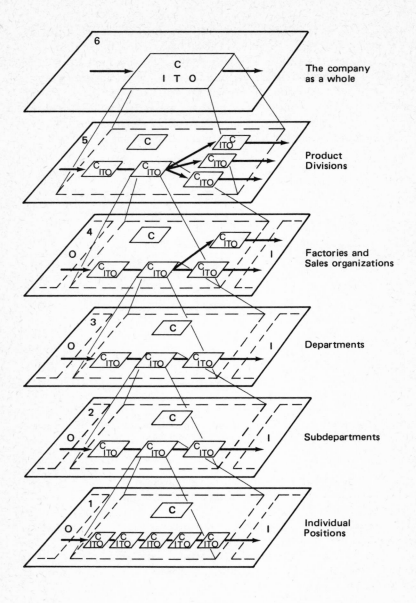

Fig. 14. The technological structure of Philips Industries as a 6-level hierarchy. Only a few of the subsystems at each level are shown.

There are also many non-conversion systems at level 5, e.g. corporate management, corporate staff departments and the corporate research department. The managements of the National Organizations can also be shown at this level.

The internal structure of the divisions (and of the other subsystems of level 5) is shown at level 4. The main subsystems at this level are factories, sales organizations, divisional headquarters (divisional management and various staff departments) and divisional product and process development departments. The factories of one product division often have proportional series connections with other factories of that division.

The internal structure of the factories and sales organizations (and the other level 4 subsystems) are shown at level 3. For instance, a factory has various production departments, usually a material management department performing most of the boundary spanning functions of the factory, a personnel department (charged with the acquisition of manpower, among other things) and factory management. These departments have often subdepartments at level 2, while finally level 1 shows the individual positions.

Control boundaries usually follow technological boundaries, for the reasons mentioned in section 6.4. The matrix structure of control was mentioned above as presenting a difficulty in this respect. In fact, the matrix structure is the result of an effort to create subsystems with a homogeneous environment (as will be discussed in chapter 13): the divisions have a homogeneous internal environment but a heterogeneous external environment (many sales and labour markets), whereas the national organizations have a more homogeneous external environment (one labour market and a few sales markets) but a heterogeneous internal environment (the 14 product divisions).

THE DYNAMICS OF COMPLEX INDUSTRIAL ORGANIZATIONS

SUMMARY OF PART III

In the present part we discuss the dynamics of complex industrial organizations, in order to gain some insight into the problems to be met by their control systems (the subject of part IV of this book). Our attention will be focussed on those phenomena in which the *complexity* of the organization plays a major role. In this context, complexity means that the organization consists of suborganizations which have interdependence of operation but a fair degree of independence of control.

Chapter 7 gives a further analysis of the control process. Apart from maintaining steady-state operation the main function of control is *interference reduction*, i.e. the promotion of adequate responses of the system to threats and opportunities. Interference reduction will be described in three phases, viz. the *sensor, selector* and *effector* phases. During the effector phase, the state of the physical part of the system is usually changed; in general some resources must be consumed to bring such a change about, because the system has *inertia*, a resistance to change. As long as the system has sufficient resources to reduce interferences it has a sufficient *interference reduction capacity*. The *controllability* of a system is defined as 'unity minus the relative adaptation costs': the lower the controllability of a system in a given environment, the harder (the more 'expensive') it is for the system to reduce interference. The chapter concludes with a discussion of interference reduction in industrial networks. Such networks must maintain an *output equilibrium* (their output should on the average be equal to the demand for this output) and various *resource equilibria* (the resources acquired should on the average be at least equal to the resources consumed). Some network aspects of the system's inertia are mentioned.

Chapter 8 discusses the maintenance of output equilibrium of an industrial system by describing it as a *network of demand servos*. A demand servo is an industrial conversion system, designed so that its output follows the demand for this output; there are usually two buffers (a production buffer and a sales buffer) between the output of the demand servo and demand. Some qualitative results of servo-mechanism theory are used to deal with the response of the system to variations in final demand; in particular the phenomenon of resonance is discussed. In this argument, we will use Philips Industries as an example of a network of demand servos. Finally some tentative remarks are made on the causes of business cycles.

69

Chapter 9 also discusses the maintenance of output equilibrium of an industrial system, in this case from sales and production-planning viewpoints. Philips Industries is again used as an example. A simulation model of a chain of factories is presented to illustrate the argument.

Chapter 10 deals with some social aspects of the phenomena discussed in chapters 8 and 9. The interactions between the subsystems discussed there are described in terms of *transfer of interference*: the reduction of interference by one subsystem can cause interferences to connected subsystems. In protecting their own mission, these other subsystems try to defend themselves against such a transfer of interference. This may cause intra-organizational conflict, which is partly solved by the interventions of coordinators and partly by a power game between the parties involved. Some examples of transfer of interference within Philips Industries are mentioned.

7. CONTROL IN INDUSTRIAL NETWORKS

7.1 Control as interference reduction

In part II we discussed the structure of industrial organizations, describing it as a hierarchic network of connected conversion systems, completed by non-conversion systems. We will now deal with the dynamics of industrial organizations from the control viewpoint.

Control was defined (definition 22) as the use of interventions by a controller to promote preferred behaviour of a controlled system. In the present part we will discuss the actual use of interventions by the controller, *Control in the Small*. An understanding of this process is necessary for the discussion in part IV of *Control in the Large*, the construction of the controller and of the system to be controlled.

This chapter will give a further analysis of the process of control, in the first three sections in a general way (applicable both to technical and to social systems) and in the last section with special reference to industrial organizations.

The analysis can proceed from the three phases of the control loop mentioned in section 5.2: the sensor phase, the selector phase and the effector phase. These phases imply that the controller must have[1]:

(i)   a *sensor* to observe the behaviour of the system-being controlled and — if desired and possible — of the systems environment

(ii) an *effector* with a *choice* of feasible interventions in the system-being-controlled (without the possibility of such a choice, there is no control problem)

(iii) a *selector*, which must include a *model* of the system-being-controlled (Conant and Ashby, 1970; Tocher, 1970) to predict its behaviour without and with interventions[2], and a set of *criteria* to evaluate the behaviour of the system-being-controlled.

---

[1] See e.g. Tocher (1970) on the conditions for control; Tocher omits the sensor, however.

[2] This model is not necessarily an explicit mathematical one, but can be any means of getting an idea of future system behaviour with and without intervention. For social systems, it usually consists predominantly of implicit qualitative knowledge of the history of the system.

The sensor, effector and selector need not be distinct *sub*systems of the controller, they can also be *aspect* systems; in the latter case all the controller's elements are involved in the control process in one way or another (as is the case for practically every social system, see section 5.2).

The core of the control process is the *information processing* during the selector phase triggered by the (physical) behaviour of the system-being-controlled through sensor activities and subsequently influencing that behaviour through effector activities.

Interventions from the controller are usually needed to start and to maintain steady-state operation of the system-being-controlled. However, in a changing environment the promotion of preferred behaviour involves not only the maintenance of steady-state operation -but above all the promotion of adequate responses to threats and opportunities. This latter process can be described as one of *reduction of interference*[1].

To define an interference, we must first introduce the concept of equilibrium.

Definition 34
A controlled system is in a state of *equilibrium* if its controller refrains from a control intervention after the evaluation of this state; the system is in a state of *disequilibrium* if its controller chooses to apply a control intervention.

Equilibrium is thus seen as essentially subjective: 'satisfaction' of the controller is a necessary and sufficient condition for equilibrium. Furthermore, equilibrium is not necessarily confined to one state of the system, but can comprise a set of states: the selector criteria can permit a certain *zone of indifference;* only if given control limits are exceeded will the controller then choose to intervene.

Definition 35
An *interference* is an event causing a disequilibrium in a controlled system.

Interferences can arise both inside and outside the system. Furthermore, as disequilibrium is defined as being subjective, one can distinguish two kinds of interferences.

---

[1] The discussion of the concepts of 'reduction of interference' and 'transfer of interference', two key issues in the present part, is strongly inspired by ideas from De Sitter (1973). However, because the elaboration of these concepts to be given here differs from De Sitter and because we do not use the rest of his paradigm, his work will not be discussed here.

Definition 36
A *state interference* is an event causing a disequilibrium in a controlled system without changing the controller criteria. A *norm interference* is an event causing a disequilibrium by changing the controller criteria.

If production according to a given plan is the criterion for the control of a production department, a machine breakdown is a state interference and a change of plan a norm interference. Of course, a change of plan is usually not a spontaneous event, but is induced by some other event inside or outside the system. The distinction between these two types of interferences for a particular case may thus depend on the way the control process in question is described.

Definition 37
Interference reduction in a controlled system is the process of restoring the equilibrium of the system.

An interference may be reduced either by changing the state of the system-being-controlled, so that this state again matches the zone of indifference, or by changing the controller criteria (or by a combination of these two measures). In the latter case the controller itself can change its criteria in e.g. an adaptation or learning process, or an outside agent can change the criteria. Following Ashby (1956, p. 213) the change of the criteria of a controller by an outside agent is often called *control* and the subsequent use of these criteria in the process of interference reduction *regulation*. This terminology will not be followed here: both actions will be regarded as Control-in-the-Small (and only changes in the *structure* of the controller or of the system-being-controlled will be regarded as Control-in-the-Large).

An event may or may not be expected by the controller, depending on the predictive ability of its model (uncertainty is thus a subjective property). Both predicted and unpredicted events may lead to a need for adaptation of the system, so interference reduction is a somewhat wider concept than coping with uncertainty. However, coping with predicted events is usually much easier than with unpredicted ones, so uncertainty is a key problem for control.

7.2 Inertia and interference reduction capacity

An intervention by the effector inducing a change in the state of the system-being-controlled usually involves the consumption of resources. This stems from the fact that most concrete systems have *inertia*. Inertia can be

73

seen as the inverse of *flexibility,* the capacity of a system to have its state changed.

The term 'inertia' suggests an analogy with mechanics: an interference or control intervention acting on a system with inertia is analogous with a force acting on a mechanical system with mass. However, in many control problems, especially where social systems are involved, it is not possible to *measure* directly a variable analogous with mass. The following definition therefore uses the resources needed for changes in the state of the system as a measure of inertia. In the mechanical analogon this would mean that the *energy* needed for a state transition is taken as measure of the 'resistance to change'[1].

Definition 38
The *inertia* of a transition between two system states is proportional to the *resources* needed to bring that transition about. This inertia is also proportional to the *time* needed for the transition.

Inertia can be expressed in any unit relevant to the resources used to realize the changes: for technical systems it may be energy, for certain animals it may be energy too, for armies manpower, for industrial organizations e.g. money or scarce materials. According to definition 38 resistance to change can also be measured as the time needed for a change.

The above-given definition is not without ambiguity, as a trade-off between time and costs is sometimes possible: in those cases one can reduce the time needed for a transisition by spending more resources. It will thus depend on the problem on hand how one operationalizes the concept of inertia.

Inertia is defined with respect to transitions between *states*. The inertia of the whole *system* can in principle be given by a table, stating for each relevant system state the various costs (i.e. resources) or times needed for all feasible transitions to other relevant states. A simpler expression for the systems inertia can sometimes be given, e.g. if the costs or times for every feasible transition are equal or can be expressed in a simple formula.[2]

---

[1] The mechanical analogue is: a force acting on a system with a certain velocity brings the system into a state with a different velocity; the 'resistance to change' is measured as the work done by the force to bring this state transition about. The mass of the system is still very relevant to the issue of resistance to change, because it determines the energy needed for a transition between two states with given velocities. The choice of energy as a measure of resistance to change is only a choice of yardstick.

[2] For instance, in the mechanical analogue the inertia can be expressed as $I = \frac{1}{2}m\Delta v^2$, where in m is the mass of the system and Δv the difference in velocities between the two states.

Events are only interferences, if they produce dissatisfaction in the selector. However, in order to survive most systems have to keep certain essential variables within assigned 'physiological' limits (Ashby, 1956, p. 196). If events threatening to push essential variables over these limits are not recognised by the controller as interferences and if there is consequently no adequate response of the system to such events, the system may not survive. There are thus some events a viable system *must* treat as interferences.

Another important condition for survival is, that the resources *available* for interference reduction should at least be equal to the resources *needed* for this purpose. This leads to the following definition of the capacity of a system to survive.

Definition 39
The *interference reduction capacity,* of a controlled system is the ratio of the resources available for interference reduction to the resources needed for interference reduction.

The interference reduction capacity, or IRC, of a system is thus a dimensionless figure between zero and infinity. In order to survive, a system must have an IRC greater than unity. If it is impossible to reduce a given interference which threatens survival, one can say that the resources needed for the reduction of this interference are infinitely large, so that the IRC=0.

The IRC of a system is defined with respect to the interferences confronting it. This implies that a system with a sufficient IRC in one environment may not have a sufficient IRC in another.

The requirement IRC⩾1 resembles Ashby's law of requisite variety, (Ashby, 1956, chapter II). However, these two concepts are not the same. Requisite variety is a property a controller does or does not have, whereas the interference reduction capacity of a system may change in the process of control. For example, a healthy antelope usually has an IRC greater than unity, but a broken leg, sickness or a prolonged period of drought may force its IRC below that value. For industrial organizations one aspect of the IRC can be the solvency of the company, a variable which can also change in the course of time. An IRC below unity means insolvency, hence bankruptcy.

A system usually consumes resources not only to reduce interferences, but also to maintain steady-state operation. Therefore it must continually acquire resources to cover both kinds of costs (with 'costs' we mean any scarce and valued resource needed by the system, thus not only monetary resources). In the following definition we divide the total costs consumed by a system in a given period into two kinds.

Definition 40

Operating costs are the resources consumed by operating a system in a state of equilibrium; *adaptation costs* are the resources spent in maintaining equilibrium. The *relative adaptation costs* are the proportion of the adaptation costs in *total costs,* i.e. operating costs plus adaptation costs.

The difference between the resources acquired in a given period and the operating costs in that period is the *operating result* for that period.

For a viable system the operating result should be at least sufficient to cover the adaptation costs. As soon as this is no longer the case, the IRC of the system starts to decrease; if this continues the system will not survive.

There are two kinds of adaptation costs.

Definition 41

The *transition costs* of a system in a given period are the resources consumed by changing the state of the system; the *disequilibrium costs* in a given period are the resources consumed by being in disequilibrium for some time during that period.

In general, the longer a disequilibrium lasts and the higher the difference between the actual state and the norm state, the higher are the disequilibrium costs.

7.3 Controllability

The interference reduction capacity of a system indicates whether the system is able to maintain its equilibrium in a given environment or not. The IRC can thus be seen as a measure of the *effectiveness* of its control. However, the *efficiency* of control is often also of interest. A measure of this efficiency can be the time average of the adaptation costs of the system or rather the relative adaptation costs: the fraction of adaptation costs in total costs. The higher the relative adapation costs, the harder (or the more expensive) it is for the system to maintain equilibrium; in other words, the higher the relative adaptation costs of a system, the worse its controllability.

Definition 42

The controllability of a system is equal to unity minus the time average of the relative adaptation costs.

The controllability of a system is thus a dimensionless figure between unity and zero. If there are no adaptation costs (no inertia or no interferences), the controllability is equal to unity. If adaptation costs are infinite (it is impossible to reduce certain essential interferences), the controllability of the system is zero.

Note, that our definition of controllability differs from the usual one in control theory, see section 8.1.

The inertia of a system is a 'closed-system property', denoting the capacity of the system for *change*. A high inertia is in itself not a bad quality; one can evaluate this property only with respect to the interferences the system faces. Interference reduction capacity and controllability are 'open-system properties', denoting the systems capacity to *adapt* its behaviour to the interferences it faces.

The inertia of the system-being-controlled determines together with certain properties of the controller (such as the dead time of sensor and selector) the adaptation costs with respect to a given set of interferences. Adaptation costs and operating costs define the controllability of the system. Adaptation costs and operating result determine the interference reduction capacity of the system.

There is often a trade-off between operating costs and adaptation costs: using a more sophisticated controller or a more flexible system-being-controlled may increase the operating costs, but decrease the adaptation costs. There is thus an *optimum* controllability in a given environment, i.e. the controllability, which gives the lowest sum of operating and adaptation costs.

7.4 Interference reduction capacity in industrial networks

The core of an industrial organization is a network of conversion systems connected by physical flows. The control of these flows is a basic issue for industrial organizations.

A thorough study of the dynamics of physical flows has been carried out by Forrester (1961) with the use of simulation techniques. His work shows that the *state* of the physical part of the industrial organization can adequately be described in terms of *levels* and *flow rates*[1]. Following section 7.1, this

---

[1] In his 'Principles of Systems' Forrester states that the levels are sufficient to describe the state of the system, because the rates can be computed from the levels (Forrester, 1968, principle 4.3–8). Although this is true for models described in his simulation language DYNAMO, a fixed relation between levels and rates is not a general property of all industrial systems. In general therefore both levels and rates are needed for describing the state of an industrial system.

system is in equilibrium if and only if all these values lie within the zone of indifference of the controllers of the pertinent values. Now the control of the *physical part* of an industrial organization can be described as a process of interference reduction, i.e. as a *process of maintaining the levels and flow rates of physical flows in equilibrium*.

Viable industrial organizations are not free to define their equilibrium arbitrarily. They should at least maintain an output equilibrium and various resource equilibria.

> Definition 43
> An industrial organization is in *output equilibrium,* if its material output is on the average equal to the demand for this output; it is in *resource equilibrium* if the resources acquired by it are on the average at least equal to the resources consumed.

As the environment of the organization is usually dynamic, both the above equilibria are also dynamic.

The resource equilibria are defined somewhat differently from the output equilibrium, because higher acquisition than consumption of resources (giving an accumulation, to be used e.g. for growth) is in principle admissible, which is not the case for a lasting difference between output and demand.

If the organization acquires its resources on markets (and not through a kind of budgetary process, see section 6.3), the monetary resource equilibrium is crucial for survival. In terms of definition 40, the monetary operating result should be sufficient to cover the adaptation costs of the organization.

Adaptation costs for industrial organizations often involve a high degree of uncertainty. Therefore the operating result should not only be sufficient to cover the current adaptation costs, but also to build up a *reserve* to be used during periods in which the operating result is not sufficient or is even negative. *Ceteris paribus,* the higher the uncertainty in future control costs, the higher this reserve (in fact the interference reduction capacity) should be.

Sometimes other resource-equilibria can become crucial for survival. If the organization has a poor social policy, it may be difficult to maintain the manpower-equilibrium; sometimes specific raw materials can be difficult to obtain.

The preceding discussion dealt with the control of physical flows. These are often in reality not continuous flows (as in the case of e.g. bulk chemicals), but consist of many individual items (as in the car industry or the electronics industry). If one deals with large numbers of indistinguishable items, a description of the system-being-controlled in terms of flow concepts will not give rise to problems. Sometimes, however, the number of items is so low that this is no longer the case. Examples within Philips Industries are electron microscopes, X-ray radiation equipment or radar systems. In analogy with physics one can say that in those cases one is dealing with 'quantum effects'[1]. One quantum effect is an increase in uncertainty: the acquisition or loss of an order for an individual item already has a noticeable effect on the total turnover. Another can be that the products often have to be customized for specific customers. Quantum effects can have a great influence on the demands made on the controller (an example of this is the use of a project organization instead of, or in addition to, a departmentalization, because the latter structure is often inadequate for handling quantum effects). The remainder of the present part will assume, however, that the quantum effects in the physical flows are negligible.

The inertia of an industrial organization is a key variable with respect to the above-mentioned process of interference reduction. As mentioned in section 1.1, this book is especially interested in *complex* industrial organizations, i.e. organizations consisting of suborganizations with a fair degree of independence of control. We will therefore conclude this section with a discussion of some network aspects of the response time and the adaptation costs of a complex industrial organization.

The time a given conversion system needs for reduction of interference is in principle the sum of the times needed for the sensor, selector and effector phases. The properties of the controller determine the first two times, the properties of the technology the third. Because the system is connected with other systems, this third time also depends on the response times of the connected systems (which again need their time for sensor, selector and effector phases).

For instance, the response time of a TV factory to a change in sales volume may consist of the time needed to observe the change, plus the time needed to decide on a new plan and the preparation of a new set-up for one or more assembly lines, plus the set-up and learning times for the actual change of production. Because the factory is connected to supplying factories, one does also need time to acquire materials. Connections with non-conversion systems may be important too. For example, the time needed for development or

---

[1]Quantum effects in physics are effects caused by the fact that matter and energy ultimately consist of particles or 'quanta'. For instance, for extremely low electrical currents or light intensities one may notice with sensitive equipment, that the current or light beam consists of distinct electrons or distinct photons.

engineering to realize changes in the assembly operations or the time needed for decision-making by divisional management may play a role.

The total response time is not the sum of the internal response time and the response times of connected systems, because the various actions are usually executed in parallel: the reduction of the interference is not a *chain* but a *network* of activities; the total response time is the longest path in this network (the 'critical path'). Reduction of the response time of the network may be obtained by various measures, e.g. by automation of information processing, by using sophisticated planning procedures, by stimulating parallization of actions (see the discussion on direct transmission of information in section 9.4), by using buffered connections instead of rigid ones, etc.

The various conversion systems of an industrial organization are connected; they form a *system* of conversion systems. This fact influences not only response times, but usually also the adaptation costs of the whole system, because the reduction of an interference by a system can cause interferences (and hence adaptation costs) to connected systems. Following an idea of De Sitter (1973) we will call this effect transfer of interference.

Definition 44
An interference is *internally reduced* by a system if this interference reduction only involves adaptation costs for the system in question; in so far as the interference reduction by a system leads to adaptation costs for connected systems, the interference is *externally reduced*. External reduction of interference causes *transfer of interference*.

For instance a mechanical breakdown in a picture-tube factory may cause interference in several TV factories, while a sales drive for shavers which was more successful than planned can cause interference in the factory supplying the shavers.

A conversion system often has several alternatives for reducing an interference. For example, the picture-tube factory may try to reduce its interference only internally by using overtime or by purchasing tubes elsewhere. In this way it *absorbs* the interference itself, so that the interference is not propagated throughout the whole network. Usually a combination of internal and external reduction of interferences is applied. In choosing this combination a system can try to minimize its own adaptation costs or minimize the adaptation costs for the whole organization. The promotion of the latter objective is one of the main tasks of coordination (see chapter 12). Note, that there is no conservation law for adaptation costs. For the network as a whole transfer of interference can both increase and decrease the total adaptation costs; one has to find an *optimum* degree of transfer of interference (see chapter 10).

The next three chapters will discuss control problems in which the complexity of the organization (as defined above) plays a major role. A complex industrial organization can be described as a network of conversion systems with *buffered* connections (if the connections are rigid, there can be practically no independence of control).

The discussion will be centered around the question of maintaining the output equilibrium of the network: how is one to control a vast industrial network with a rather high inertia to meet a varying and uncertain demand for its output. Various examples taken from Philips Industries will be used. The analysis will concentrate on level 4 of the hierarchy of Fig. 14: the factories and sales organizations level (at lower levels there is usually less independence of control and higher levels do not show sufficient detail to allow us to understand the phenomena).

8. THE DYNAMICS OF A NETWORK OF DEMAND SERVOS

8.1 Introduction

The maintenance of output-equilibrium by a set of economic systems, or the adaptation of supply to demand, is a subject extensively discussed in economics. To a first approximation, classical theory is not interested in the dynamics of such a process, but in equilibrium states. Because supply is an increasing function of price and demand a decreasing function, price variations and the resulting entering and leaving of the market by customers and suppliers cause equilibrium: if supply exceeds demand, the price goes down, some suppliers leave and some customers enter until equilibrium is reached. If supply is too low, the reverse happens.

A step towards dynamics is the introduction of a time lag between the decision to initiate production and the availability of the commodities. The result is the famous cobweb model, which still deals with equilibrium states, but now different successive states (Ezekiel, 1938). Using Forrester's simulation approach, Meadows (1970) also considers intermediate states. His model is essentially a 'demand servo' (as introduced in section 8.2), but he does not use control theory nor is he able to clarify the basic mechanisms governing the fluctuations his models generate.

Another approach to the study of the dynamics of the equilibrium between supply and demand is the use of macro-economic models at the level of the national economy as a whole (see e.g. Kalecki, 1968). However, it is somewhat difficult to link these models to the behaviour of economic agents. As this latter issue is of interest in this book, a different approach to the maintenance of output equilibrium will be used, viz. control theory.

Control theory has developed a rather impressive set of mathematical tools for the analysis of the behaviour of dynamic systems. However, this chapter will use the results of control theory in a more qualitative way. The present section will discuss some of these results, which will be applied to industrial systems in subsequent sections.

One can distinguish two types of controlled systems (see e.g. Elgerd, 1967, p. 119).

Definition 45

A *servomechanism* is a controlled system, designed so that its output will follow a given 'reference signal' (a certain time function or time series) as closely as possible. A *regulator* is a servomechanism with a constant reference signal.

Section 7.1 introduced the concepts of 'state interference' and 'norm interference'. The reduction of state interferences by industrial systems can be considered as a regulator activity, and the reduction of norm interferences as a servomechanism activity. Maintaining output equilibrium in a changing environment can be described as a servo-mechanism activity, the demand for output forming the reference signal.

We will now discuss some properties of regulators and servomechanisms with reference to a simple example: the thermostat.

Fig. 15 shows a diagram of a thermostat, controlling the temperature of a room. Instead of the usual on-off action the thermostat considered here uses a continuous command signal to control the flow of heat to the room. We will first discuss this device as a regulator.

Fig. 15 shows the classical feedback loop (sensor, selector, effector activities): the temperature T_r of the room is measured and compared with a preset norm T_n. The deviation from the norm $(T_n - T_r)$ is used by the controller to operate a valve in the flow of heat to the room: if T_r is too high, the flow of heat is decreased, while if T_r is too low the heat flow is increased.

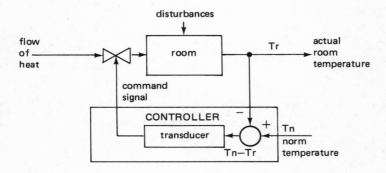

Fig. 15. A thermostat for the control of room temperature T_r.

If the norm T_n is constant, the temperature of the room will be more or less constant. On account of disturbances T_r will show small variations around the equilibrium value T_n[1]. The frequency of these variations depends on the time constants of the control loop and on the capacity of the heater (how fast the latter can raise the temperature). Such variations will be called *autonomous* variations. Their frequency is called the eigen-frequency or resonant frequency f_r of the system[2].

The thermostat can also be driven as a servomechanism; in that case the norm-temperature T_n is no longer constant but a function of time. The behaviour of the room temperature T_r will then depend on the amplitude of the variations in T_n and on their frequency. Very low frequencies, e.g. changes by $1°C$ a day, are simply followed by T_r. Very high frequencies, e.g. an increase and subsequent decrease of T_n by $1°C$ every second, are not followed at all: the system is too 'slow', has too high an inertia, to follow variations of such high frequencies. And medium frequencies, i.e. frequencies in the neighbourhood of the resonant frequency f_r of the system, are found to be amplified: this is the well known phenomenon of *resonance*.

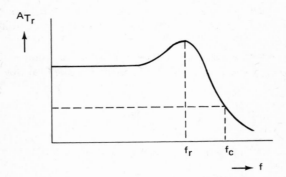

Fig. 16.   The amplitude of the induced variations in room temperature T_r as a function of the frequency f of the inducing variations in norm temperature T_n (the amplitude of the variations in T_n is kept constant).

[1] If there is no dead time in the control loop, it is in principle possible to suppress these variations too by using a more sophisticated control procedure, than that described here.

[2] These variations are not really autonomous, but in fact disturbances with frequencies in the neighbourhood of the resonant frequency of the system, which are amplified by the system. They are called 'autonomous variations' to contrast them with the 'induced variations', to be discussed below.

84

The variations due to variations in the norm-temperature T_n will be called *induced* variations. Fig. 16 shows the amplitude of the induced variations in T_r as a function of the frequency of the variations in T_n. This figure shows that the servomechanism is a 'low-pass filter', i.e. the low frequencies ($f \ll f_r$) are followed and the high frequencies ($f \gg f_r$) are suppressed. An important characteristic of a servomechanism is its 'bandwidth'. In Fig. 16 this is the interval between $f = 0$ and f_c, f_c being the frequency at which the amplitude of the variations induced in T_r begins to fall below a prescribed level. The bandwidth of a servomechanism is a measure of its ability to follow fast changes in the reference signal.

One can define various criteria for assessing the quality of a servo-mechanism. The bandwidth of the system is one example. Other criteria are often based on the response of the system to a step in the reference signal, see e.g. Elgerd (1967, chapter 7).[1] An example of such a response is given in Fig. 17. Common step-response criteria are:
(i) *accuracy* determined e.g. by the time needed to reach the new equilibrium $(t_2 - t_0)$ and by the final value of the error between reference signal and output
(ii) *stability* and the *suppression of disturbances*.

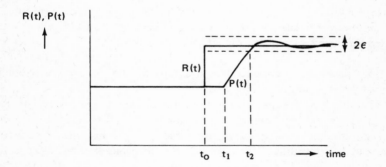

Fig. 17   Response P(t) of a servomechanism to a step in its reference signal R(t). After a dead time $(t_1 - t_0)$, P(t) starts to rise; after the rise time $(t_2 - t_1)$ P(t) reaches the interval $\pm \epsilon$ around the equilibrium value and then remains in this interval; however, it exhibits overshoot and there remains a residual difference between P(t) and the norm R(t).

[1] This set of criteria is chosen because a step is usually easy to realize and because the step response determines the entire system performance if the latter is linear: any reference signal can be described as a series of positive and negative steps and, if the system is linear, its response to such a series can be found by superposition of the responses to individual steps.

With classical control the servo-mechanism is designed to follow a given reference signal as closely as possible. With optimal control it is to maximize a given object function of reference signal and system behaviour.

Accuracy, stability and disturbance suppression are important in the latter case too.

An important factor determining the response of a servomechanism is its *damping*. If the servomechanism is 'overcritically' damped, it does not show overshoot and oscillations as in Fig. 17, but creeps up gradually to its end value; if it is 'undercritically' damped, it does show overshoot and oscillations. These are often undesirable, but on the other hand the response time of an overcritically damped servomechanism is relatively high, giving a poor accuracy.

The response time of the servomechanism of Fig. 17 is the sum of the dead time and the rise time. Not only this sum, but also the dead time and rise time themselves are important, because they have different effects on the behaviour of the system. One often demands a fast, but damped response to variations in the reference signal, i.e. as short as possible a dead time but not too short a rise time. A short rise time is often associated with excessive overshoot and many oscillations, or may even endanger the stability of the system.

In the terms of chapter 7 one can say in many cases, that the time needed for the sensor and selector phases has the effect of a dead time and the time needed for the effector phase, the effect of a rise time.

Control theory pays considerable attention to the concepts of stability, observability and controllability.

The *stability* of industrial organizations is usually, not a very important issue, because the requirements for instability are rather severe and because potential instabilities are soon suppressed by 'non-linearities', such as a shortening of control dead times when crisis situations arise and interventions from higher levels of management or suppliers of (monetary) resources.[1] Undercritical damping may be a problem (as will be shown in section 9.2), but instability in the sense used in control theory is rare.

Observability may be a problem for very large organizations or for the economy as a whole (e.g. for a government trying to damp the business cycle). This concept will, however, not be used here.

---

[1]This remark does not apply to purely technical processes, such as in chemical installations; in such cases the potential instability of the process can indeed be a serious problem.

Controllability in control theory is a property like Ashby's requisite variety: a system is either controllable or it is not. For example, Kwakernaak and Sivan (1972, p. 54) define controllability more or less in the following terms: a system is completely controllable if its state can be transferred from any initial state to any terminal state within a finite time. Defined in this way controllability is a closed system property. However, as Van der Grinten (1968, p. 55) puts it, '...control procedures should always be evaluated against the background of the disturbance properties'. He defines a controllability factor, which is an indicator of the ability to suppress disturbances. Controllability, as defined above in definition 42, therefore resembles Van der Grinten's concept much more than that generally used in control theory.

8.2 The Demand Servo

Servomechanism theory can be applied to industrial organizations, which try to maintain output equilibrium. To this end, we introduce the concept of 'demand servo'. A demand servo is an industrial conversion system applying a special type of interference reduction; thus only a special class of control problems can be considered with the aid of this concept.

Definition 46
A *demand servo* is an industrial conversion system designed so that its material output follows the external potential demand for this output.

Fig. 18 shows a diagram of such a demand servo. The production of the conversion system is eventually sold, but there is a buffer (the production buffer) between production and sales. This buffer can be a stock of finished products or an order portfolio.[1] Sales need not be equal to the potential demand. The latter is determined by demographic factors and the general price level of the goods concerned among other things. Differences between sales and potential demand can be caused e.g. by price variations, the activities of competitors, and lost sales due to increasing delivery times; these effects are described in our model by inserting a buffer between sales and potential demand, the sales buffer.

The control of the demand servo is based on two signals:
(i) the difference between production and potential demand, often simplified in actual production control to the difference between production and

---

[1]The rigid connection between production and sales can be seen as a special case in which the content of the production-buffer is fixed or zero.

sales, because of the unreliability of the available information on potential demand (of course, this simplification can cause problems).

(ii) the difference between the contents of the production buffer and the sales buffer and their desired levels (if information on final demand is insufficient, only the first buffer is explicitly taken into account).

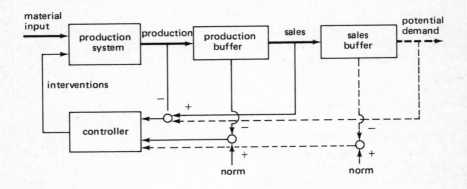

Fig. 18.   A demand servo   ➡ material flow   → information

The adaptation costs of the demand servo consist of transition costs (the costs of changing production, such as set-up costs, costs of hiring and training personnel, etc.) and disequilibrium costs (the costs of excess stocks or lost sales, etc.).

The behaviour of a demand servo can be analysed by making a mathematical model of it and applying the tools of control theory to this model (a simple example of such a model is given below). However, the characteristics of the behaviour of a demand servo can also be given without the use of mathematics.

Because the conversion system has inertia, it will not be able to follow the high-frequency variations in demand or sales; these frequencies are absorbed by the buffers. The low frequencies (low with respect to the resonant frequency of the demand servo) will be followed quite correctly; the final value of the 'error' between sales and production is zero, due to the feedback from the production buffer. The demand servo can be seen as a low-pass filter with a frequency response resembling that of Fig. 16.

As long as there is no dominant frequency in the variations in demand (no seasonal variations, no business cycle, only random variations), the demand servo will exhibit *autonomous* oscillations with frequencies in the neighbourhood of its resonant frequency. This resonant frequency depends on the rise time and the dead time in the step response of the demand servo.

If there *is* a dominant frequency in the variations of demand, the system will also show *induced* variations of the same frequency, the amplitude of the induced variations being determined e.g. by the amplitude of the inducing variations and by the difference between its frequency and the resonant frequency of the demand servo (see Fig. 16). Inducing variations in the neighbourhood of the resonant frequency of the system are amplified: the phenomenon of resonance.

Section 8.3 will give an approximate treatment of the resonant frequencies of demand servos which describe the behaviour of a whole factory. The bandwidth of a factory is usually too small to follow adequately a seasonal variation in demand, but large enough to follow (or even to amplify) a business cycle.

The demand servo is a 'flow concept'. It is especially suited for description of the adaptation of aggregate production to aggregate demand, but not so well for description of adaptation to variations in the composition of demand. Quantum effects can also limit the applicability of this concept.

Control can have objectives other than the maintenance of output equilibrium. One could imagine an optimum control approach, in which the objective is e.g. to maximize profit. However, in complex industrial organizations this may be too difficult. Profit maximization may be pursued by trying to maximize the long-run steady-state operating result, but for actual aggregate production and sales control the maintenance of output equilibrium often receives much more attention than short-run profit maximization (the resource equilibrium being used as a constraint: only a loss situation produces an interference for the controller).

A demand servo approach is only useful if sales is the restricting factor. If the acquisition of a certain resource (such as certain basic chemicals during the oil crisis) is the restricting factor, control activities could be described in terms of a 'resource servo' (designed to follow the supply of the resource in question). However, in a mature economy every demand with sufficient purchasing power is eventually satisfied (until now), thus sellers markets tend to become buyers' markets. In the long run therefore, demand is usually the restricting factor, rendering the demand-servo approach appropriate.

We will now discuss a simple mathematical model of a demand servo by way of illustration. This is a version of the production-smoothing model of Holt et al. (1960), described by Grünwald (1965, 1972) and Van Aken (1970).

The model describes a production unit, producing one kind of products on stock. The model contains no sales buffer. The state of the unit at the end of period t is given by the flow of production P_t in that period and by the stock level I_t at the end of the period. S_t is the flow of sales in period t and I^* is the stock norm (the norm for the content of the production buffer); I^* is constant. The system is in equilibrium if

$$P_t = S_t \text{ and } I_t = I^*$$

The behaviour of the system is described by the changes in the flow of production

$$\Delta P_t = P_{t+1} - P_t \tag{1}$$

and by a continuity equation for the flow of products

$$I_t = I_{t-1} + P_t - S_t \tag{2}$$

ΔP_t is the control variable, which the controller has to choose at the beginning of each period.

Now, P_t has to follow a changing and usually uncertain S_t. As the system has inertia, one has to expend transition costs to change P_t. On the other hand, one incurs disequilibrium costs for deviations of I_t from the norm I^*. The total adaptation costs in period t are given by

$$C_t = C_1 \Delta P_t^2 + C_2 (I^* - I_t)^2 \tag{3}$$

Holt et al. (1960) claim that equation 3 describes the actual costs of aggregate production and inventory control in many cases. Although one may doubt whether this is true, this expression gives a very useful criterion for maintaining output equilibrium. By assigning a more than proportional penalty for large deviations from the equilibrium (both for P_t and I_t), it produces a smooth following of S_t by P_t, without too large variations in the content of the production buffer (such a quadratic criterion is very common in control theory).

The minimization of the sum of the adaptation costs over a large period T, subject to the restriction of the above-mentioned continuity equation and with given sales figures S_t, produces the following *linear control rule* for the demand servo (see e.g. Van Aken, 1970).

$$\Delta P_t = \alpha (I^* - I_t) + \alpha \sum_{\tau=1}^{T} (S_{t+\tau} - P_t) g_\tau, \qquad 0 < \alpha < 1 \tag{4}$$

90

This rule proposes that the change in the flow of production should be equal to a fraction α of the deviation of the stock from its norm $I^* - I_t$, plus the same fraction of the weighted sum of $S_{t+\tau} - P_t$ (the differences between future sales and current production; the weighting factors g_τ are smaller than unity and decrease exponentially: differences far in the future have only a small influence on present changes in production). This control rule is not only optimum with respect to criterion 3 for given future sales S_t; it is the optimum rule too in the case of uncertain future sales if one uses unbiased estimates for S_{t+1}, S_{t+2},... S_{t+T} in equation 4 (the theorem of certainty equivalence, see e.g. Simon, 1956, and Theil, 1957).

The control rule combines feedback with feedforward: the second term of equation 4 produces feedforward on expected sales, while the first one produces feedback on the accumulated difference between production and sales (any difference between P_t and S_t gives a change in the stock level I_t through equation 2, which is subsequently fed back to P_t through this first term of equation 4).

The values of α and g_τ depend only on the ratio C_1/C_2, the *relative* penalty on production-level changes. This ratio, which we will call r^2, determines the *damping* of the response of the demand servo. *Ceteris paribus,* the higher the inertia of the controlled production system, the higher one will choose this *damping factor* r^2. The higher r^2, the lower is α so the slower P_t reacts on changes of S_t and the lower the bandwidth of the demand servo. A procedure for the optimalization of the response of the system is to calculate the adaptation costs for various values of r^2 with the help of a realistic cost function and then to choose the damping factor which gives the lowest adaptation costs, see e.g. De Leeuw and Grünwald, 1971 (this procedure is to be preferred to that of Holt et al. (1960), who try to cast the real costs directly into a quadratic form).

The combination of control rule and continuity equation gives a linear second-order difference equation. This demand servo is thus a second order system, which can easily be analysed with the mathematical tools of control theory. This will, however, not be done here. To give an impression of the behaviour of the system its response to an unpredicted step in sales and to a predicted one is given in Fig. 19 (the figure is taken from Van Aken, 1970).

8.3 Philips Industries as a Network of Demand Servos

Philips Industries as a whole can be seen as a demand servo: one objective of its control is the smooth adaptation of its production to final demand. An

91

indication of its performance as a demand servo is given in Fig. 20. This figure shows the input and output of the production buffer, respectively the production plus purchases and sales (as there is no reliable information on demand for the company as a whole, the sales buffer is not taken into account in Fig. 20).

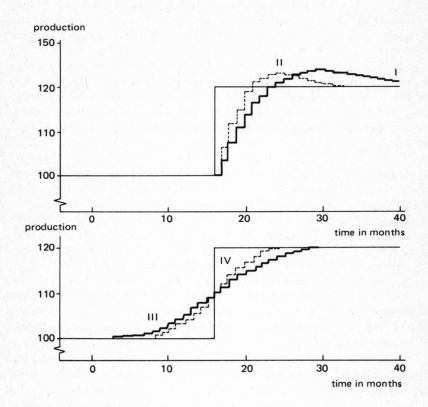

Fig. 19.   The response of a demand servo to an unpredicted step in sales of 20% (curves I and II) and to a predicted one (curves III and IV).
The production is controlled by equation (4); the damping factor r (the square root of C_1/C_2) was about 40 months for curves I and III and about 12 months for curves II and IV.
With an unpredicted step, overshoot is unavoidable:
the temporary excessive production is needed to build up the stocks, which fell below the norm during the period sales exceeded production.

The figure demonstrates that the performance of the company as a demand servo is not very good: the input of the production buffer shows much higher oscillations than the output, which results in strong variations in its content, i.e. in stock levels. Both the variations in stock level and the changes in production level are very expensive, which results in strong variations in company profit (Table 2 of section 3.2, giving the Philips balance sheet, shows that inventories are a very important part of total company assets). The phenomenon of oscillating production plus purchases, which may be called the company's *internal business cycle,* is a serious control problem for the company (Van Aken, 1973). The fact that competing firms are also plagued by an internal business cycle (Polderman, 1971) is only a small consolation.

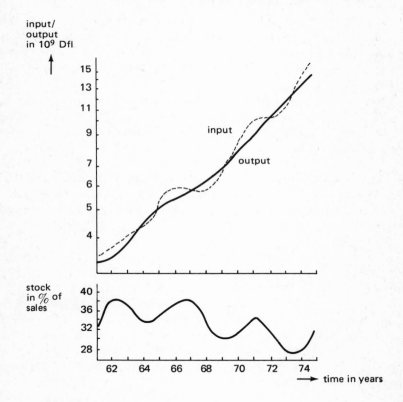

Fig. 20.   Philips Industries as a demand servo.
The top graph gives the moving annual total of the input and output of the production buffer: respectively production plus purchases and sales (both input and output are measured at standard cost-price).
The bottom graph gives the net stock level as a percentage of sales in the preceding year.

Fig. 20 suggests a rather simple control situation: steadily growing sales, so easy to follow by production. This is, however, not the case, due to the following factors among other things:

— the logarithmic scale gives a somewhat distorted picture of the variations in sales; in particular, we do not see the variations in the *growth* of sales, a signal for which the marketing sector (and hence the sales plans) is very sensitive

— the aggregate sales figures do not show the variations in composition of sales, giving adaptation problems which are not visible in Fig. 20 (but on divisional and sub-divisional level the variations in production and purchases are usually higher than the variations in sales too)

— the variations in demand (influencing the reference signal for production planning) are higher than the variations in sales, due to the use of the sales buffer made by the marketing sector (price variations, sales drives, etc. influence the content of this buffer and can have a stabilizing effect on sales)

— last but certainly not least, the company is not one monolithic demand servo (or a system of rigidly coupled demand servos), but a very complex network of demandservos with buffered connections, a system which is difficult to control.

One can analyse the production and sales planning procedures to find the causes of the cyclic behaviour shown in Fig. 20. This will be done in chapter 9. Here a somewhat more abstract approach will be followed, using the demand servo concept.

The company can be seen as a large network of demandservos, each trying to adapt its output to the demand for this output. This demand can come from outside the network or from other demand servos in the network.

Demand servos serving only outside demand will show *autonomous* oscillations if there are only random variations in demand or sales and also *induced* oscillations if there are dominant frequencies in the variations of demand (provided that the bandwidth of the demand servo is large enough to follow these frequencies; as mentioned above, this usually means that seasonal variations do not — or practically not — induce oscillations, but that business cycles *do*).

Demand servos serving internal demand (components and parts for the above-mentioned demand servos), face a quite different demand pattern. Their demand is more or less proportional to the production levels of their customers. This means that the variations in final demand with frequencies higher than the bandwidth of their customers are suppressed, that the low frequencies in final demand are still present in their demand and finally that the medium frequencies (about the resonant frequency of their customers) are amplified. So their demand spectrum has roughly the shape of Fig. 16.

Unfortunately, the amplified variations have frequencies to which also the 'second-echelon' demand servos are most sensitive: their resonant frequency usually does not differ very much from the resonant frequencies of their customers (see below). This means that the medium frequencies are further amplified by the second echelon and transmitted to their suppliers. These give a further amplification of the oscillations and transmit them to the next echelon, and so on. These phenomena are illustrated by the simulation model of section 9.2.

The worst situation is to be found at the end of the production chain, the suppliers of means of production. Not only are they hampered by the above-mentioned amplification effects in various echelons, but they also have a *differential* connection with their customers, instead of the usual proportional one (see section 6.3). As is well known in control theory, this causes amplification of the higher frequencies, in this case the frequencies in the neighbourhood of the resonant frequencies of their customers. The result of this is shown in Fig. 21, which represents the flow of orders to the internal machine works of Philips Industries as a function of time.

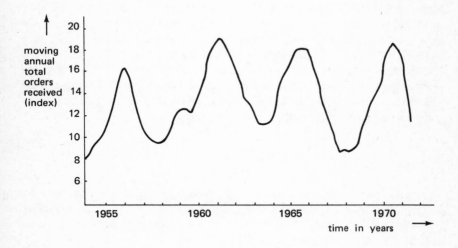

Fig. 21. The orders issued to the Philips Machine Works by the internal customers in index figures (the original measuring unit was the number of processing hours demanded by the orders).

95

The troubled situation of the investment-goods industry has of course already attracted much attention from students of business cycles, hence the – perhaps too strong – emphasis on investment in many business-cycle models.

An important parameter of a demand servo is its resonant frequency. A way of determining this frequency is to make a model of the industrial system concerned and to analyse its behaviour (with analytical methods or by simulation). An estimate of the resonant frequencies of Philips' factories can be obtained from investigations in various Product Divisions, which used the linear control rule discussed in section 8.2 (Grünwald and Smit, 1965; Grünwald, 1972; Braat, 1973; Van Aken et al., 1974; Abels, 1976). In these cases the availability of unskilled or semi-skilled labour determined the production level. The damping factor r (as defined in section 8.2) at factory level was usually some 30 to 60 months (at lower levels of aggregation, viz. capacity group level, the value of r is often roughly a factor three lower). Without a dead time in the response of the factory or variations in the discharge from its production buffer, the resonant periods for these values of r are some 50 to 70 months; dead times decrease these values somewhat (Grünwald, 1973).

The resonant frequency and bandwidth of the machine works are much lower. This is because its production level is determined by the availability of highly skilled labour, which is much more difficult to vary than unskilled or semi-skilled labour. Owing to this small bandwidth, the machine works are not able to follow the variations in their demand, which have a period of 4 to 5 years (see Fig. 21). Its production level thus reacts to these variations more or less in the same way as its customers react to seasonal variations: the production level is kept practically constant and the variations in demand are absorbed by the production buffer (strong variations in delivery times) and to some extent by farming work out to outside suppliers.

8.4 Business Cycles

The cyclic phenomena discussed in the previous section and in chapter 9 are not confined to a few electrical companies, but are present in practically every industrialized economy. The approach of the previous section may thus be used to discuss other situations as well.

The industry of a country can be described as a vast network of demand servos, serving final private and public demand. Final demand shows random fluctuations and possibly seasonal variations, a business cycle and a long-term trend. The output of an industrial sector, trying to follow its final demand, will show variations. There will usually be autonomous variations in the neighbourhood of the resonant frequencies of the demand servos constituting the sector[1] and also induced variations if there are dominant frequencies in the demand spectrum below the bandwidth of the demandservos.

An example of such behaviour is the man-made fibre industry. Langereis (1975) gives the frequency spectrum of the production in this sector for a certain country and compares it with the frequency spectrum of the total industrial production of that country, see Fig. 22. The total production spectrum shows a strong peak at the frequency of the 'normal' business cycle (with a period of about 5 years). The spectrum of the man-made fibre industry, however, shows two peaks: one with the familiar period of 5 years and one with a much shorter period, about 3 years, the so-called 'textile cycle'. The explanation for this phenomenon may be that the 5-year cycle is an induced cycle and the 3-year cycle an autonomous one, determined by the resonant frequency of the demand servos in this sector (a sector, by the way, in which strong variations in the content of production buffers is customary). Such a separation of induced and autonomous variations is not possible for Philips Industries, because its resonant frequency lies close to the frequency of the inducing variations, the general business cycle.

The business cycle discussed in section 8.3 is essentially an inventory-employment cycle, produced by demand servos for which employment determines output. We saw that the resonant frequency of the Philips Machine Works, employing highly skilled labour, was lower than that for a typical Philips assembly factory. On the other hand, the above-mentioned factories of the man-made fibre industry appear to have higher resonant frequencies, which may indicate that their inertia is lower than for Philips factories (perhaps due to the fact that the output level of the former factories is not so closely linked up with the size of the workforce as it is for Philips factories).

Institutional pressures on companies in Western Europe to stabilize employment tend to increase the period of the autonomous inventory-employment cycle (in the terms of the model of section 8.2: C_1 increases, so r^2 increases and hence the resonant frequency of the demand servo decreases). On the other hand, tightening market conditions and high inflationary interest rates increase the disequilibrium costs (inventory costs) and hence tend to compensate the above-mentioned effect on the inventory-employment cycle (in terms of the model of 8.2 : the increase in C_1 may be offset by the increase in C_2, so r^2, and hence the resonant frequency, may not change very much).

---

[1] As mentioned above, such variations are not really autonomous, but are variations in demand, amplified by the system; they form a peak in the production spectrum (see Fig. 22), but not necessarily in the demand spectrum.

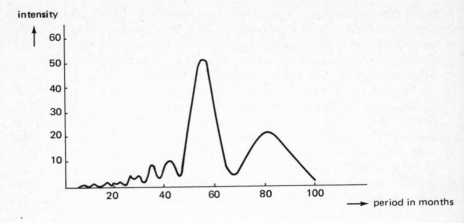

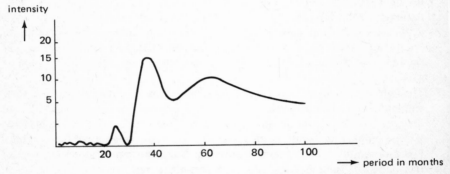

Fig. 22. The spectrum of total industrial production in Western-Germany, top graph, and
of the production of the man-made fibre industry in that country, bottom graph
(after Langereis, 1975).

The time lags for adaptation of capital equipment to changes in demand are
often longer than those for adaptation of employment. If the equipment costs
in a given sector represent a high proportion of total costs, equipment instead
of employment can be the limiting factor for the output of the demand servos
in that sector[1], which may result in a lower resonant frequency. (or perhaps
even in a double cycle: an inventory-cycle having a period of several years and
an equipment-cycle having a much longer period). For example, the transport-
building cycle, which has a period of some 17 years (Isard, 1942), is perhaps an
equipment-cycle.

[1] This is not the case for Philips Industries. Because equipment costs are relatively low, see
Table 3 of section 3.2, one is often somewhat more liberal with capital equipment, than
companies for which equipment is relatively more expensive.

The autonomous variations in the various sectors do not necessarily produce a nation-wide business cycle, even if the resonant frequencies of the majority of the demand servos are of the same order of magnitude. If the *phases* of the cycles in the various sectors were randomly distributed, total industrial production might show only a long-term trend without the 4 to 5 year cycle. Unfortunately, there are various mechanisms which *synchronize* the autonomous cycles in the various sectors. One of these are the connections due to intersector deliveries. Another is government policy (changes in taxes, changes in total expenditure, etc.), which usually has a nation-wide impact on final demand. Once there *is* synchronization (and hence a general business cycle), synchronization is intensified by psychological factors, especially by the attitude of business policy makers towards risk: the general optimism during boom periods promotes in all sectors production increases, whereas during slack times all are hampered by the general pessimism.

As discussed above, a general business cycle can be generated by the synchronized autonomous variations in the various sectors of industry, even without cyclic variations in final demand. In pre-Keynesian times variations in final demand amplified the cycle, because there was a closed loop between final demand and industrial production which gave strong positive feedback. Autonomous variations of production generated variations in employment and hence in consumer income with the very frequencies to which industry is sensitive (its resonant frequency) and practically in phase with the autonomous cycle. The resulting variations in final demand boosted the amplitude of the business cycle. This vicious loop was cut by the social security laws, which stabilized final demand. Nowadays, variations in final demand at the frequencies to which industry is sensitive are rather caused by government policies, trying to control the business cycle; if their timing is poor (see e.g. Post (1973) for the Dutch case), such policies of course only increase the amplitude of the business cycle.

Different rise and dead times of the demand servos in a country produce different autonomous variations in industrial production. It seems that many of them have resonant periods of 4 to 5 years. As mentioned above, it is also possible that the frequency response of (some) demand servos has two or more peaks instead of one as in Fig. 16, for example one for an inventory-employment cycle and one for a capacity expansion cycle (see e.g. Forrester, 1976, on these two types of cycles).

Following earlier writers, Schumpeter (1939) proposes a three-cycle scheme: the Kitchin cycle (period 3-4 years), the Juglar cycle (period 10 years) and the Kondratiev cycle (period 60 years). The first could be the above-mentioned inventory-employment cycle and the second a capacity expansion cycle[1]. If the Kondratiev cycle exists[2], it may be caused by the introduction of fundamentally new technologies and the subsequent satiation of the economy by them (see e.g. Freeman, 1977). If that were true, the first Kondratiev cycle was caused by the steam engine, the second by the railroads, the third by the electrical and automotive technologies and the present-day fourth Kondratiev by electronic and data-processing technologies. It is not the discovery itself, but its introduction and subsequent full exploitation, needing an entire new generation of highly skilled workers *both* on the supply side and on the demand side (creating positive feedback from demand to supply), that would cause the Kondratiev cycle. In that case the long period of this cycle may be explained by the relatively large time constants involved in the creation of such a new generation of highly skilled workers and in the creation of employment for them. The period of the Kondratiev cycle may even increase because of some present-day tendencies which hamper the functioning of the labour market (such as a lack of incentives for occupational resettlement and labour union pressures against displacement of employment).

The discussions on the Kitchin, Juglar and Kondratiev cycles are usually confined to the age of industrialization. However, cyclic behaviour is perhaps fundamental to society. In this connection one may mention the long established tradition in classical Chinese thought (going back at least 2000 years), which explained many phenomena from medical ones to political economy, in terms of cyclic behaviour. One of their major cycles has a period of 60 years (Porkert, 1974).

[1] Schumpeter attributes all three cycles to the introduction of technological innovations.

[2] In a thorough study Weinstock (1964) concludes that its existence is still not sufficiently proven and that its generating mechanism is still unclear. Nevertheless, its possible existence still attracts the attention of many students of economic activity.

9 THE DYNAMICS OF A NETWORK OF PRODUCTION SYSTEMS

9.1 The Generation of Cyclic Behaviour

Section 8.3 discussed the maintenance of output equilibrium in Philips Industries in the 'frequency domain'. The present chapter will discuss the same issue in the 'time domain': instead of treating the sensitivity of the system to various frequencies in the demand process, the effects of changes in demand or sales on the variation of production and inventory with time will be studied. The central problem is again the internal business cycle discussed in section 8.3, i.e. the generation of cyclic behaviour as illustrated in Fig. 20. The analysis will again be confined to the level of the factories and the sales organizations: a network of conversion systems with buffered connections.

Capital investment plays only a minor role in the cycles of Fig. 20, so only inventory-employment questions will be dealt with.

Every conversion system of the network tries to follow with its output the perceived demand for this output. Information on demand is obtained by the units own efforts, from customers within the organization and/or from non-conversion systems such as planning departments and market research departments. The control of the output of a conversion system (and of the input needed to produce this output) can be described as being a function of the deviations of levels and flows from their desired values.

The changes in the volume of the production P of a factory can be described by

$$\Delta P = f_1 (I^* - I) + f_2 (S^* - P) \tag{5}$$

This means that the change in production is a function f_1 of the deviation of the inventory level I from its norm plus a function f_2 of the deviation of the flow of production from the estimated flow of sales (the planned sales S^*). An example of the functions f_1 and f_2 is given by equation 4 of section 8.2, but other, e.g. non-linear responses of P to deviations from the norm are of course also feasible. The norms I^* and S^* may change with time. S^* is a function of demand (insofar as demand is known) and of actual sales S (i.e. that part of demand that is satisfied). An example of S^* as a function of S is the exponential smoothing equation of the next section (equations 7 and 9), but again various other functions are also possible.

Variations in demand and/or sales induce variations in the planned sales S* and consequently in production P via the production control equation 5 (as long as these variations have frequencies below the bandwidth of the production and supply system in question). As discussed in the previous chapter, there will also be autonomous variations in production, even if there are no dominant frequencies in demand, because the inertia of production prevents an instantaneous adaptation of supply to demand.

Now we can discuss in more detail the role of the buffers in the network, especially the production buffers. The production buffer of each production system amplifies the variations in the production of the system through three mechanisms, while in the lower-echelon production systems further amplification takes place through three types of 'chain effects'.

The three amplification mechanisms are:

(i) Dead times in sensor and selector activities (decision-making in complex organizations can take much time, see e.g. chapter 10) often make production changes to lag behind changes in sales. Such lags cause the inventory to deviate from its norm. The production will thus have to be made temporarily too high or too low to compensate for this, so the changes in P will in the short run have to be greater than those in S (the overshoot effect, discussed in connection with Fig. 19 above).

(ii) Further amplification takes place if one uses dynamic stock norms, as is usual. In that case I* is a function of S or S*, e.g. the following linear relation (with k as a dimensionless constant).

$$I^* = k.S^* \tag{6}$$

This relation gives rise to positive feedback from S to P: the temporary overshoot of P has to be even greater than indicated under (i) above, because I* has been increased (or decreased if the change in S* was negative).

(iii) Finally, the constant k may also be dynamic and subsequently cause further amplification. If there is a business cycle of some magnitude, delivery times tend to become longer and less reliable in boom periods and shorter and more reliable in slack times. Each unit thus has a tendency to increase its safety stocks in boom periods and to decrease them in slack times. This intensifies the positive feedback from S to P via I*: if S increases, I* increases not only because S* increases but also because k increases (if S decreases, the reverse takes place).

In a network of conversion systems further amplification takes place through three types of 'chain effects':

(i) the *pipeline effect*: as discussed above, the cyclic behaviour of a factory is amplified by variations in the content of its production buffer. Now further amplification takes place if two demand servos have a buffered connection: the production of the second one suffers not only from the amplification by its own production buffers but also from amplification by the production buffers of its customers. Lower echelon factories thus suffer from variations in the content of the entire pipeline between them and final demand.

(ii) the *distortion effect*: the reference signal which lower-echelon factories use for their production control is in principle the demand from their direct customers. However, this demand is a distorted representation of the final demand because of the pipeline effect: besides changes in final demand it contains a temporary component, viz. the demand caused by a desired variation in inventories higher up along the pipeline. If lower-echelon units are not able to separate these two components, as is often the case, they misread changes in their total demand as being due to changes in final demand; they thus tend to set their production level continuously too high in boom periods and too low in slack times.

(iii) the *peristaltic effect*: information on variations in final demand are not transmitted directly through the whole network, but step by step by each echelon; this process can be compared with the peristaltic movement of the gullet, transmitting food or drink to the stomach. Owing to this peristaltic transmission of information, it can take a very long time before the lowest echelons get to know about variations in final demand. Because of this long time lag, total pipeline inventory deviates strongly from its norm, so the production changes in the lower echelons have to be greater than they otherwise would.

It should be noted, that the first chain-effect mentioned above is a 'real' one, (lower echelons *do* have to compensate for variations in the content of the pipeline in one way or another), while the last two are 'control effects', which can in principle be eliminated (see section 9.4).

Chain effects can occur in any compound system with buffered connections. An example is a column of trucks. Random variations in the speed of the first truck are amplified throughout the column, because each driver reacts only after some dead time to a deviation of his buffer (the inter-truck distance) from its norm. So each driver has to correct his speed more than his predecessor to compensate for the varying inter-truck distance. The distortion effect here is the fact that a driver cannot discriminate between the acceleration of his predecessor in order to decrease his inter-truck distance from an acceleration of the whole column: in the first case he can take his time in responding because his predecessor's action is only temporary, while in the second case he should respond as soon as possible. One can see that the pipeline effect and the peristaltic effect are also present in this example.

Finally, there are also intentional and unintentional majorating effects, which amplify the internal cycle of the network further. In boom periods suppliers cannot always follow their increasing demand quickly enough, so they cut their deliveries (usually distributing the cuts more or less proportionately over the various customers). To safeguard themselves against such cuts, customers tend to order more than they need (and their needs were already higher than the final demand), thus causing further amplification. They can safely do so, because in boom periods a possible full delivery of the excessive quantities ordered does not matter so much. On the other hand, in slack times customers tend to order less than they need, because it is possible that the quantities needed at the time of delivery are still lower than expected (and again they can safely do this, because the now high stock levels of their suppliers make it possible to obtain extra quantities if the orders were indeed too low). In addition to these intentional majorating effects, there are also unintentional majorating effects caused by different attitudes towards uncertainty: in boom periods the sales plans (and consequently all other activity plans) tend to overestimate future demand and in slack times to underestimate it.

9.2 A Simulation Model

A simple simulation model of a chain of factories has been developed to study the generation of cyclic behaviour (Van Aken, 1971). The objective was to get some qualitative insight into the dynamics of compound industrial systems and their sensitivity to various parameters. The model was not intended as a tool to generate solutions for specific control problems (as e.g. Forrester's industrial dynamics models). We therefore modelled not a specific situation, but a rather general system of factories connected by flows of products.

As the purpose was to study inventory-employment problems, the model is essentially a multi-echelon production smoothing model.[1] The adaptation of the production volume of the system to changes in final demand are studied; variations in the composition of demand and production are not taken into account.

Unless expansion of capital equipment is needed, the production level of a factory is determined by its work force. Changes in the work force of an entire factory have to be smooth: sharp increases give many control problems and usually a considerable loss of efficiency, whereas decreases are – at least in Western Europe – hardly ever allowed to exceed natural turnover. The linear control rule of section 8.2 is well suited to describe such situations, so the core of the model consists of a set of such rules.

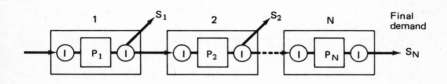

Fig. 23   A model of a chain of factories.
Apart from the first one, each factory needs components from the preceding one for its production. Each factory holds a stock of these components and also of its own end product. Components are not only supplied to the next factory in the chain, but also to outside customers.

Fig. 23 shows the basic structure of the model. It consists of a chain of identical factories, each producing one kind of products on stock. The control of each factory consists of three elements: sales planning, production-level control (which together with sales planning also furnishes the inventory control for its own end products) and the inventory control for the components it needs. Control rules and parameters are the same for all factories. Further, there are of course many operational activities in the model, such as the issuing of

---

[1] A survey of multi-echelon inventory models is given by Clark (1972) and of production smoothing models by Silver (1972). Combinations are rare. One might consider the work of Burns (1970) as an example; although he discusses essentially only an inventory pipeline, he uses a linear control rule (containing only the inventory term of equation 4 of Section 8.2) for inventory control, which produces behaviour with some resemblance to that discussed here.

orders, and the shipment and reception of goods. Although a 4-month planning cycle for production-level control is customary in Philips Industries, there are so many changes during the planning period, that actual control is better described in terms of a monthly cycle. This monthly cycle was simulated on a computer.[1]

Exponential smoothing was used to model sales planning (Brown, 1963). With single exponential smoothing the sales plan for month t+1, as determined at the start of that month, is

$$S^*_{t+1} = S_t^* + \beta_1 (S_t - S_t^*), \quad 0 < \beta_1 \leqslant 1 \tag{7}$$

The sales plan is equal to the previous plan plus a damped response to the forecast error. A trend correction is often used. In that case the correction R_{t+1} follows from the previous correction R_t and the S_{t+1} and S_t^* from equation 7:

$$R_{t+1} = R_t + \beta_2 (S^*_{t+1} - S^*_t - R_t), \quad 0 < \beta_2 \leqslant 1 \tag{8}$$

With this correction, the sales plan for month t+τ made at the start of month t is:

$$S^*_{t+\tau} = S^*_{t+1} + \left(\frac{1-\beta_1}{\beta_1} + \tau \right) R_{t+1}, \quad \tau = 1,2, \ldots \tag{9}$$

The trend correction can be suppressed by putting β_2 equal to zero. All the sales plans are recalculated every month. S_t is the sum of the internal and external orders received. If these orders exceed the stock of end products of a factory, the excess is put in a backlog and delivered as soon as possible in one of the next months.

Production-level control is simulated with a version of the linear control rule of section 8.2 (equation 4). The inventory norm I* is variable; equation 6 of section 9.1 is used to calculate it. In this case, therefore, the linear control rule also contains a term through which the production also anticipates changes in inventory due to predicted changes in the norm (see Van Aken, 1970). There is a dead time T_c between the moment of decision-making with respect to the production level and the implementation of the change in this level.

---

[1] A Philips P1400 computer was used, together with a graphical display terminal. The parameters for a simulation run were fed into the computer via this terminal and the results could be studied on the display after a short time interval.

Finally, a very simple rule is used for the control of the stocks of components: each factory tries to keep its stock level at k times its need for the next month (in the simulations the value of k for the inventory norm for components was the same as for end products). If the need for components is A times P_{t+1} and if the inventory level of components at the start of the period is I_t^c, the orders to the next factory are:

$$O_{t+1} = \text{Max } (0, k.A.P_{t+1} - I_t^c) \tag{10}$$

The model describes the *results* of planning, not the planning process itself (as the Forrester models usually intend to do). Exponential smoothing and the linear control rule are used not because decision-makers within Philips Industries predominantly use these rules, but because they give a fair description of the *results* of complex (political) decision processes: if sales increase, the sales plans will eventually increase too (with a certain speed of response, which can be varied by varying β_1 and β_2); if sales plans increase and/or if stocks decrease, the production plans will eventually increase too (again with a certain speed of response which can be varied by varying the value of r^2 used in the linear control rule).

The model contains various potential non-linearities (such as production stops due to lack of components and non-negativity constraints for production, stocks and plans). As long as these non-linearities do not occur, the system is linear and can also be studied using analytical methods instead of simulation. This has been done for a somewhat simpler version of the model by Grünwald (1973).

9.3 Simulation Results

The behaviour of the system described in the previous section can be studied for various patterns of final demand and various settings of the control parameters. Table 4 gives a survey of the usual setting, which is fairly typical for many Philips situations (with the exception perhaps of the chain length, which is more often 4 than 5).

N = 5	chain length
k = 3	constant for inventory norm
$\beta_1 = 0.2; \beta_2 = 0.1$	smoothing constants for sales planning
$T_c = 3$	dead time for production-level control in months
r = 40	damping constant for production-level control in months

Table 4 The 'standard' setting of the parameters of the chain model.

In the case that final demand shows random fluctuations around a constant level (having a uniform distribution and an amplitude of 10% of the mean), the behaviour of the first and last factory is shown in Fig. 24 (the parameter setting is as in Table 4). Two inferences can be drawn from this figure:

(i) Without any dominant cyclic component in final demand, the system shows strong cyclic behaviour: the autonomous internal business cycle. The causes for this have been discussed in section 8.3 in the frequency domain and in section 9.1 in the time domain

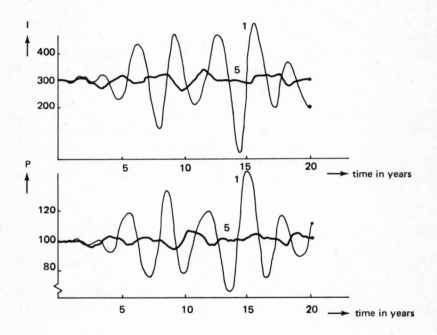

Fig. 24.   The behaviour of the chain model when the final demand shows random fluctuations around a constant level.
Factory 5 faces final demand, factory 1 is at the beginning of the production chain. For t = o the system is in equilibrium:
$P_i = S_t^* = 100$ and $I_i = I_i^* = 300$ for $i = 1,2, ..., 5$

108

(ii) The autonomous internal business cycle arises despite optimum local control. No mistaken or suboptimum behaviour is built into the model, each factory reacts optimally to its environment. It is the combination of the local optimalizations that gives the poor overall behaviour. The major cause for this is the distortion of the reference signals for local control (S* and I*) by chain effects.

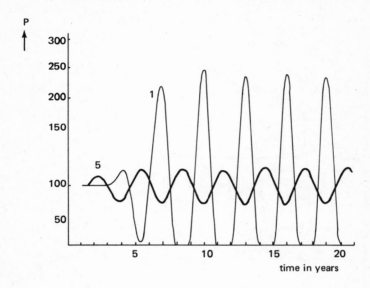

Fig. 25. The response of the production of factory 1 and factory 5 to a sinusoidal variation in final demand for factory 5. The period of the sinewave was 3 years, its amplitude was 10% and the parameter setting according to Table 4. It may be seen that the variations for factory 5 are so large that this factory has to be shut down from time to time.

As was to be expected, the system is very sensitive to variations in final demand, which lie near the resonant frequency of its subsystems. Fig. 25 shows the response of the system to a pure sinusoidal variation in final demand with a frequency near the resonant frequency of the individual factories.

In order to gain more insight into the behaviour of our system, we studied its response to a constant sales level with only once a deviation of 5% from this level (the pulse response of the system). The production of the first and last factories in the chain for the standard values of the parameters is shown in Fig. 26. The system is stable (equilibrium is reached eventually), but shows strong undercritical damping. There were no non-linearities in this case.

The pulse response will be used to investigate the influence of various parameters. The maximum value of the production of the first factory P_{max} for a pulse of 5% in final demand will be used as reference (in the standard situation shown in Fig. 26, P_{max} is 10% of the equilibrium value of P).

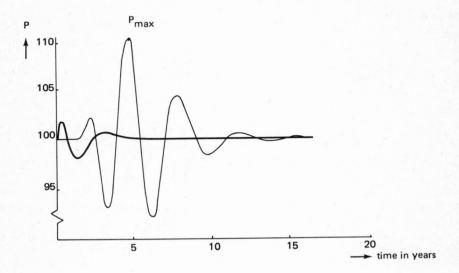

Fig. 26   The response of the production of factory 1 and 5 to an unpredicted pulse in sales in month 1 for factory 5.

Of course, increasing chain length increases the amplitude of the variations in production of the factories with the greatest distance to final demand. Fig. 27 shows P_{max} as a function of chain length N; for $N \geqslant 7$ the fluctuations in production are so high that the last factories have to be shut down from time to time (in order not to violate the non-negativity constraint on P).

Increasing the dead time of production-level control gives an increase in P_{max} too, see Fig. 27.

One of the main causes of cyclic behaviour suggested in section 9.1 was the variation in the content of the production buffers of the various units. It is therefore not surprising that P_{max} depends strongly on the stock norm constant k, as is shown in Fig. 27. The higher the value of k, the higher the positive feedback from S to P and the more underdampened the whole system is.

110

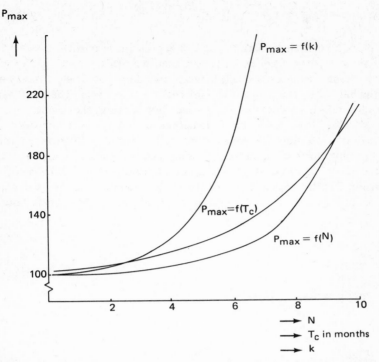

Fig. 27.   The influence of chain length N, production-control dead time T_c and inventory norm constant k on the maximum value P_{max} of the pulse response of the first factory in the chain.

Fig. 28 shows the dependence of P_{max} on r^2, the damping factor for the response of each individual factory. The higher this damping factor, the lower is P_{max} i.e. the less is the underdamping of the whole system. Of course the factor r^2 also influences the frequencies of the fluctuations in production. This is shown in Fig. 29.

The influence of β_1 and β_2 is not shown. Between 0.2 and 0.8 the influence of β_1 is weak; P_{max} drops sharply for $\beta_1 < 0.2$, above 0.8 it shows a strong increase. The dependence of P_{max} on β_2 is strong: the higher β_2, the stronger the variations in production and stocks.

These simulation results have given some insight into the behaviour of compound industrial systems and provide some support for the verbal reasoning of sections 8.3 and 9.1. The model has sharpened our intuition and to some extent enabled us to understand formerly counter-intuitive behaviour of industrial systems.

111

9.4 The Damping of Cyclic Behaviour

For production systems with inertia it is in principle impossible to avoid cyclic behaviour, if they face an uncertain demand. This is not serious if the amplitude of the cycles is small; if the amplitude is not small, it is very much worthwhile to try to dampen the internal business cycle. There are various measures, which can be used to this end. For instance, shortening the sensor and selector dead times by automation of information processing and sophisticated planning procedures can help (see Fig. 27). Decreasing the total pipeline inventory by improved ordering and scheduling procedures and a limited use of dynamic stock norms also improves the overall behaviour (see again Fig. 27). Increasing the damping of the response of factories to changes in sales (a higher r^2, see Fig. 28) in principle also improves the behaviour, but

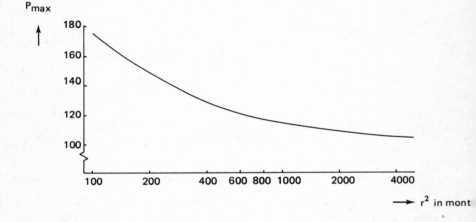

Fig. 28. P_{max} as function of the damping factor r^2 of the response of each factory.

this is an example which shows that the damping of the internal business cycle cannot be isolated from other control problems: a higher damping may mean a lower accuracy of the system as a demand servo and hence higher and perhaps unacceptable disequilibrium costs (such as a loss of market share, which can have far-reaching consequences). Therefore an *optimum* value of r^2 must be chosen.

112

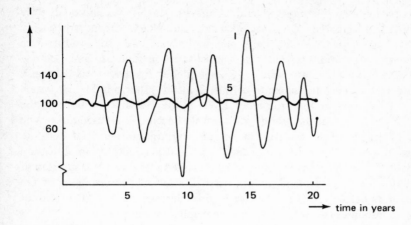

Fig. 29. The response of the stocks of the first factory to random fluctuations in final demand when r has the improbable low value of 17 months (cf. the top graph of Fig. 24, for which r = 40 months). A lower damping gives higher frequencies (and also higher amplitudes) in the variations of production and stock levels.

A more fundamental way of improving the overall behaviour of the system is the removal of the distortion of the local reference signals S* and I* which is caused by chain effects. If the lower-echelon factories base their production

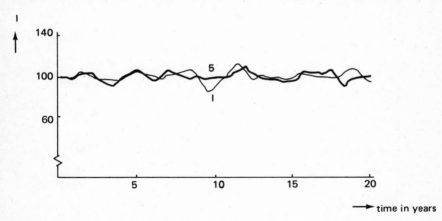

Fig. 30. The effect of direct transmission of information on finald demand.
The response of the stocks of the first and last factory on random fluctuations in final demand is shown for the system of Fig. 24, but now with a direct transmission of information on final demand, whereas for Fig. 24 only local information on demand was used for production control.

113

control not only on the orders from their direct customers but also on directly transmitted information on final demand, the chain effects are largely eliminated: the pipeline effect is still present, but not nearly so harmful if one can discriminate inventory changes from changes in final demand (see e.g. Magee, 1958, who uses essentially the same idea in his 'base stock system'). The effect of a direct transmission of final demand is shown in Fig. 30, which plots as a function of time the stock levels in the first and last units of the chain for the case, that the production control of each unit is based not on the orders of its direct customers but on directly transmitted final demand. Because this removes the distortion and the peristaltic effect, the amplification of variations is eliminated. It may also be remarked that direct transmission of information on final demand gives a parallelization of the responses of the various units of the chain to changes in final demand instead of a series of successive responses (see section 7.4 on the parallelization of responses).

Direct transmission of information on final demand in complex industrial organizations is more easily said than done. Therefore, we will discuss in chapter 16 the PROSPECT project, which developed a design for such a procedure for one of the Product Divisions of Philips Industries.

10. THE DYNAMICS OF A NETWORK OF SOCIAL SYSTEMS

10.1 Transfer of Interference

The previous chapters gave a rather dispassionate and sometimes rather abstract description of variations in production and sales levels: each conversion system simply tries to follow its demand and, after some amplification of variations, it transmits this demand to the conversion systems which supply it and which in their turn behave in the same way.

The conversion systems were described as demand servos. Such a description gives some insight in the dynamics of an industrial network but it is a rather mechanistic approach to control. Industrial conversion systems can also be described as groups of people exploiting a technology or, in the terms of chapter 5, as occupied compound positions. Now the amplification of variations in production and sales levels causes serious intra-organizational stress and conflict, so the interactions between the conversion systems are not so cool and automatic as the preceding discussion might suggest. Some social aspects of these interactions can be described by using De Sitter's concept of transfer of interference, as introduced in section 7.4.

An interference generated somewhere in a compound system consisting of rigid subsystems with rigid connections, will be propagated throughout the whole system. In this case transfer of interference is an automatic process. For social systems, however, the situation is in general quite different. There are often buffered connections between the subsystems, which have drawbacks (as was seen in section 9.1) but which also have the capacity to absorb interference (to some extent). Furthermore, social systems may be able to use (to some extent) internal reduction of interference, which gives a further absorption. Transfer of interference in social systems is therefore not an automatic process but to some extent a matter of *choice*.

The possible absorption of interference is extremely important for large organizations. Among other things it is this capacity that makes departmentalization worthwhile. Thompson (1967) states that organizations tend to protect their technical cores by establishing 'boundary spanning units'; this means that the latter units have the mission of absorbing many of the external disturbances in order to ensure undisturbed and hence efficient operation of the technical core.

This argument can be extended to every compound position in an organization. In general such a subsystem (department, division, etc) is established to perform a certain task, which is of importance for the organization. This means that subsystem control has to protect the execution of this task against interference, *be it externally generated interference or interference from inside the organization* (if the protection of this task was unimportant, it would not have been necessary to establish a *separate* subsystem to perform it). So each subsystem will try to use its power over its (intra- or extra-organizational) environment on the one hand to protect itself against transfer of interference and on the other hand to obtain external reduction of interference (to the extent that this can decrease its own adaptation costs).

From the viewpoint of the organization as a whole there will in general exist an *optimum degree of transfer of interference*. Full absorption of external interferences by the boundary spanning functions of a subsystem means that its technical core never adapts its operations, which is clearly impossible and undesirable if the organization operates in a dynamic environment. On the other hand, full transfer of interference harms the efficiency of the technical core of the subsystem. To find the optimum compromise between these two extremes in a complex organization, however, is extremely difficult. One reason is the fact that the trade-off's between internal and external reduction are usually unclear. The transfer of interference in complex organizations thus poses a true dilemma; using a classical figure of speech, it may be called the *pars pro toto dilemma*. On the one hand an organizational subsystem has to protect its own technical core (it should serve the 'pars'); on the other it should serve the organization as a whole because its task is not an end in itself (it should operate 'pro toto'). As long as the trade-off's between the protection of the 'pars' respectively of the 'totum' are unclear, each subsystem may defend its own interests by equating them with the interests of the organization as a whole (like 'what is good for General Motors is good for the country').[1]

The discussions around transfer of interference within an organization are the more difficult, because the actors often have a tendency to identify themselves with the subsystem they belong to and because their personal interests may coincide with subsystem interests.

[1] In the literature on organizations the problems associated with the pars pro toto dilemma are often referred to as the problem of *suboptimalization*. We will not use this term, because it suggests that the suborganizations pursue the wrong objectives and should know better, whereas we feel that in many cases these problems pose true dilemmas.

Of course it is one of the objectives of coordination to overcome the 'pars pro toto dilemma' as well as is possible (see chapter 12). Intra-organizational conflict generally takes place in a 'triangular setting', consisting of the two conflicting subsystems and a coordinator. The coordinator usually has some degree of power over the coordinated subsystems and can use this power to settle the conflict.

However, in complex and turbulent situations the control of many intra-organizational interactions has to be left to the selfcontrol of the subsystems concerned. Bargaining processes and the use of power thus play an important role in the transfer of interference. The power of coordinators is predominantly based on the official control structure, while the power relations between subsystems are more based on the technological structure, depending on the centrality and the substitutibility of the inputs to one another (see section 5.4 and 5.5).

The organizational control system (in particular the accounting system and the reward system) also effects the 'pars pro toto dilemma'. In theory, the accounting system should be able to show (some of) the trade-off's between internal and external reduction of interference, while the reward system should motivate the actors to act 'pro toto'. Unfortunately organizational reward systems tend to judge the performance of an organizational subsystem more in local than in global terms, i.e. more in terms of the (financial) results of the subsystem itself (according to the accounting system), than in terms of its contribution to the rest of the organization (one reason being that the latter results are often much more difficult to assess than the former).

Section 10.3 will discuss some examples of transfer of interference within Philips Industries to give an impression of the problems the organizational control system (to be discussed in part IV of this book) has to solve. This section is based on 'participative observations', made in the course of the BIC projects (see section 1.2). It should thus be borne in mind that the argument may suffer from selective perception and selective retention. To prepare for this discussion, the next section will mention some of the major intra-organizational interfaces, across which transfer of interference can take place in Philips Industries.

10.2 Some intra-organizational interfaces of Philips Industries

The control of sales, production and acquisition by the Product Divisions of Philips Industries is usually executed in a series of negotiations, during which the following intra-organizational interfaces are crossed in succession:

(i) *Sales organizations – end-product factories*

There is usually no direct contact between these two types of organizations; first the sales organizations negotiate with Divisional Headquarters (in which Divisional Management, Divisional Sales Department and Divisional Planning Department play the main role) and then Divisional Headquarters (in particular the Divisional Planning Department) negotiate with the factories in question. An iterative procedure between these two types of negotiations is sometimes necessary.

(ii) *End-product factories – components factories*

The component factories may either be in the same Product Division as their customers or in another. Most of the latter cases are found in the ELCOMA Division, (see Table 1) but the internal Machine Works also belongs to this category. In the case of aggregate production planning, the negotiating parties are the factories concerned and the Divisional Planning Department (sometimes also Divisional Management). Ordering is often performed via direct contacts between the factories concerned.

(iii) *Factories and other organizations – resource acquisition departments*

Manpower acquisition is predominantly a local affair. This means that the factories usually do it themselves; in areas, however, where there are several company organizations (as in Eindhoven), manpower acquisition is often centralized. The acquisition of material resources is in general performed at the factory level, but there is a corporate purchase department to support such activities. The acquisition of capital is almost exclusively performed by the corporate finance department (of course under close supervision of the corporate management).

10.3 Examples of transfer of interference

If there are strong cyclic variations in sales and production, the transfer of interference across the boundary between sales organizations and the rest of a Product Division depends on the phase of the cycle. If demand exceeds production capacity, the sales organizations tend to protect themselves against cuts in deliveries by majorating their sales plans or the orders to Divisional Headquarters (intentional or unintentional, see section 9.1) and by using their power in the negotiations with Divisional Headquarters (sources of power are size and profitability). Because of the parallel connections between the sales organizations, such actions cause transfer of interference among these organizations.

If production capacity exceeds sales, Divisional Headquarters may on the one hand try to induce the sales organizations to increase their sales and on the other to obtain an optimum distribution of production decreases (optimum from a divisional standpoint).

A sales drive (additional sales promotion, price cuts, etc.) often only influences the content of the sales buffer: it shifts some demand forward in time, but does not create new demand. In the case of too low sales levels, this can nevertheless be important for the Production Division, which thus gains some time to adapt its production level to the sales level. However, this internal reduction by the sales organizations of the interferences caused by disappointing sales is expensive for them, so they are reluctant to use it. They are the more reluctant, because these problems arise in slack times, which are the very periods in which the sales organizations are under pressure from corporate management to maintain profit levels.

The actions of Divisional Headquarters in the other direction (the end-product factories) also meet opposition. Production decreases confront the factories concerned with serious problems, so such questions often have to be resolved in a difficult bargaining process between Divisional Management and the National Organization Managements concerned. The triangular setting in this case is completed by the corporate management, but the latter is rather reluctant to play the role of arbiter regularly in such conflicts (see also the discussion on internal international relations in section 3.4). The result of the bargaining process may thus be a compromise, which is not always optimum from a corporate standpoint (another important consequence of such bargaining processes can be a considerable increase in the dead time between the occurence of the interference and its reduction, which amplifies the variations in production levels, see chapter 9).

As already mentioned in section 3.2, most Product Divisions have a dual management: they have a commercial and a technical manager. One of the consequences of this is that the benefits of the triangular setting of conflicts between commercial and technical subsystems are not fully reaped: the very conflict in which the coordinating subsystem should arbitrate is also operative *within* this subsystem.

The core of the conflict between the commercial and technical sectors (consisting of the sales organizations and commercial oriented divisional departments on the one hand and of the factories and technically oriented divisional departments on the other) is the question of who has to bear the burden of entrepreneurial uncertainty, or in other words, how much of the interference from the market should be internally reduced by the commercial sector (by e.g. sales drives and variations in the stocks of end products) and how much should be transferred to the technical sector (to be reduced by adaptation of production).

119

The internal reduction of interference by the commercial sector costs money. Furthermore, the commercial sector is not too happy about using marketing instruments to adapt sales to production; they would prefer to use them to promote commercial objectives, which are expressed in terms of growth of turnover, market share and profit rather than in terms of output equilibrium. The commercial sector will thus often try to transfer interferences from the market to the technical sector.

On the other hand, adaptation of production can be painful to implement and tends to decrease efficiency, while the technical sector is already under constant pressure from the same commercial sector to increase efficiency so that the company can stand up to intercontinental competition.

Another way of describing the conflict between the commercial and technical sectors was mentioned in section 9.4, during the discussion of the damping factor r: the technical sector wants a high value of r to stabilize employment and maintain efficiency, whereas the commercial sector wants a low value, so that it can follow changes in demand quickly. These conflicts constitute a good example of the 'pars pro toto dilemma': both parties pursue their own objectives, which are in some way connected with overall objectives, but these connections are not sufficiently clear to settle the argument (an interesting discussion on conflicts between marketing and production, including some of the above-mentioned problems, is given by Shapiro, 1977).

If component factories are in the same Division as their customers, the bargaining accompanying transfer of interference is usually not too trenchant. One reason for this is that the triangular setting works relatively well, due to the lower uncertainty and lower complexity of the problems involved.

If component factories are in another Product Division, the situation is different. The triangular setting functions less well, because it is completed at corporate level instead of at divisional level, so the 'distance' of the coordinating subsystem to the conflicting parties is greater. Furthermore, in such cases the components are often also sold to some outside parties, which does not only increase the uncertainty for the supplier, but which can also produce very difficult 'pars pro toto dilemmas' in case of shortages during boom periods: if one cuts external deliveries to deal with these shortages, the component division must do without the related profit and may lose some of its market share; if internal deliveries are cut this may cause costly production stops in the factories supplied. This dilemma is the more difficult to solve, as the corporate accounting system gives distorted information on this issue: the transfer prices for intercompany deliveries do not contain a profit margin, so the accounting system shows a higher income to internal suppliers for external deliveries than for the same deliveries to internal customers. This can produce a tendency to promote external deliveries rather than internal ones.

120

With relation to the acquisition of resources, only the capital acquisition aspect will be discussed here. The disequilibria between sales and production, shown in Fig. 20 cause strong interferences to the corporate finance department. When production exceeds sales, this department has to acquire the capital needed for financing the resulting higher stocks (Table 2 of section 3.2 shows that stocks amount to about one third of total company assets, so the variations in stocks shown in Fig. 20 have a considerable influence on the company's need for capital). Especially if the extra capital has to be acquired at short notice, a positive feedback mechanism can come into action, as this signal may induce the corporate management to increase the pressure on the divisions to decrease their production levels rapidly. In the short run this only increases costs, so still more money has to be acquired. The decrease in production will eventually be sufficient to reach an equilibrium in stock levels, but the extra pressure from the above mentioned process tends to amplify the down swing of production.

An interesting aspect of the conflicts discussed above is that they tend to be regarded as 'taboo' within the organization. The 'pars pro toto dilemma' is not considered as a true dilemma, in principle present in any organization which uses some degree of decentralization of control to cope with complexity and uncertainty. One of the results of this taboo is that the development of control systems tends to underestimate the consequences of the pursuit of self interest. For instance, one proceeds from the idea that materials managers do not majorate, because they know the highly adverse effects this has on the company as a whole. In our view he faces a *true* dilemma: it is difficult for him to choose between protection of the interests of his own factory and of the interests of many other factories within the company.

PART IV

CONTROL SYSTEMS FOR COMPLEX INDUSTRIAL ORGANIZATIONS

Here we discuss some aspects of control systems for complex industrial organizations. The central theme will be *integration of control,* by which we mean the mutual adjustment of the control interventions in the various parts of an organization to get satisfactory overall behaviour.

First we describe the view of organizations which forms the background of this book. Since control is seen here as the basic organizational problem, this view may be called a *control paradigm.* In line with this control paradigm, the optimalization of the *integral controllability* of the organization (i.e. the controllability of the organization as a whole) is put forward as a major objective for control-system design.

The structure of an organizational control system is derived by way of a discussion on *decomposition* and *integration.* To cope with the complexity of the overall control problem, this problem is decomposed into small homogeneous subproblems. This conjures up an integration problem, viz. that of combining the solutions of the subproblems to a satisfactory solution for the overall control problem. Homogeneous control subproblems can be obtained by pursuing unity of time, place and action in decomposition. The first operation creates a *control Ablauf with various control levels,* while the search for unity of place and action creates the *Aufbau.* Both structures combined give an *Aufbau-Ablauf framework,* which usually has a specific structure in order to facilitate integration of control.

Integration can be obtained through the *selfcontrol* of the actors assigned to the various (compound) positions of the Aufbau. However, complexity and conflict necessitate complementation of selfcontrol with *coordination* in order to ensure satisfactory overall behaviour.

In chapter 12 we discuss *four coordination modes.* Coordination can be *direct,* modifying actual selfcontrol in suborganizations directly, or *indirect,* preparing actual selfcontrol. It can also be *stratified,* if the coordinator has power over the coordinated groups, or *non-stratified,* if he has only influence. The combination of these criteria produces four coordination modes. These modes are dealt with in some detail and the chapter is concluded with a discussion on the *coordination mix,* i.e. the combination of selfcontrol and the four coordination modes to be used in specific situations.

Chapter 13 discusses some design considerations related to the Aufbau, in particular the use of various *specialization principles* and of the two defining characteristics of a line-organization, *hierarchy* and *stratification.*

The decomposition of the control Ablauf is treated in chapter 14: *vertical decomposition,* creating the above-mentioned control levels and *horizontal decomposition,* determining the extent to which the boundaries between compound positions play a role in control procedures. After a discussion of the concepts of *futurity, decision horizon* and *control period,* the control levels and their interactions are discussed. The chapter is concluded with a discussion on horizontal decomposition: the relations between control procedures in different compound positions can show various *degrees of connectiveness;* they can be *disjoint, adjoining, coupled* or *fused.*

In chapter 15 we discuss some aspects of control-system design. This indirect mode of control is driven by the dissatisfaction of influential members of the organization with the existing control system, in particular with respect to the controllability it produces. After a plea for a holistic approach to control-system design, we discuss various ways in which this activity can create favourable conditions for integration of control.

Finally, chapter 16 discusses the application of various concepts dealt with in this book in a project, aimed at developing a blueprint for a part of the control system for one of the Product Divisions of Philips Industries.

11 CONTROL-SYSTEM STRUCTURE

11.1 A control paradigm

In part II we described the structure of an industrial organization as a hierarchic system of conversion systems, completed by non-conversion systems. Some dynamic aspects of the behaviour of such a system, in particular the consequences of *complexity,* were discussed. In this context, complexity means that the organization consists of suborganizations with *interdependence of operations,* due to technological connections, but with some degree of *independence of control.*

In part III we also described the control process, i.e. the use of interventions by a controller to promote preferred behaviour of a system-being-controlled. Control has to maintain steady-state operation and to ensure the proper response of the organizational activities to *interferences,* i.e. threats and opportunities.

In the present part we will discuss some aspects of the organizational control system used by the actors of the organization to provide the above-mentioned control interventions. We will first describe the view on organizations and on organizational control that forms the background of our considerations.

A discussion on organizational issues usually proceeds from an implicit or explicit *paradigm*[1] of the phenomenon of 'organization'. The organization may, for example, be seen as a device for attaining certain given goals (such as the maximization of profits on behalf of shareholders or getting a man on the moon), as an institution providing goods and services for society, as a marketplace where people exchange contributions and incentives, as a set of people exploiting a certain technology, as a legal corporation acting as a contracting party etc., etc.

The paradigm used in this book takes the organization itself as the main frame of reference (and not for example its function with respect to society or its contribution to certain outside stakeholders). Furthermore, it will take the

---

[1] See Hofstede and Kassem (1976, p.41): 'the word paradigm (,...) stands for a set of concepts used to build a theory. The same paradigm may be found in different theories. A paradigm is not a theory itself, but a basic way of ordering reality, which inevitably has to precede any theory formation'.

control process as the central organizational problem and will use control concepts to order reality. Hence we may call it a control paradigm.[1] As we have seen above, it is far from the only paradigm possible; however, it is used here because it gives a useful perspective on control-system design issues.

In this book the organization is conceptualized as a set of human beings who combine their efforts in a relatively stable network of social relations. According to definition 18 (section 5.1) an organization is *a system of occupied positions with their physical means of operation*. The positions, or the roles of the actors in the organization, thus constitute its defining characteristics.

An organization has a 'Gestalt' of its own. Paraphrasing the French saying 'un journal est un monsieur', we can say 'une organisation est un monsieur'. It is a 'monsieur' not only through various identification processes on the part of its members (see e.g. Simon, 1957), but also through the expectations of its social environment (this can be seen most clearly for incorporated organizations; for instance, a banker does not loan money to some set of individuals but to the organization as such, and he is acutely aware of the fact that once the 'monsieur' is gone his money is gone).

While the organization can be seen as a 'monsieur', it still consists of individual actors. The behaviour of these actors can be described at various levels of aggregation. At higher levels the interactions between suborganizations are discussed, often without explicit reference to individual behaviour (the suborganizations are more or less treated as black boxes; the analysis of interdepartmental conflict in chapter 10 is an example).

However, when using such a 'higher level approach' we should bear in mind Thompson's warning: 'there is obvious danger in reifying the abstraction 'organization' by asserting that it, the abstraction, has goals and desires' (Thompson, 1967, p.127). We interpret this statement as a warning against the use of concepts applicable at the level of individual behaviour (such as thought and action, see Silverman, 1970) in higher-level discussions, not as a claim that higher-level discussions are impossible: the choice of the level of aggregation depends on the problem on hand. For some problems the level of the individual is best but for others higher levels of analysis may give better insight. No level gives a complete picture of all phenomena.[2]

[1] Another type of control paradigm is presented by De Leeuw (1974, p.171).

[2] One can compare this position with physics, where some phenomena are treated at the atomic level, others at higher levels (e.g. mechanics, thermodynamics) and still others at lower levels (e.g. nuclear physics). I therefore disagree with authors (see e.g. Silverman, 1970), who claim that the analysis of organizational behaviour can only adequately be performed at the level of individual actors.

128

As mentioned above, the organization as such is the focus of interest here. An organization is an open system. A viable organization must be able to acquire resources, such as manpower, materials and money, from its environment. In chapter 7 this demand was described by stating that the organization must maintain various *resource equilibria*. These resources are often acquired in exchange for a certain output to the organization's environment, in which case the organization must also maintain an *output equilibrium.*[1]

These equilibria are dynamic, they are continually threatened by *interferences*, so the actors in the organization must control the organization's activities in order to reduce these interferences (section 7.1). Reduction of interference usually involves the consumption of resources by the organization (*adaptation costs,* section 7.2). A necessary, but not sufficient, condition for an organization's survival is that it should have sufficient resources for the reduction of interference; this is expressed in section 7.2 in the demand that the *interference reduction capacity* of the organization as a whole should remain above unity.[2]

It is of crucial importance for the organization to have a technology and a control system which give it sufficient *controllability* (section 7.3). An organization with an insufficient controllability is not able to keep its interference reduction capacity above unity.

It is the task of 'Control in the Large' to create a technology and a control system with at least a sufficient, but preferably an optimum, controllability: it should try to decrease the average adaptation costs as long as the possible resultant increase in operating costs (e.g. due to a more flexible but more expensive technology, or to a more sophisticated control system) is less than this reduction.[3]

Because of the connections between the various technological processes in an organization (see chapter 6), the reduction of an interference somewhere in the

---

[1] This discussion of the organization as an open system, which has to secure its resources from its environment, is inspired by Thompson (1967). See also Yuchtman and Seashore (1967, p.898), who see as the organization's basic objective the optimalization of its 'bargaining position' as reflected in its ability to exploit its environment in the acquisition of scarce and valued resources.

[2] The condition IRC$>$1 is not a sufficient condition for survival as, among other things, it does not exclude the possibility that the organization does not recognize some essential threats and hence fails to cope adequately with them.

[3] Whenever we speak of an *optimum* controllability, we only mean that in control-system design the costs of the control system should be weighed against its advantages, not that one should always use an explicit quantitative optimalization; a satisfycing approach to the above-mentioned weighing may be quite acceptable in many cases.

organization often has effects on other processes (discussed as transfer of interference in chapter 10). The demand for satisfactory controllability of the organization thus has both *local* and *overall* aspects: the maintenance of local output equilibrium and local resource equilibria should not aim exclusively at minimization of local adaptation costs, but should at the same time try to optimalize the transfer of interference. Control-system design should thus be aimed at optimalizing not local controllability but rather the controllability of the organization as a whole, the *integral controllability*.

Our control paradigm may be summarized as follows: *the organization is a set of human actors in a stable network of social relations with a 'Gestalt' of its own. It is an open system which must maintain various resource equilibria and usually an output equilibrium in order to survive. These equilibria are threatened by interferences, which must be reduced by Control in the Small. Control in the Large must create a technology and a control system with an optimum, or at least sufficient integral controllability to enable Control in the Small to carry out this task.*[1]

11.2 The integral control system

As discussed in part II, the technology of an industrial organization consists of various *physical conversion functions* (such as the acquisition of physical resources, production and sales) and *support functions* (such as research and development, engineering and training). These technological functions must be controlled so that the organization can respond to externally and internally generated interferences. Thus throughout the whole organization interventions are continually chosen and applied, ranging from e.g. the interventions of a worker at an assembly line controlling his own programme to the decision of top management to issue a large debenture loan.

It is the task of the organizational control system to enable the actors of the organization to select and apply the interventions through which they control their technology (see Fig. 8). It should provide them with information on the state of the system being controlled and its environment, on the expected evolution of this state in the absence of intervention, on the

---

[1]One can make several other demands on organizational control systems apart from optimum integral controllability (which may also depend on one's value-system), such as the promotion of motivation, the use of participative decision-making, the inclusion of external societal effects in decision-making, etc. However, sufficient controllability will always be a necessary condition for survival. The controllability will therefore receive most attention in our subsequent arguments.

consequences of possible interventions (local consequences and consequences for connected subsystems) and it should provide them with the means to apply interventions (directly on the technology or indirectly through other actors). The control system can also provide or influence the criteria or preferences used in control.

In section 5.2 an organizational control system was defined as 'the system of formal and informal rules of behaviour, information systems and physical expedients, used by the actors of an organization to control the technology of that organization'. These rules of behaviour include the specification of the programmes of the various positions within the organization and of their mutual relations (the Aufbau of the organization) as well as the control procedures (the Ablauf structure of control). They are partly routine-official and partly non-routine and/or unofficial (see section 5.1 on the formalization mix).

An organizational control system usually has various subsystems and aspect systems, such as the accounting system, the budget system, the planning system, the materials management system, the cash management system, the personnel system (including the reward system), etc. It contains a vast number of information systems, some of which may be automated, while many are manually operated.

If the control system is to contribute to the integral controllability of the organization, it should be an 'integral control system'.

Definition 47
An *integral organizational control system* is a control system that enables and stimulates all actors in the organization to promote the minimization of both local and integral adaptation costs.

The separate mention of minimization of local adaptation costs[1] in the above definition might seem superfluous: minimization of integral costs implies the minimization of local costs under the constraint that the reduction of local costs is not carried on at the expense of larger increases of costs elsewhere in the organization. However, the majority of the control interventions are to be selected by actors with a prime responsibility for only a part of the organization. Owing to cognitive limits the trade-off between local and integral costs is often unclear to them, so the weighing of local against integral interests

---

[1] Note that 'costs' refer to any scarce and valued resource consumed by the organization; they are thus not restricted to purely monetary resources (see section 7.2).

131

is a major issue in control (see the discussion on the pars-pro-toto dilemma in section 10.1). Now definition 47 states that the more the control system contributes to a proper balancing of local and integral costs the more it can be said to be an integral control system.

The main objective of the present part is to contribute some ideas to the design of integral control systems, in particular by developing a holistic approach to organizational control systems. To this end we will discuss a framework for analysis and design of organizational control systems (the Afbau-Ablauf framework) together with some of its essential structural traits (such as hierarchy and stratification) and the basic coordination mechanisms that are embedded in it. Such a framework enables the designer to describe the place of the various control subsystems within the overall control system and their mutual relations and interfaces.

In our opinion an overall view of the essentials of control systems for industrial organizations is needed because of a number of socio-economic trends as well as because of trends in information-processing technology.

Higher demands are being made on control systems because of the increasing complexity of control (increasing size, diversification and internationalization of operations) and because of a decreasing profit margin in many industries (necessitating among other things better controllability of the organization). Another trend which may threaten the controllability is the tendency for the power ratio (see section 5.4) to drop in organizations in many (Western) countries: middle management and specialists as well as workers, e.g. through work councils, claim more influence on company decisions[1] (see chapter 12 for the functions of power in coordination).

On the other hand there are ever increasing technic/economic possibilities of electronic data-processing and communication, which provide some of the tools to meet the above mentioned demands. Computers can perform complex manipulations on vast amounts of data on a routine basis at very high speeds; the control systems of the various parts of the organization can be linked through computer networks, which can nowadays be extended practically down to the level of the individual thanks to the drastic decrease in hardware costs.

However, organizational control is much more than data handling, so insight into the essentials of control systems is needed to decide what has become obsolete in the existing control system and which new solutions

---

[1] A decreasing power ratio does not always result in a lower organizational controllability, see section 12.5.

should be implemented. Such insight is also needed because the diffusion of automated information processing often implies more routine-official control (sub) systems (more use of field 1 of the formalization mix as shown in Fig. 5, section 5.1) and more explicit design of control systems, which may decrease the flexibility of *both* Control in the Small and Control in the Large. Control in the Small can become less flexible because non-routine and non-official control procedures used to handle exceptions and emergencies tend to be driven out by automated official-routine procedures; Control in the Large can become less flexible because changes in control systems (both Aufbau and Ablauf structure) now often involve high investments in adapted or new automated information systems.

It is for these reasons that the following discussions will not take the well known control structures of existing organizations for granted, but will probe for their essential functions in the control process.

11.3 Decomposition and integration

As · discussed in chapter 7, Control in the Small follows in principle a three-phase cycle (the sensor, selector and effector phases). The core of this cycle is the choice of intervention, made during the selector phase. Control in the Small consists essentially of a sequence of a vast number of choices, or decisions, made everywhere in the organization.[1] Control system design is therefore essentially the design of the decision-making system, defining the types of decisions to be made, the conditions for each type of decision and the relations between the various types.

To solve the overall control problem, Control in the Small should ideally be able to survey all possible interventions at any given moment and to evaluate their effects (both local and elsewhere through transfer of interference), so that the best one can be chosen. Of course cognitive limits of human decision-makers make it impossible for them to carry out this task, even with the most sophisticated information processing tools. Therefore, in coping with the complexity of the overall control problem, Control in the Small is preceded by Control in the Large, which structures (or 'organizes') the former to make it manageable for human decision-makers. Decomposition techniques play an essential role in this.

---

[1] Focussing the attention on decision-making does not imply that a decision is always a well defined event, a clear-cut choice made by someone at a specific moment of time. Decision-making in complex organizations is often more like a condensation process, taking much time, with many actors contributing to it, while afterwards it is not always clear when the choice was actually made.

Definition 48A
Decomposition of the overall control problem by Control in the Large is the partitioning of the problem into subproblems involving the control of technological subsystems or aspect systems.

Decomposition thus aims at the creation of subproblems which are *smaller* and *more homogeneous* than the overall problem and therefore easier to solve by Control in the Small.[1]

However, decomposition conjures up an *integration problem*. As there are usually technological connections between the subsystems or aspect systems mentioned in definition 48A, the solution of one subproblem depends on the solutions of related subproblems and *vice versa*. Thus Control in the Small has not only to solve the subproblems, but also to *integrate* the partial solutions of these subproblems in one way or another.

Definition 48B
Integration by Control in the Small is the combination and subsequent mutual adjustment of the partial solutions of control subproblems in order to arrive at a satisfactory solution of the overall control problem.

When solving one subproblem, one has to use estimates of the influence exercised on it by the solutions of the related subproblems. The subsequent integration can be direct or indirect. Direct integration means that the partial solutions are combined to a solution of the overall problem and then adjusted to arrive at a better overall solution (possibly following an iterative procedure: if the overall solution is still unsatisfactory the partial solutions are changed once more, a procedure which is repeated until the overall solution is satisfactory). Indirect integration means that the control of the subsystems is based on the partial solutions, which are only adapted when the difference between the estimated and actual solutions of the related subproblems produces a local interference.

Different actors can be assigned to solve different control subproblems. The integration of control, i.e. the mutual adjustment of the various local control interventions in order to arrive at satisfactory overall control, can in principle be left to their *selfcontrol*. However, as will be discussed in section 12.1, selfcontrol is often not sufficient, in which case there is also a need for *coordination* to solve the integration problem.

---

[1] Decomposition is used in several fields to handle complex large-scale problems. The standard example is the decomposition of linear programming problems (Dantzig, 1963, chapter 23).

Control in the Large has the task not only of decomposing the overall control problem into manageable subproblems, but also of creating the conditions for integration (this interdependency of decomposition and integration is well reflected by Kosiol's term 'integratieve Strukturierung'; Kosiol, 1962, p.23). Thus the creation of subproblems should not only satisfy a *decomposition requirement*, i.e. the subproblems should be small and homogeneous, but *at the same time* also an *integration requirement*, i.e. the subproblems should have few, stable and homogeneous mutual relations (another formulation of this integration requirement is that the creation of the control subproblems should as well as is possible follow the near-decomposability, see section 4.2, of the organization's technology). These two requirements may impose conflicting requirements on control-system design, see e.g. section 13.2. Furthermore, Control in the Large should create a *control system,* which enables selfcontrol and coordination to solve the integration problem.

11.4 The Aufbau-Ablauf framework

One of the objectives of decomposition is the creation of small and homogeneous control subproblems. Homogeneity can be achieved by making the same demands for decomposition as for a classical drama: the subproblems should deal with activities with unity of time, place and action. *Unity of place* means that the subproblems involve the control of technological functions with an as *small* as possible *geographical dispersion*. *Unity of action* means an as *small* as possible *diversity* of these technological functions. *Unity of time* means that the subproblems should deal with interventions which have as much as possible the *same 'futurity'* (see below).

Decomposition creating subproblems with unity of place and action is in fact the well known process of departmentalization, the creation of the Aufbau, the *system of positions.* Departmentalization decomposes both technology and control (see also chapter 13). In the present section we shall be considering mainly control decomposition; the (compound) position is used to label a set of mutually related control problems (in section 13.2 we shall discuss decomposition from the viewpoint of technology).

As will be discussed in chapter 12, control-system design usually arranges the positions of the Aufbau in a specific way in order to help coordination to solve the integration problem: the positions form a *stratified hierarchy,* viz. a hierarchic system of (compound) positions with at each level at least one coordinating (compound) position, which has official power over the (compound) positions it has to coordinate.

The creation of the *Aufbau* decomposes the overall control problem into subproblems, which are (to a certain extent) homogeneous with respect to place and action. Decomposition of the *control Ablauf* (the control procedures) can produce a further homogenization of control. With respect to this decomposition, the criterion of 'futurity' can be used.

'Futurity' is a concept taken from Drucker (1974-a, chapter 43). In his terminology the 'degree of futurity' of a decision indicates the time over which it commits organizational resources. This interpretation is sufficient for our present purposes (in section 14.2 we will give a different definition, one that still has the same tenor as Drucker's interpretation). Thus the ordering of a batch of resistors has a lower futurity than the acquisition of new production machines, which in its turn has a lower futurity than the take-over of a company.

Now Ablauf decomposition with respect to time means that interventions with diverging futurities should be chosen in different decision procedures.

These decision procedures can also be arranged in a specific way in order to facilitate integration. As will be discussed in chapter 14, it is advantageous to arrange them in a *stratified system* of procedures with the futurity of the interventions as priority criterion, decisions with higher futurities being dominant over ones with lower futurities.

Decomposition of the control Ablauf thus clusters decision procedures according to the futurity of the interventions concerned. This creates various *levels of control*. Such levels may be labelled as: long-term control, medium-term control and short-term control (if a three level decomposition is used). Other labels are strategic planning, managerial control and operational control (see Anthony, 1965[1]).

Just as the concept of hierarchy has already been used for centuries in military organizations, so has the idea of a stratified system of control levels been used there for a very long time. Military decision-making distinguishes the levels of strategy and tactics, strategic decisions taking precedence over tactical ones (see e.g. Liddell Hart, 1954, who uses a three-level decomposition: grand strategy, military strategy and tactics; or Van der Laan, 1967, who decomposes the third level further into grand tactics, tactics and minor tactics).

---

[1] Anthony's levels do not necessarily correspond with those used in this book, because the Ablauf levels are used here as a level-*in*dependent concept: 'long-term control' for a production department does not have the same meaning as 'long-term control' at corporate level. Anthony's concepts are level-*de*pendent; his strategic planning level, for example, has the same empirical content for every organization or every part of an organization.

Through the decomposition of the overall control problem and the creation of suitable conditions for integration, Control in the Large creates the structure of the organizational control system: the *Aufbau-Ablauf framework, a stratified hierarchic system of (compound) positions, combined with a stratified system of control levels.* This framework constitutes the skeleton of the overall control system.

A further discussion of the Aufbau-Ablauf framework will be given in chapters 13 and 14. Here we will confine ourselves to an illustration. Fig. 31 shows the Aufbau-Ablauf framework of the infantry brigade discussed in section 4.3.

Aufbau / Ablauf-level	General with staff	batallion 1	batallion 2	batallion 3	batallion 4	batallion 5	batallion 6
Military Strategy							
Grand Tactics							
Tactics							
Minor Tactics							

Fig. 31. The Aufbau-Ablauf framework for an infantry brigade. The figure shows the control structure at the batallion level of the Aufbau (containing one coordinating compound position: general with staff). It may give sufficient detail to 'fill in' the boxes at the higher Ablauf levels with control subsystems, but possibly not at the lower levels: to design control systems at lower Ablauf levels one may need a further partitioning of the boxes shown here, e.g. to show companies or platoons (cf. section 14.4).

This framework is essentially an *array of empty, labelled boxes.* The label of each box gives the (compound) position and Ablauf level in question and thus defines roughly the types of decisions to be made and the place of these decisions in the overall control structure. Subsequent Control in the Large activities have to 'fill' these boxes with control procedures (formal and/or informal), information systems and physical expedients and they have to create the interfaces between the boxes.

So far, we have introduced the Aufbau-Ablauf framework in a descriptive manner: nearly every organization uses decomposition of the overall control problem according to place and action (i.e. departmentalization) and uses stratified hierarchies for its line management. It is also nearly always possible to distinguish various levels of control.

However, the Aufbau-Ablauf framework also has a prescriptive element. Decomposition and integration, hierarchy and stratification, the Aufbau and Ablauf of control are not always used explicitly in control-system design, but are often only implicitly present in long established structures. We would suggest to use these elements more explicitly in control-system design, in order to make optimum use of their control functions.

12.1 Integration through coordination

Decomposition of the overall control problem in order to get manageable subproblems is in principle a straightforward activity. It is the creation of satisfactory conditions for integration, which forms the core of the organization problem.

Different actors are usually assigned to the task of solving different control subproblems. In the first instance, one could leave the solution of the integration problem to selfcontrol. In that case integration is obtained through direct consultations among the actors, assigned to the various subproblems. Now selfcontrol is essentially a *local* activity, based on the (limited) information locally available to the actors involved and on their preferences, which are often predominantly expressed in terms of local behaviour. Therefore the free play of selfcontrol cannot guarantee satisfactory overall behaviour: local selfcontrol has to be supplemented by an overall mode of control, i.e. *coordination*.

As already implied above, there are two basic sources of a need for coordination to supplement selfcontrol, viz. *complexity* and *conflict*.

A need for coordination due to complexity arises if the suborganizations are quite willing to cooperate in such a way that overall behaviour is satisfactory, but are not able to do so because their local information is insufficient (an example of this is the suboptimum behaviour of the chain factories, discussed in chapter 9, due to a distortion of information on final demand and pipeline inventory).

A need for coordination due to conflict can arise if local interests do not coincide (sufficiently) with overall interests. When there is no coordination, possible conflicts among suborganizations (often caused by transfer of interference) are solved in a free power play between the conflicting parties, which does not guarantee satisfactory overall behaviour if local interests differ from overall ones. This phenomenon was discussed as the pars-pro-toto dilemma in chapter 10 and is the direct consequence of departmentalization (which is essentially the formation of suborganizations, each with the task of exploiting *and protecting* its own technology). Such conflicts can arise along physical connections (chapter 6). A series connection demands a mutual balancing of physical flows and capacities; conflicts can e.g. arise with regard to the speed of this mutual adaptation or with respect to the risks to be taken for an expansion. Parallel connections can lead to conflicts with respect to *distribution questions*: the suborganizations can compete for certain scarce resources (such as investment funds or certain components, which are in short supply) or they can compete with respect to output diposal (if they have overlapping missions).

Coordination is the control of the execution of the programmes of specified (compound) positions by actors in coordinating (compound) positions, see section 5.3; it is the control of the behaviour of people (or groups of people) by other people, using influence and/or power, see section 5.4 (remember, according to our definition control does not mean complete determination of behaviour; it only promotes certain preferred behaviour).

The objective of coordination is to modify local selfcontrol in order to promote satisfactory (according to the preferences of the coordinators) overall behaviour: the organization as a whole should be able to respond well to threats and opportunities, output and resource equilibria should be maintained for the whole and not only for some parts and control interventions should lead to an optimum − or at least satisfactory − amount of transfer of interference. *In short, the 'raison d'être' of coordination is its contribution to the solution of the integration problem.*

12.2 Four coordination modes

Coordination activities can be classified according to two criteria. In the first place coordination can be direct or indirect.

> Definition 49
> *Direct coordination* promotes preferred behaviour of coordinated groups by intervening directly in the ongoing process of local selfcontrol; *indirect coordination* promotes preferred behaviour by conditioning local selfcontrol before actual decision-making takes place.

In the case of direct coordination the interventions are chosen in a process of interaction between selfcontrol and coordination; the coordination activities are based on the current situation. In the case of indirect coordination, coordination activities have rather the format: *if* (situation i occurs), *then* (act according to instruction set j). In this way coordination controls selfcontrol without directly participating in its decision making. For instance, traffic regulation can be seen as a kind of coordination, modifying the selfcontrol of individual cardrivers. Traffic regulation by policemen or by traffic lights is an example of direct coordination, whereas the modification of selfcontrol by the highway code is an example of indirect coordination.

In the second place, coordination can be stratified or non-stratified.

Definition 50
Stratified coordination is coordination by coordinators who have official power over the coordinated groups; *non-stratified coordination* is coordination by coordinators who officially have only influence over the coordinated groups.

Stratified coordination can use its power to modify the local selfcontrol to such extent that local behaviour is in conflict with local preferences.[1] Non-stratified coordination is in principle not able to do this, as it only uses influence.

The two classification criteria introduced above are independent of one another. They can be combined to give *four coordination modes* (see Figure 32):

mode 1, stratified direct coordination
mode 2, non-stratified direct coordination
mode 3, stratified indirect coordination
mode 4, non-stratified indirect coordination

stratified	non-stratified	
mode 1	mode 2	direct
mode 3	mode 4	indirect

Fig. 32.   The four coordination modes.

---

[1] The fact that social system S_i has power over social system S_j does not mean that S_i can induce any behaviour of S_j; it only means that S_i is able to induce some degree of conflict within S_j. This capacity can be used by S_i to promote preferred behaviour of S_j. The amount of power S_i has over S_j can be said to be equal to the degree of conflict it can induce in S_j (see also section 5.4 on power).

141

Mode-1 is in fact the traditional, powerful and well tested mode of coordination by line management, almost as old as the phenomenon of organization itself. This mode is the backbone of the whole coordination process in virtually every industrial organization. However, as we will see, in complex and turbulent situations the use of this mode is not sufficient to guarantee satisfactory overall behaviour and it has to be supplemented by other measures.

Mode-2 coordinators have no official power over the coordinated groups, although they may have some amount of expert power (i.e. power based on having expertise). They influence behaviour by providing additional information to decision-makers and by participating in the process of decision-making. Examples are planning departments, liaison officers and coordination committees consisting of managers from the same level.

Mode-3 coordination is indirect; it uses regulations, instructions, standards, etc. to constrain the local selfcontrol *before* actual decision-making takes place. It is not based on information on the current control situation, but on the image the coordinator has of the repetitive elements of that situation. Mode 3 is also a stratified type of coordination; this means that the instructions are issued (or at least supported) by a coordinator which has the power to impose them; this also means that it can, in principle, induce behaviour which is in conflict with the preferences of selfcontrol.

Mode-4 coordination is indirect too, thus it does not intervene directly in decision-making. It is also non-stratified, so the interventions chosen by selfcontrol are in principle always in agreement with the latter's preferences. Mode-4 coordination tries to create such conditions for selfcontrol that the decisions of the latter are 'automatically' in agreement with the preferences of the coordinator. The classical example of mode-4 coordination is Adam Smith's 'invisible hand', i.e. the coordination of the activities of independent economic agents by the price mechanism. This 'invisible hand' can be simulated in organizations e.g. by using the concept of 'profit centres' (see Anthony, 1964). However, there are various other mechanisms for conditioning selfcontrol on behalf of the organization as a whole, for example intra-company management training.

The four coordination modes will be discussed in greater detail in the next two sections. To conclude this introduction, we will discuss by way of illustration various ways in which the government can control industrial pollution, which can be seen as a modification of the selfcontrol of industrial companies.
Mode-1 coordination here would mean the use of a permit system: for

each discharge a company would have to apply for a permit, which a pollution agency can decide to grant or not. Mode-2 coordination would mean e.g. that companies would have to report intended discharges to the pollution agency, which could advise them on the environmental consequences, on the timing of the discharge and on technical possibilities for purification of waste. Mode-3 coordination could be a general prohibition of discharge above a certain amount per period and Mode-4 a tax on discharges. In the latter case the companies are still free to exercise their selfcontrol to decide on whether to discharge waste, but the tax provides a pressure on them to decrease the amount of such discharge.

12.3 Mode-1 coordination

As we mentioned above, mode-1 coordination (i.e. stratified direct coordination) is in many cases the backbone of the whole organizational coordination structure; it provides the basis for integration of control.

The modification of selfcontrol by mode-1 coordination is direct and thus based on the (limited) information on the current situation available to the coordinator. It is also stratified; this means that mode-1 coordination can induce a choice of intervention which is contrary to the discretion of selfcontrol.

The essential function of mode-1 coordination is its capacity to settle conflicts among the coordinated groups on behalf of the whole. Without stratified coordination, the conflicts among coordinated groups are settled by a power play among the conflicting parties and hence usually to the advantage of the most powerful (which will in general not produce minimum total adaptation costs). The use of mode-1 coordination to settle conflicts can increase the integral controllability of the organization in two ways, viz. by *promoting optimum transfer of interference* and by *decreasing control dead times*. As discussed in Chapter 10, too little transfer of interference produces a sluggish response to changing external circumstances, but too much transfer threatens the efficiency of technology. The selfcontrol of a suborganization will tend to protect its own technical core too much (the pars-pro-toto dilemma); it is therefore the task of mode-1 coordination to promote optimum transfer. Furthermore, a free play of power between conflicting parties will also tend to increase control dead times, because then the settling of conflicts often needs prolonged bargaining, especially if some parties do not need a quick decision. Long control dead times can strongly increase the adaptation costs as is well known in control theory (see also chapter 9), thus if mode-1 coordinators use their power to accelerate decision procedures, they increase the organization's controllability.

Mode-1 coordination can on the one hand induce conflicts in coordinated groups, if overall interests do not coincide with local ones. On the other hand it can also help a coordinated group to reduce certain interferences, which would otherwise cause difficult problems, e.g. by settling a conflict with a more powerful group or by allotting resources to it which it cannot acquire by itself (an example is a temporary non-profit situation for a suborganization, which would lead to bankruptcy for an independent company, but which can be survived by a suborganization if it is temporarily 'subsidized' by the overall organization). This means that mode-1 coordination can produce *ultra-stability* for the coordinated groups 'Ultrastability' is a concept introduced by Ashby (1952), which in the terms of this book can be defined as follows:

Definition 51
A system is *ultrastable* if it can reach an equilibrium state even after the occurrence of an interference which its normal mode of control cannot reduce.

Ultrastability thus implies that the system is able to switch to a different mode of control in special circumstances, or to obtain support from outside (as in the above-mentioned case).

Next to the internal role of mode-1 coordinators discussed so far, they usually also perform an important *external role*: they can represent the coordinated groups to their (intra- and extra-organizational) environment. For instance, when the general of Fig. 4, coordinates the actions of batallions, he does not interact with the batallions as such, but with the lieutenant-colonels representing them. It greatly facilitates control if such representatives are mode-1 coordinators, because in that case they are in a better position to implement internally the agreements made with external parties.

If a mode-1 coordinator has to coordinate many actors, he faces a very complex coordination problem. A specific arrangement of coordination relations is therefore almost always used to cope with this complexity, viz. a *hierarchic* one.
    In the case of analysis it is the *black-box property* through which a hierarchy reduces complexity: at any level of detail the intricacies present at lower levels are veiled under the cover of the black-box, so the analysis can be confined to the properties of the black-boxes as a whole and to their interactions. In the case of coordination of activities in an organization, the same function is performed by *selfcontrol*. At any level of the hierarchy the complexity of coordination is reduced, if the control of interactions *within* the suborganizations at that level is left to their selfcontrol so that the coordinator

144

can concentrate on the interactions *among* suborganizations. The suborganizations are thus treated more or less as black-boxes and coordinators deal predominantly with inputs and outputs, i.e. the contributions of the suborganizations to the whole, the resources needed to produce these contribution and the interactions among suborganizations (this is what Miller and Rice discuss as 'boundary control', see e.g. Miller, 1976). Without proper use of selfcontrol one cannot reap the benefits of hierarchy[1].

Not only hierarchy but also the decomposition of control itself becomes powerless if no adequate use is made of selfcontrol. The creation of the boundaries between selfcontrol and mode-1 coordination is thus a key issue in control. This boundary is defined by the issues which are left to selfcontrol respectively subjected to coordination, and with respect to the latter category to what extent selfcontrol is constrained. Decisions by mode-1 coordinators can still leave a fair amount of variety to selfcontrol, e.g. if they are expressed as aggregate plans or budgets, which have to be detailed by selfcontrol, or if they use control limits.

   Another aspect of the constraining of selfcontrol by mode-1 coordination is the power ratio, the ratio of the power of the coordinator over the coordinated groups to the power of the latter over the coordinator (see section 5.4). In particular because the boundary between selfcontrol and coordination is not static, but often subjected to *ad-hoc* changes due to changing circumstances, it is the power ratio which in many cases determines the extent to which selfcontrol is constrained.

When introducing the Aufbau-Ablauf framework in section 11.4, we stated that the Aufbau is usually a stratified hierarchic system of positions. We have now seen that this statement refers essentially to the mode-1 coordination structure. There are many other relations between the various positions in an organization, so the mode-1 coordination structure is only an aspect system of the organizational structure. However, as will be seen in Section 13.1, this

---

[1] This point is well illustrated by the history of army organizations. After the reorganizations by Marius, the Roman army had the following hierarchic structure. It consisted of 20 to 30 legions of about 6000 men, each having 10 cohorts, in their turn divided in 3 manipels. Each legion had a high degree of selfcontrol at strategic and tactical levels; the cohorts and to some extent the manipels had selfcontrol at the tactical level (see e.g. Encyclopaedia Britannica, volume 19, p.575, 1974).
   After the fall of the Roman Empire, armies still frequently used hierarchic structures, but the essential supplement, selfcontrol of the parts, was lost. It took 10 centuries before selfcontrol regained its proper place next to hierarchy in the pre-Napoleontic reorganization of the French army, which created independently operating divisions (Lidell Hart, 1954). Since then the question of what is the appropriate degree of selfcontrol at each level of any army's Aufbau has remained a key organization issue (see e.g. Van der Laan, 1967).

aspect system is so important and so many other relations coincide with it, that it is understandable that in practice the mode-1 coordination structure (as represented e.g. in an organigram) is often regarded as *the* organization structure.

We have also seen that hierarchy is used to cope with complexity, and stratification is used to cope with conflict (in order to promote optimum transfer of interference and short control dead times).

12.4 Mode-2, -3 and -4 coordination

Coordinators using *mode-2 coordination* modify local decision-making by providing the coordinated groups with information, by stimulating information exchange and direct consultations among them and/or by directly participating in the decision-making process. They may play a role comparable to a barrister, promoting certain specific interests, or comparable to a real-estate agent, bringing together demand and supply. Mode-2 coordination usually pertains to one or more *aspects* of control (e.g. cost control, control of the flows of materials), not to the *total* control problem of a suborganization.

Mode-2 coordinators have by definition no official power over the coordinated groups; they use officially only influence to modify selfcontrol. Their constraining effect on selfcontrol is thus much less than that of mode-1 coordination: the interventions are ultimately chosen according to the discretion of selfcontrol. Mode-2 coordinators may still have some power, e.g. expert power based on the fact that they have more information on a certain subject or power because responsible line managers need their approval on certain issues (e.g. the mode-2 coordinator could be a product manager who has to sign certain investment proposals before they can be submitted to top management). However, this kind of power differs greatly from the power of a mode-1 coordinator, because in the latter case all parties involved in a conflict expect the coordinator to prevail (at least officially), whereas a mode-2 coordinator sometimes has his way and sometimes not.

Planning and budgeting often involve a great deal of mode-2 coordination. Although plans and budgets may need approval of mode-1 coordinators, the major part of the efforts involved often consists of discussions of planning or accounting departments with the suborganizations concerned[1]. In such cases it

---

[1] However, if plans or budgets are drawn up by the planning or accounting departments themselves and submitted to management for approval after only a minor degree of participation of the suborganizations concerned, one should regard this process rather as mode-1 than mode-2 coordination.

can be the task of the coordinator to ensure the mutual balancing of plans of budgets by providing information to the parties concerned on possible misfits.

Examples of mode-2 coordinators are:
— liaison officers with the task of promoting communication among suborganizations
— committees comprising members from various suborganizations at the same Aufbau level, with a coordinating role with respect to a specific problem
— planning departments
— accounting departments
— material managers, who use mode-2 coordination with respect to production control, supplementing the mode-1 coordination by the managers of production departments (with respect to the purchase department and the warehouse of the factory they are usually mode-1 coordinators)
— officers with integrating roles (Galbraith, 1973), with the task of coordinating suborganizations at the same Aufbau level with respect to a specified issue; they may carry labels such as product managers or program managers (project managers may also fall into this category, if they only have the task of guarding the schedule and/or the specification of the results of the project; if they have full — albeit temporary — authority over the deployment of the resources put at the disposal of the project, they are rather to be considered as mode-1 coordinators; see also section 13.2).

The examples given above of the product manager with some power, the material manager (combination of mode mode-1 and 2) and the project manager show that the boundary between mode-1 and -2 coordination can be complicated. The criterion for classification is always the stratification: who has the final say in case of conflict, according to the official power structure.

Mode-3 coordination modifies selfcontrol through rules, regulations, standards etc. It is a stratified mode, i.e. it can induce control interventions which are contrary to the discretion of selfcontrol. It is also an indirect mode, i.e. the modifications it brings about are not based on information on the current situation but on *a priori* information available to the coordinator. These two points limit the applicability of mode-3 coordination; it usually concerns only specific aspects of a situation.

As is the case with the direct version of stratified coordination (mode-1) the variety remaining to selfcontrol after the modification by mode-3 coordination can vary widely. For instance, the constraining of selfcontrol of citizens by legislation is less than the constraining of the behaviour of members of military forces by military instructions (which may even try to control their social behaviour outside the organization, see e.g. VVKM 229, 1963).

Mode-4 coordination is non-stratified, so it constrains the exercise of discretion by selfcontrol much less than the stratified modes-1 and 3. It tries to modify selfcontrol in such a way that the latter 'automatically' chooses its interventions in the best interest of the organization as a whole.

In principle the budget/accounting system combined with a system of transfer prices, making lower-level managers responsible for the costs and benefits of their suborganizations within the constraints of an approved budget, tries to do this. But as accounting systems usually show only *local* costs and benefits and not the costs of transfer of interference, this only works well if the suborganizations are independent. If there are no, or only weak, dependences between suborganizations the optimalization of *local* financial results also produces *optimum overall* results; but if there *are* dependences this is in general not true. In the latter case it depends to a great extent on the reward system whether the budget/accounting system promotes satisfactory overall behaviour. If the reward system stresses local results, it intensifies a 'chacun pour soi et dieu pour nous tous' attitude and thus promotes suboptimum transfer of interference. If the reward system stresses the contribution to the organization as a whole this effect will be much less. This might be attained if the reward system were to be based not only on the opinion of superiors, but also on that of officers from related suborganizations[1].

There are several other, albeit less formalized, examples of mode-4 coordination. 'Automatic' behaviour in the best interests of the whole can also be obtained by consistent decision-making by mode-1 coordinators, since in that case the coordinated groups can anticipate the interventions from the coordinator and will tend to solve their problems without needing explicit interventions. The French call this phenomenon 'penser patron' (Mayntz, 1976, gives an interesting example of this for the administration of Western Germany, where a change of political leadership produces a change in the behaviour of civil servants after a certain time, without many explicit interventions from the new ministers). In legal matters, case law is an example of mode-4 coordination of lower-level judges, because it coordinates without

[1]Hofstede (1967) gives an example of this with respect to the reward system for accountants. When the opinions of line management on the contribution of their accountant played a role in determining rewards, the relations between line management and their accountant were indeed much better than when only corporate accountants appraised the performance of these accounting managers.

148

stating explicit rules (which would be mode-3) and without overruling specific lower-level sentences (which would be mode-1). In complex organizations, years of management practice yield the same results (see e.g. Gloor, 1972).

Intra-company training programmes and 'organization development' activities can also be regarded as mode-4 coordination; another example is the training of soldiers. A very elaborate version of mode-4 coordination can be found in Chinese organizations, where some 6 to 12 hours a week are spent on 'ideological training' (Laaksonen, 1975).

12.5 The coordination mix

The four coordination modes do not exclude one another but are usually used in combination. The combination practically always includes mode-1 coordination, while the other modes are added in appropriate amounts. We will call the extent to which the activities of a suborganization are controlled by its own selfcontrol and by a combination of coordination models the *coordination mix*. This concept is illustrated with reference to three imaginary examples in Fig. 33 (one should see this figure only as a mental exercise, as we do not have yet a measure for the contribution of each mode of control).

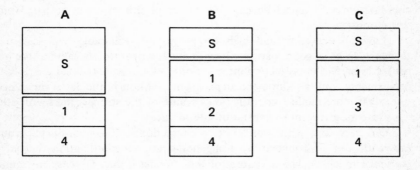

Fig. 33.   The coordination mix for three imaginary examples.
The figures stand for the various coordination modes, the S for selfcontrol.

A: a research department
B: a commercial department
C: an accounting department

The benefits of coordination should come from improved overall behaviour, leading to lower integral adaptation costs. On the other hand coordination involves operating costs, i.e. the costs of manpower and physical resources used by coordinating agencies, which can be quite substantial. Another kind of coordination costs are the costs of imperfect decisions due to incorrect prediction of the local adaptation costs resulting from coordination interventions (due to the limitations of the coordinator's knowledge of the local situation).

In principle, selfcontrol is in a better position to judge the local consequences of decisions, but may have little information on the consequences elsewhere and may thus tend to pursue predominantly local interests. The proper mix of selfcontrol and one or more coordination modes will depend on the situation. We will close this section with some tentative remarks on the right choice of this mix.

Among the factors which influence the desired coordination mix are the complexity and predictability of the technology of the coordinated groups, the complexity (especially the heterogeneity) of the technological dependences between the coordinated groups and the degree of conflict involved in their interactions, the complexity of the relations with the organizational environment and the rate of change in this environment, the quality of the communications between coordinator and coordinated groups, the operating costs of coordination and the properties of the actors in the coordinated groups. The various factors may impose conflicting demands on the coordination mix, in which case the choice of this mix will be based on a compromise.

Low predictability and high complexity of technology will lead to a tendency to use a coordination mix with much selfcontrol, because of the high risk of imperfect coordination interventions in this case (examples are research departments and development departments, although the latter may need somewhat more mode-1 coordination because of the stronger links with other departments, giving more transfer of interference).

One may cope with complexity of interactions among coordinated groups and with the environment by using non-stratified coordination modes (in particular mode-2). The advantage of these modes is their limited constraining effect on the exercise of discretion by selfcontrol. Disadvantages are the low conflict-resolving capacity and possibly long control dead times (one example is the mode-2 coordination by planning departments; another is the direct transmission of information on final demand and pipeline inventory, mentioned in section 9.4 and elaborated in chapter 16).

If the need for coordination is due to conflict one may want a high amount of

150

stratified coordination (especially mode-1) in the coordination mix to promote optimum transfer of interference and short control dead times.[1] The higher the degree of conflict and the higher the need for short control dead times (e.g. in crisis situations), the higher the power ratio one may need. A disadvantage of mode-1 is the risk of imperfect coordination interventions due to the constraining of selfcontrol, while excessive use of mode-1 may also have motivational disadvantages (an example of a suborganization using in general relatively much mode-1 coordination is a commercial one, because it is subjected to frequent interferences from the market and needs a high speed of response).

If the communication between coordinators and coordinated groups is poor, one may tend to use much indirect coordination, combined with relatively much selfcontrol.

Indirect coordination is especially powerful in placid situations (as for example often found in accounting departments), because in that case the fact that coordination is not based on up-to-date information on the current situation does not matter too much. In some cases, where mode-3 coordination is used very extensively and has a very constraining effect on selfcontrol, one may get the impression that the driving force behind this is not only a desire for an efficient use of organizational resources but also a strong distrust of selfcontrol (and of human nature) or a fear of the uncertainty selfcontrol causes the coordinator (see Van Gunsteren, 1976, chapter 5, on the psychological basis of the quest for tight coordination).

The operating costs of mode-3 coordination are often relatively low, usually much lower than mode-1. The costs of mode-2 and 4 coordination can vary widely, because one can apply them to practically any desired extent. In complex organizations mode-1 coordination is often largely supplemented by mode-2, in which case the operating costs of the latter mode can be much higher than those of mode-1.

Finally, one may mention cultural influences on the coordination mix. One gets the impression that there is a tendency in China and Japan to use more non-stratified coordination than in the West (Laaksonen, 1975, Sasaki, 1973), whereas the differences among countries in the West with respect to the power ratio in organizations (Hofstede, 1976), may indicate differences in the

---

[1] Mode-1 does not always give a short control dead time. If the mode-1 coordination structure uses a 'tall' hierarchy (due to a small span of the hierarchy) or a matrix structure (see chapter 13), control dead times may be quite long; in those cases a larger span of the hierarchy or a one-dimensional structure, combined with mode-2 coordination might give shorter control dead times.

amount of mode-1 coordination in the coordination mix (more mode-1 in Latin countries than in Germanic ones). In this context we can remark that the decreasing power ratio in many organizations in the West, mentioned in section 11.2, does not of necessity result in a lower organizational controllability. If the coordination mix is sufficiently adapted to the lower power ratio (i.e. more use of non-stratified modes), it is in several situations possible to maintain the controllability or even to increase it through a possible higher motivation and a better utilization of selfcontrol.

13. THE AUFBAU

13.1 The nature of the Aufbau

The Aufbau of an organization was defined in section 5.1 as its *system of positions.* It can be seen as the static anatomy of the organization, determining its task and control structure. The programmes and relationships as defined by the Aufbau have a strong influence on the behaviour of the actors in the organization. As March and Simon (1958, p.143) put it: 'knowledge of the programmes of an organization permits one to predict in considerable detail the behaviour of the members of the organization'. The Aufbau is thus an essential part of the organizational control system.

The Aufbau provides not only a division of control tasks (as discussed in sections 11.3 and 11.4) but also a division of labour. Hence Aufbau design is not only control-system design, but at the same time technology design; it must thus be based on both control considerations and technological considerations.

Many technological considerations boil down to the demand of low operating costs, i.e. high steady-state efficiency. Low operating costs can be obtained by *task specialization* and by *combination of tasks,* which can give synergy (see Ansoff, 1965, chapter 5), economies of scale, efficient use of common resources, etc.

The main control consideration is the above-mentioned *integral controllability*, or in the terms of Ansoff and Brandenburg (1971) the 'operational and strategic responsiveness' of the organization as a whole (the first property refers to its ability to adapt the mix and volume of the output to changes in demand, the second to its ability to adapt the nature of the output).

Aufbau design pertains to the definition of individual positions *and* to the definition of their mutual relations. In part II we introduced the concept of the clustering of individual positions to a hierarchic system of *compound positions,* such as departments and divisions (see Fig. 14 for an example of such a system). With the concepts introduced in chapter 12 we can now define the clustering criterion: *a set of positions belongs to the same compound position if and only if they are coordinated by the same mode-1 coordinator.* As compound positions can be defined at various levels of aggregation, we can make for them an analogous statement: a set of compound positions belongs to the same 'higher level compound position' if and only if they are coordinated by the same mode-1 coordinator.

There are many relations between positions — both technological (physical and information support connections) and control relations. However, it is the system of mode-1 coordination relations (a subset of the latter category) that constitute the core of the Aufbau — not only because these relations are so important in themselves, but also because many other relations coincide with them. The mode-1 coordination structure, i.e. the structure of line management, is usually designed in such a way that the resulting compound positions have a homogeneous technology, while the technological relations within such compound positions are more numerous and stronger than those with positions from different compound positions. These technological relations also involve control relations, not only in connection with the above-mentioned mode-1 coordination, but also in connection with selfcontrol ('horizontal relations') and possibly other coordination modes (and this applies not only to the official-routine relations, but also to the unofficial and/or non-routine relations). Thus the mode-1 coordination structure coincides with the near-decomposability of both technology and formal and informal control.

13.2 Some design considerations

Because the core of the Aufbau is the mode-1 or line management structure, Aufbau design usually starts with this aspect system of the Aufbau. After that other coordination and control structures can be filled in.

Of course the choice of an Aufbau configuration depends on the organization's situation, i.e. its technology and environment. But even in a given situation there is usually no 'one best way of organizing'. A situation usually has a certain degree of 'indifference', i.e. there are several feasible solutions to the problem of designing a mode-1 coordination structure. As will for example be seen below, the complete control system contains a combination of control and coordination mechanisms, so the shortcomings of each of the above-mentioned mode-1 coordination structures can often be compensated by combining it with other control elements.

Another point is that the situation itself is usually not immutable, but is also subject to design and control. Technology is artificial (although by no means having dispensation from natural laws), so its design can use control considerations (such as flexibility) in addition to technological ones (such as effectivity and steady-state efficiency). The organization's environment can be chosen, within limits (for instance, manufacturing sites can be situated in politically stable countries), or controlled (e.g. by seeking support from

154

government agencies, by making coalitions or cartels or by negotiating long-term delivery contracts).

The design of the mode-1 coordination structure has a dual objective. On the one hand it should satisfy the *decomposition demand* (see section 11.3), i.e. it should create compound positions with a homogeneous technological core, which can be protected by its boundary spanning functions. On the other hand it should at the same time satisfy the *integration demand*, i.e. it should create compound positions with few, stable and homogeneous technological relations with other compound positions. Satisfaction of the decomposition demand promotes steady-state efficiency and local controllability, while satisfaction of the integration demand promotes integral controllability (or overall responsiveness).

Compound positions with homogeneous technologies and/or technological relations with their environment can be obtained by using one or more of the following *specialization principles* (already discussed in various versions by the 'classics' such as Gulick and Urwick, 1937):
— *transformation specialization:* combination of positions occupied with the same physical transformation or function
— *object specialization:* combination of positions occupied with different transformations on the same object (product or service)
— *geographical specialization:* combination of positions located in the same geographical area
— *environment specialization:* combination of positions obtaining their inputs from the same type of suppliers or disposing of their outputs to the same type of customers.

Unfortunately, a technology which is homogeneous with respect to one of these principles often gives heterogeneous relations with respect to others and hence a difficult control and coordination problem, because every relation can give rise to interference. For example, one can organize a multinational company according to the countries in which it operates (geographical specialization), or use the classical functional organization in sales, manufacturing, R&D, etc. (transformation specialization) or use a divisional organization (object specialization). In each case homogenization according to one principle gives heterogeneity according to the others.

This problem can be solved partly by efficient use of the hierarchy and the stratification of the mode-1 coordination structure; it can also be solved partly by complementing this structure with other coordination and control mechanisms.

155

The homogenization problem exists at every level of the hierarchy, but one can use different specialization principles at different levels. For example, Product Divisions (the result of object specialization) have often a functional internal structure, which means that on the level below the divisional level they are organized according to the transformation specialization principle. At the next level down one has a choice again: should one for example organize the divisional sales department according to the countries where the products are sold or according to types of clients (two versions of environmental specialization) or according to the different types of products made by the division (object specialization)? Thus heterogeneity at one level can be tackled by using the appropriate specialization principle at the next level down.

Of course, this usually does not solve the problem of heterogeneity with respect to different principles completely. Another possibility is to use a specific type of stratification, viz. a *multidimensional stratification,* usually called a matrix organization. In this case there are at least two types of mode-1 coordinators at a given level of the Aufbau, each type having the mission of controlling interferences connected with one type of technological relations. Thus, instead of solving the heterogeneity problem at different Aufbau levels, one tries to solve it at the same level.

Multidimensional stratifications, or matrix organizations, can be of a static or a dynamic nature. A static version is the structure of Philips Industries, discussed in section 6.5, which uses both geographical and object specialization at the same time: each (compound) position is always coordinated both by a National Organization Management and by a Divisional Management (see Fig. 13). Another example of a static matrix organization is the system of functional bosses proposed by Taylor (1911).

The project organization is a dynamic version: positions are combined in competence or functional groups, while the actors occupying these positions are temporarily assigned to projects and then coordinated by a project manager.

Matrix organizations are increasingly popular as devices to cope with heterogeneity of interaction (see e.g. Knight, 1976, Sayles, 1976 and also Goggin, 1974), but have of course one major shortcoming: the possible conflicts between the various types of mode-1 coordinators (the more vexing, because the very mission of mode-1 coordination is to cope with conflict).

The mode-1 coordination structure does not need to provide a complete solution to the control/coordination problem. If, for example, the interferences involved in a certain type of technological relation do not cause acute conflicts, they can often very well be dealt with by mode-2 coordination. As discussed in section 12.4, there is a great variety of mode-2 coordinators, such as planning groups, liaison officers, product managers etc. The use of

156

mode-2 coordination to deal with certain complex interactions has the advantage that it hardly affects the clarity and conflict solving power of mode-1 coordination (as opposed to solutions which use a complex mode-1 structure such as matrix organizations).

Heterogeneous relations can also be controlled by mode-3 coordination. An example is the coordination of accounting or EDP departments through standardization of systems and procedures. Another example is the organizational personnel policy, which is often largely coordinated through mode-3 coordination too.

There are also scores of possibilities of using the Ablauf organization to cope with some of the possible shortcomings of a particular mode-1 coordination structure. An example is the introduction of the PPB-System (Planning Programming Budgeting System, see e.g. Lyden and Miller, 1967) in the United States Department of Defence. This can be seen as the introduction of object specialization (the PPB-System prepares budgets for missions rather than for departments) by means of the Ablauf organization, while leaving the Aufbau, predominantly organized according to transformation specialization (i.e. functionally) unaltered. Another example is the use of integrated or fused (or 'vertical', see Galbraith, 1974) control systems to be discussed in section 14.4. A final example is the separation of decision-making on policy from decision-making on operations (centralizing the former, decentralizing the latter), mentioned by Ansoff and Brandenburg, 1971 (see section 14.3).

14. THE ABLAUF STRUCTURE

14.1 Ablauf decomposition

Decomposition and integration of control and technology in order to create an Aufbau, i.e. departmentalization, is performed in every organization and studied by practically every student of organizations (in fact we used the Aufbau, the system of positions, as the defining characteristic of an organization in definition 18).

The explicit use of decomposition (and integration) of the control Ablauf as an element of organization design, is somewhat less common but still well known in the literature. For example, the following authors have described a multilevel structure for organizational control procedures (apart from the military use of this concept mentioned in section 11.4):

- Parsons (1960): technical level, management level, institutional level
- Ansoff (1965): operational decisions, administrative decisions, strategic decisions
- Anthony (1965): operational control, management control, strategic planning
- Mesarovic et al (1970): control, learning and adaptation, self-organization
- Sagasti (1973): short-range planning, medium-range planning, long-range planning
- De Leeuw (1974): routine control, adaptive control, strategic control

These authors introduce their multilevel control structure predominantly to discuss the differences between the various levels in the *nature* of decision-making itself and in the *norms* or *goals* used. They use these differences as criteria for clustering different types of decisions. Furthermore, the levels of Parsons, Ansoff, Anthony and Sagasti are level-dependent concepts (see section 1.1), i.e. they have a fixed empirical content.

The Ablauf levels discussed here are level-*in*dependent concepts: the control Ablauf is decomposed according to a single criterion, the futurity of the decisions concerned; the empirical meaning of these levels (and the number of levels used) depends on the situation (see the next sections). This decomposition is not proposed as a descriptive classification scheme, but as a design method; it can help the designer to create *homogeneous classes of decisions,* each class having a specific *place* in the overall control structure, which makes it possible to design the proper relations among these classes of decisions from the viewpoint of this overall control structure.

This decomposition of the control Ablauf in order to create various control levels can be called *vertical Ablauf decomposition* (if we take the Aufbau-Ablauf framework as shown in Figs. 31 and 34, as our frame of reference for determing what is vertical and what is horizontal). A second way of decomposing the Ablauf is *horizontal decomposition,* which partitions control procedures according to the boundaries of (compound) positions, see Fig. 34.

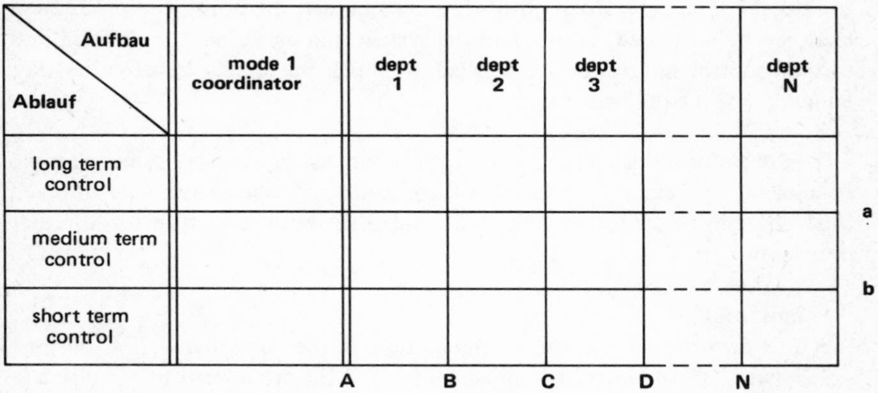

Ablauf \ Aufbau	mode 1 coordinator	dept 1	dept 2	dept 3		dept N	
long term control							a
medium term control							b
short term control							
	A	B	C	D	N		

Fig. 34. Vertical and horizontal Ablauf decomposition.
The figure shows an Aufbau-Ablauf framework. Vertical Ablauf decomposition creates the interfaces a and b, horizontal decomposition creates the interfaces A, B, C, etc.

14.2 Futurity

A discussion of the vertical Ablauf decomposition requires more insight in the concept of futurity, introduced in section 11.4. In chapter 5 we defined control as a continuous process, promoting preferred behaviour of a system-being-controlled. Control thus implies a *sequence of control interventions* (decision-making for unique situations is not regarded as control here). In chapter 7 the control process was discussed as interference reduction; the sequence of interventions produces an *equilibrium-seeking process* (where the equilibrium in question may be static or dynamic). The system-being-controlled was defined as being in equilibrium if the controller refrained from control interventions (definition 34). Now we need to define two types of equilibria (unlike definition 34 this definition requires knowledge of the criteria or preferences of the controller).

Definition 52
A system-being-controlled is in *ultimate equilibrium* if its state is in accordance with the preferences of its controller; it is in *provisional equilibrium* if its state is not in accordance with the preferences of its controller, but the latter nevertheless refrains from control interventions.

For example, in production-level control the system-being-controlled may be in ultimate equilibrium if the production level equals the sales level and the stock level equals the stock norm. If stocks exceed the norm, the production level can be decreased, whereupon the system is in provisional equilibrium: no further control intervention is applied, although the stocks are of course not immediately in equilibrium again.

The application of a control intervention will usually aim at some ultimate equilibrium. Owing to the inertia of technology it takes some time to reach this ultimate equilibrium. We will call this time the futurity of that intervention.

Definition 53
The *futurity* of a control intervention is the expected period of time between the moment it is implemented and the attainment of the ultimate equilibrium state aimed at.

For example, the futurity of a decision to invest in new production equipment covers the time needed to acquire the equipment plus the period it is used in production during its (economic) life. The system is in provisional equilibrium as soon as the equipment is ordered (until the time has come to hire or train personnel for it, which necessitates control actions). The futurity of a decision to start a project is the expected time needed to complete the project plus the time during which the benefits of the project are reaped.[1]

The fact that it takes time to reach ultimate equilibrium after an intervention is selected, often has the important consequence that the decision in question is not irrevocable, but can be reversed or adapted after some time. We will call this time the control period.

[1] The futurity of a control intervention should not be confused with Jacques' concept 'time span of discretion' (Jacques, 1956). The latter concept is rather to be compared with our 'control period', to be defined in definition 54.

Definition 54

The *control period* of an intervention is the time that has to elapse after it is implemented before a new or adapted intervention can be implemented.

One can compare the control period with the refractory period of a nerve (after a nerve has transmitted a pulse it needs some time, the refractory period, before a new pulse can be triggered). The length of the control period depends both on the technology and on the control system. Short control periods decrease control dead times but increase the operating costs of the control system and may lead to too many interventions in the system-being-controlled, which threatens its efficiency. Finally, in complex organizations the time needed for negotiations to adapt current plans sets a lower bound for the control period (for example, in several divisions of Philips Industries the control period for divisional production level control is four months, which is practically equal to the time needed to prepare the plans: as soon as a set of production plans has come into force, the Divisional Planning Department starts a new planning cycle).

The concept of control period applies to routine control activities. In special circumstances it is almost always possible to bypass the routine control procedures in order to arrive at a quick response. However, in complex organizations this bypassing can produce considerable transfer of interference, so it is often more profitable to design routine control procedures with short response times than to permit many exceptions.

The horizon used in decision-making on a specific type of interventions will be called the *decision horizon*. In principle the decision horizon should be equal to the futurity of the interventions in question. A longer horizon would be superfluous, while a shorter one gives problems: ultimate equilibrium is reached via successive provisional equilibrium states, but if the state of ultimate equilibrium does not fall within the horizon it will be difficult to determine whether a state is a provisional equilibrium state or not. Too short decision horizons produce suboptimum control interventions, but in general the longer the decision horizon the higher the operating costs of the control system. An optimum value of the decision horizon should thus be sought.

It follows from the above discussion that control consists in principle of a sequence of interventions (the intervals between interventions being the control period) aimed at reaching ultimate equilibrium through successive stages of provisional equilibrium. Now ultimate equilibrium is never actually reached, not only because new interferences continually cause new disequilibria, but also because the ultimate equilibrium state itself usually changes (cf. the discussion on the demand servo in chapter 8: it tries to follow demand, but as the demand level changes the equilibrium state changes too). The pursuit of ultimate equilibrium in industrial organizations is therefore often performed via a *revolving planning system* (see Fig. 35). At time t_1 one aims at reaching ultimate equilibrium at time t_T (or earlier), at time t_2 one aims at reaching a (possibly different) ultimate equilibrium at time t_{T+1}. Revolving planning combines feedforward with feedback; it contains feedforward because it anticipates the events expected until t_T and feedback because the differences between the plan for the first period (t_1 to t_2) and the realization are fed back to the new plan through the new values of the initial state of the system-being-controlled at t_2.

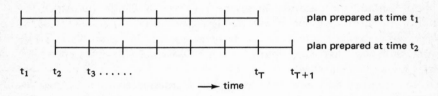

Fig. 35.   Revolving planning.
At time t_1 a plan with a decision horizon of T control periods comes into force. One control period later, at time t_2, a new plan with the same decision horizon, i.e. terminating one control period later, comes into force.

Ceteris paribus, the higher the inertia of the system being controlled the higher the futurity of the interventions which control it, and usually also the longer the control period (a revision of an intervention is only meaningful, if the relevant variables have changed sufficiently, and for systems with a high inertia the rate of change of the relevant variables is usually low). The higher the futurity of an intervention, the longer in general the time that organizational resources are committed. It is this property that Drucker used to describe the futurity of a decision (see section 11.4). We prefer definition 53, because it has somewhat less ambiguity.

Decisions with high futurity (i.e. concerned with slow-moving subsystems or aspect systems) often apply to larger parts of the organization and can often be taken at higher aggregation levels (see also the next two sections).

Some of the concepts discussed in this section can be illustrated with the linear control rule of section 8.2. This is an example of revolving planning: the rule only determines the production level for the first period, but this is done in anticipation of the development of the sales level (through the second term of

162

equation 4). The futurity of this decision cannot be determined exactly, because the weighting factors g_τ tend to zero but never reach this value. Nevertheless, the decision horizon T can be chosen in such a way that the remaining error is smaller than any arbitrary value (because the prediction of S_t naturally becomes less accurate with increasing T, very high values of T are senseless).

The higher the inertia of the system being controlled the higher will be damping factor r^2 be chosen. The rule shows that the higher r^2, the slower the factors g_τ decrease, thus the longer the decision horizon T should be (other things being equal).

14.3 Vertical Ablauf decomposition

Vertical Ablauf decomposition clusters control procedures according to the futurity of the interventions to be chosen, thus creating various control levels. Fig. 36 gives an example of such a multilevel structure for one of the divisions of Philips Industries (taken from the PROSPECT-blueprint to be discussed in chapter 16). The higher the level of control the longer the control period and the decision horizon, and the higher the level of aggregation.

level of control	control problems	control period (in months)	decision horizon (in years)	lowest level of aggregation
long-term control (LTC)	— innovation of technology — investment in fixed assets — size and structure of organization	12	4-10	market section
medium-term control (MTC)	— aggregate production and sales-level control — budgeting	4-12	2-3	capacity group
short term control (STC)	— ordering — scheduling	1/30-1	1/12 - 1/4	item

Fig. 36.   An example of a multilevel Ablauf structure.
(taken from the PROSPECT-blueprint, discussed in chapter 16).

At each level there may be a set of formalized (revolving) planning procedures, but it is also possible to have procedures which are only used when triggered by some event (e.g. procedures with respect to investment in fixed assets). Each level also has many non-routine and/or non-official control activities (which are of course less amenable to explicit design than routine-official procedures). Higher-level decisions are not restricted to issues in the more distant future: every procedure starts from the present situation (although control dead times may be longer for higher Ablauf levels). The number of levels depends on the situation and on the discretion of the control-system designer; of course the often used three-level structure has the appeal of simplicity.

The empirical content of the terms 'long-term control' (LTC), 'medium-term control' (MTC) and 'short-term control' (STC) is not fixed, but depends on the context. It often happens that the greater the distance to actual operations, the longer the control time constants. For example, in Philips Industries STC at factory level may have a decision horizon of a week, for a divisional planning department one to four months and for financial planning at corporate level a year.

Every control level has its own impact on technical operations. For instance, the LTC of Fig. 36 determines the capacity of fixed assets, MTC is used among other things to determine the size of the work force and to negotiate delivery contracts for parts and components and STC is used for ordering and scheduling (it is misleading to state, as e.g. Emery, 1969, section 5.5, does, that lower levels only have the task of spelling out higher-level decisions and that on the other hand organizational activities are only controlled at the lowest level). In Fig. 36 LTC provides strategic responsiveness (changes in the *nature* of the output) and MTC and STC operational responsiveness (MTC for changes in the *volume* of the output and STC for changes in the output *mix*).

This also means that each level needs its own information systems, because the information needed at higher levels is not just the aggregate of lower level information. Higher levels need not only additional information on the expectations for the more distant future, but also information on other subjects (e.g. prediction of the growth of consumer income in a country may be needed for aggregate sales control, but not for ordering). Finally, it is often possible to prepare better predictions for aggregate variables than for the items separately; one may call this phenomenon the *aggregation effect* (the predicted sum is more accurate than the sum of the predictions; we once encountered a situation, where the sum of the sales plans for the individual items of a division showed an increase of 22% over the figure for the previous year which was, as all planners agreed, far too much; at the same time each planner was reasonably sure that *his* detailed plans were not too optimistic). In view of the fact that different Ablauf levels require different information systems, automation of the information processing for higher Ablauf levels need not always be postponed until much of the information processing for lower levels has been automated.

An important task of higher Ablauf levels is to produce *ultrastability* (see section 12.3) for lower levels, i.e. they should control the slower-moving subsystems of the organization in such a way that they do not constrain the lower-level control too much. In the example of Fig. 36, LTC has to ensure that the aggregate production control by MTC is not unduly hampered by insufficient machine capacity and production space.

Higher Ablauf levels control the slower-moving subsystems of the organization over longer decision horizons. Decisions taken at higher levels must thus have *priority* over decisions taken at lower levels; lower levels should not be allowed to overrule higher-level decisions, because they cannot oversee the consequences of the latter. The interactions between levels thus often take the form that higher-level decisions set *constraints* for lower-level decision-making, while the lower levels have the task of *reporting* to the higher levels when these constraints seem too tight (see Fig. 37). On receipt of such a report, the higher level may change the constraints, but may well not do so in view of the longer-term consequences. It is because of this priority of decisions from higher Ablauf levels that we introduced the Ablauf structure as a *stratified system of control levels* in section 11.4.

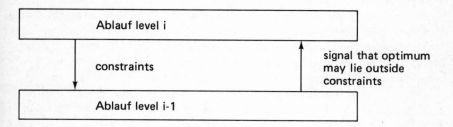

Fig. 37.   Relations between Ablauf levels.

Decisions, taken at level i have priority over decisions taken at level i-1; they set constraints for the latter. For instance, LTC determines the capacity with respect to manufacturing space and thus sets an upper bound on the aggregate production level to be controlled by MTC. MTC can report to LTC that this constraint will become too tight in next year view of the expected sales level for that year, whereupon LTC can decide whether a capacity expansion is worthwhile in view of the expected sales and profit for perhaps the next ten years.

The decomposition of decision-making in such a way that some decisions have priority over others can have a strongly simplifying effect on decision-making, because it *bounds iterations*. Many planning problems in complex organizations are solved iteratively: a provisional solution is prepared for a particular suborganization and passed on to connected suborganizations, where it is adapted and passed on to further connected suborganizations, etc. The proposed plans are finally returned to the first one and adapted again. In principle, this cycle continues until a satisfactory solution is found (an example is the divisional medium-term sales and production planning in Philips Industries, which involves sales organizations, divisional headquarters, end-product factories, component factories within the division and outside suppliers). Such procedures can take an enormous amount of time, which leads to long control dead times and possible suboptimum solutions (because it is often impossible to use more than two iterations). If some decisions have priority over others, decision-making can be performed *sequentially*, which takes less time than iterative decision-making (all other things being equal).

Vertical Ablauf decomposition creates homogeneous control subproblems (homogeneous with respect to the control period, decision horizon and aggregation level). This decreases the complexity of decision-making and permits specialization of people, procedures and information systems. Specialization with respect to people has the additional advantages of protecting higher level decision-making in turbulent situations. In such situations a version of Gresham's law ('bad money drives out good money') is often applicable, which can be formulated: *'today drives out tomorrow'*[1]. If the same man has to solve both short-term and long-term problems, he will tend (especially in turbulent situations) to give most of his attention to the short-term and to shelve long-term problems until they become so urgent that they have to be treated as short-term ones.

Integration of control is also simplified by explicit vertical Ablauf decomposition; decisions from various levels are then integrated through the above-mentioned sequential decision-making (instead of through iterative procedures), while the homogeneity of the control period, decision horizon and aggregation level facilitates the coupling of control procedures from different suborganizations (see the next section).

---

[1] We prefer this formulation to Simon's (1960, p.12–13) 'Gresham's law of planning', which states that 'programmed activity drives out unprogrammed activity'. Simon's version of the law is violated if unprogrammed activities become urgent. For example, the unprogrammed activities of handling the consequences of a breakdown of the electric power generator of a plant, will drive out a plant manager's programmed activities of writing his monthly report to divisional management.

14.4 Horizontal Ablauf decomposition

There appear only a few *Aufbau* levels at each level of the Ablauf structure, discussed in the previous section. For instance, in the PROSPECT-blueprint described in chapter 16, medium-term control deals with three Aufbau levels, viz. the capacity-group level, the production-department level and the factory level (Aufbau-levels 2, 3 and 4 in Fig. 14 of section 6.5). Decision procedures with respect to investments in fixed assets (LTC in Fig. 36) usually operate in particular at the factory and divisional levels.

As already mentioned in section 14.3, higher Ablauf levels tend to deal with larger parts of the organization and consequently with higher Aufbau levels. It should be noted, however, that (vertical) Ablauf decomposition assigns in the first instance *decisions* with respect to certain technological control problems to the various Ablauf levels, not *positions* The positions are assigned to the appropriate types of decisions during the specification of the decision procedures. Of course, the mode-1 coordinators of the suborganizations, appearing at a given Ablauf level, will usually be given a role in the decision-making procedures in question. Thus, the higher the Aufbau level of a suborganization, the higher in general the Ablauf levels where its mode-1 coordinator plays a role (which does not mean that mode-1 coordinators of large suborganizations *only* play a role at higher Ablauf levels; e.g. the board of management of a large company will not only deal with strategic questions, but will also be very interested in monthly reports on the status of their company).

An important design issue is the choice of the lowest level of aggregation to be used at a given Ablauf level (and consequently the smallest suborganization to be discerned at that level) and furthermore how and to what extent the control procedures for the various suborganizations *at that Ablauf level* should be connected in order to obtain integration of control. This is the question of *horizontal* Ablauf decomposition and integration.

We can distinguish various 'degrees of connectiveness'. If control procedures at corresponding Ablauf-levels in different suborganizations are totally unrelated, one can say that they are *disjoint*. If there are routine control inputs and outputs between suborganizations, but no mutual adjustment of procedures, these procedures may be called *adjoining* (e.g. suborganizations with a technological series connection, exchanging only orders and confirmations of orders). If there *is* mutual adjustment between control procedures e.g. by using corresponding timetables and by precisely defining the interfaces (with respect to aggregation level, planning horizon, etc.), one can say that the procedures are *coupled*. Finally, if the control interventions for different suborganizations are chosen in one integrated control procedure, one can say that the procedures are *fused*.

The 'degree of connectiveness' can vary for the different Ablauf levels. Long-term control (as defined in e.g. Fig. 36) of the production departments of a factory may be fused, whereas the scheduling procedures (STC in Fig. 36) for these departments may be disjoint or only adjoining. The degree of connectiveness may also be chosen differently for different aspect systems of the organizational control system. For instance, in designing a materials management system one may have the choice between designing an integrated (or fused) system for a whole Product Division or for the factories separately (only adjoining at divisional level) or even for separate production departments (possibly coupled at factory level). Although this question is certainly not unrelated to other aspects of the organizational control system, one still has some freedom of choice.

Higher degrees of connectiveness will usually improve the integration of control and will thus promote optimum transfer of interference. On the other hand, they may restrict local selfcontrol and consequently decrease local controllability. One has to choose, therefore, an optimum degree of connectiveness.

15.1 Control in the Large

The control paradigm discussed in section 11.1 can be roughly paraphrased as *'to Organize is to Control'*. Thus, changing the Aufbau or the Ablauf structure is regarded here as a form of control. This was expressed in section 5.2 by using the term *Control in the Large* for such activities.

The process of control was described in chapter 7 as one of interference reduction. Interferences are normally reduced by Control in the Small (CS), but sometimes Control in the Large (CL) is used as well in order to cope better with similar interferences in the future. If e.g. the factories of a company have increasing difficulties in obtaining certain materials, the company may set up a central agency to purchase such materials. If the settlement of damages by an insurance company is continually hindered by incomplete information from the insured, the company may change the control Ablauf by introducing forms for the declaration of damages. Thus CL can be regarded as an indirect mode of control.

CL belongs to the everyday activities of a manager. Apart from making decisions on various control issues (CS) he is also engaged in assigning tasks to his subordinates or in establishing procedures to deal with certain matters. However, this chapter will be mainly concerned with major CL efforts, such as major reorganizations of the Aufbau or the design and implementation of (large) automated information systems.

In chapter 7 we described interference reduction as an equilibrium-seeking process driven by the *dissatisfaction* of the controller with the existing situation. That discussion dealt chiefly with Control in the Small, but the same approach can be used to characterize Control in the Large. A control system is practically never designed and implemented starting from scratch, but evolves from one steady state to another (in several small steps or in larger ones), this evolution being driven by the dissatisfaction with the existing control system of one or more powerful organizational participants.

Dissatisfaction can be caused by a decreasing interference reduction capacity due to financial losses, by high adaptation costs or by ever recurring problems of a similar nature, which may indicate that the controllability is too low. Such situations may occur because of environmental changes, such as the appearance of powerful competitors, increases in the price of resources, or an increased rate of change in the demand on output markets. Another reason can be a change in corporate strategy, such as the start of a diversification programme or the expansion of activities to new geographical areas. This second cause is well expressed in Chandler's (1962) adage 'Structure follows Strategy'.

CL efforts with respect to control systems are often 'reactive', a result of dissatisfaction with the *present* situation (this is not so much the case with CL efforts with respect to technology). The reason may be that it is very difficult to predict the impact of environmental changes or changes in strategy on the organizational controllability[1]. A reactive CL strategy, however, can cause an evolution of the control system marked by recurrent crises, as is well described by Greiner (1972): only a crisis produces sufficient dissatisfaction to start a major CL effort.

Control in the Large involves initial costs for development and implementation, which have to be recouped during the life of the new control system. This means that the futurity of decisions to start major CL efforts is often of the order of five years or more (unless the benefits of the new system are very high or the initial costs very low). In the context of fig. 36 this means that such decisions belong to the Long-Term Control level.

A major CL effort may pass through a succession of various phases, for instance
— *initiation*: problem definition, orientation on possible solutions (or feasibility study), planning of the CL effort
— *analysis and design*: analysis of requirements and of the present situation, design of the new control system (or of a new subsystem of the control system)
— *implementation* of the new (sub)system
— *maintenance*: audit of the project and of the performance of the new system, maintenance and possibly implementation of minor changes (called 'control of the control system' by Ackoff, 1971) eventually resulting in initiation of a new CL effort to design and implement the next-generation system.

---

[1] Chandler (1962) shows that the trend towards divisionalization in corporate structure is not so much caused by deliberate actions in view of intended diversification programmes, but rather by dissatisfaction with the results of controlling diversified operations with the 'old-fashioned' functional organization structure. This is only to be expected: a simultaneous change of strategy *and* structure would involve a dual risk, so one tries first to run new operations with the existing organizational structure.

Explicit control-system design will deal predominantly with field 1 of the formalization mix (see section 5.1), i.e. with the creation of the routine-official parts of the Control System. Control subsystems belonging to the other three fields are much less amenable to explicit design. They are strongly effected by changes in the routine-official system, but the actors of the organization themselves have to supplement this subsystem to a large extent with effective unofficial and/or non-routine subsystems. It is therefore crucial to obtain efficient participation from them in the design and implementation process. When their participation is gained, 'an awful lot of things just organize themselves' (Beer, 1972, p16); this is also extensively discussed in the literature on 'organization development' (see e.g. Bennis, 1969, and Argyris, 1971).

15.2 Design Aspects

It is advantageous to use a holistic approach to Control in the Large. Such an approach has three aspects. In the first place CL should not be separated from CS: major CL efforts for industrial organizations should fit their strategic plans with respect to e.g. sales and production; new control systems are in principle built to solve not present-day control problems, but those to be expected for the coming years.

In the second place, Control in the Large should be based on a view of the control system as a whole. As mentioned above, a control system is practically never designed and implemented starting from scratch; CL efforts are usually directed at the replacement of a subsystem of an existing control system. However, changing one subsystem usually affects others. Using a holistic approach means that one analyses and designs not only the subsystem in question, but also the interfaces and relations with connected subsystems, from a perspective of the control system as a whole.

A holistic approach to control in the large means in the third place a holistic view of the evolution of the organizational control system. It is wise to execute actual organizational change in relatively small steps. In the words of Banbury (1975), paraphrasing two cosmogenetic theories, the emphasis should be on the 'continuous creation' of control systems instead of on one 'big bang'. A major reason for this is the difficulty of creating the necessary supplementary unofficial and/or non-routine control subsystems and of erasing the existing ones, if one makes too drastic changes in the official-routine system. However, one has to find the proper balance between the dangers of the 'big bang' and the hazards of using too many obsolete solutions from the present (trouble-ridden) situation. It is therefore advantageous to have a master plan for the development of the control system as a whole, which can be used to derive the CL projects of today. Just as the ultimate equilibrium of Control in the Small, discussed in section 14.2, may change with time, so can this masterplan be adapted on the basis of the experience with the new control subsystem, or changing CS strategies. In this way one gets a kind of revolving planning for Control in the Large.

A holistic approach to Control in the Large does *not* mean that one should always aim at designing large-scale automated information and control systems for the whole organization or large parts of it. For such endeavours Dearden's (1972) statement 'MIS is a mirage' is still valid in our opinion (especially if the step from the present situation to the new system is a large one).

As discussed in section 1.1, design is the activity of making artificial things with desired properties. 'A design is a structure within a situation' (Gregory, 1966). In this case the situation consists of the technology and the environment of the organization.

Design activities take place in the second phase of a CL effort. One can distinguish three stages in the design process (see e.g. Nadler, 1967, and Simon, 1969):

— determination of the function of the artefact to be designed (Simon: specification of the outer environment of the system)
— information gathering and search for alternative solutions (Simon: specification of the inner environment of the system)
— evaluation of the alternatives

Once the function of the artefact is specified the design process moves between two poles: the *synthesis* of solutions and the evaluation, testing or *analysis* of these solutions. These synthesis-analysis iterations continue until an optimum (or satisfactory) solution is found.

A key role in these iterations is played by the *representation* of the design problem (Simon, 1969). Only with the aid of an adequate representation, or model, can the designer handle his problem (Nadler, 1967, p18 'models are the alphabet and language of design'). It is one of the objectives of this book to develop concepts (such as stratified hierarchy, compound position and coordination mix) which can be used to represent elements of the organizational control system in order to help designers to handle their design.

A special function in this respect may be performed by the Aufbau-Ablauf framework discussed above, because it provides a coherent overall picture of the organizational control system. In designing a new control subsystem one can use such a framework to determine the position of the new subsystem (see Fig. 39 for an example), which can help the design of the interfaces with adjacent control subsystems.

Control is essentially a kind of information processing (linked through sensor and effector activities to the physical system-being-controlled). Control system frameworks in literature, therefore, often stress the information processing aspects. An example is the framework of Gorry and Morton (1971), who use a combination of Anthony's (1965) levels of control with Simon's (1960) distinction between programmed, semi-programmed and non-programmed decisions. Their framework is basically a taxonomy of information processing functions, not a coherent model of the organizational control system.

Another example in this field is the 'Kölner Integrationsmodell' (see e.g. Grochla, 1970), which is a very detailed descriptive model of the information processing functions in industrial organizations, providing also the relations between these functions. It is oriented towards the development of computerized information systems. Our Aufbau-Ablauf framework is not nearly as comprehensive as this model; we only propose to make a rough picture of the overall control system in terms of this Aufbau-Ablauf framework and to fill in the details only as far as is necessary in order to design the interfaces of the newly designed subsystem with other subsystems. Furthermore we may remark that the 'boxes' of the framework do not only contain official-routine control procedures but also procedures in the other three fields of the formalization mix and manually operated information systems as well as automated ones.

Finally we may mention the approach of Van de Wouw (1977), who describes the organization at various 'strata' in order to help the design of a coherent set of information systems. These 'strata' are: the goal-task stratum, the control stratum, the communication stratum, the automated message stratum, the files and programmes stratum and the data elements and actions stratum. The first two strata correspond roughly with the Aufbau and the Ablauf structure of control, whereas the next strata give more details of the information processing functions, in particular the automated ones.

15.3 Integration of Control

Control in the Large should create the conditions for integration of control, i.e. for obtaining sufficient mutual adaptation of the control interventions in the various suborganizations. This is particularly important if the control system faces complexity, uncertainty and a high rate of environmental change. In placid and simple situations there is ample opportunity to preplan activities and to secure their mutual adjustment beforehand. Long control dead times and a high technological inertia may nevertheless result in a sufficient controllability in those cases. However, if complexity, uncertainty and change make preplanning difficult, one has to rely much more on local responsiveness, i.e. one has to use a coordination mix with much selfcontrol. But this threatens at the same time the integral controllability (as discussed in section 12.1), so one also has to invest more in various coordination mechanisms.

173

We will conclude this chapter on control-system design with a summary of various ways of tackling the integration problem, discussed above (see also Galbraith, 1973 and 1974, for an interesting discussion of such issues; some of his ideas are incorporated in this section). Various aspects of the control integration problem are presented in Fig. 38.

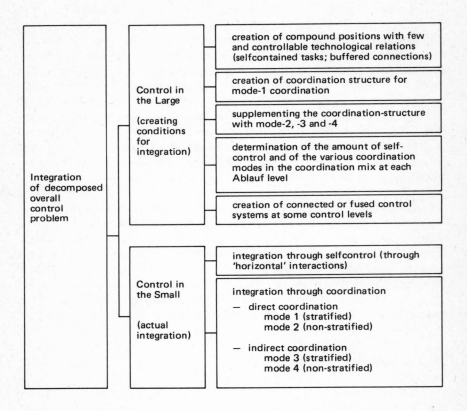

Fig. 38.   Integration of Control

Integration of control can firstly be facilitated if Control in the Large creates an Aufbau having compound positions with few and controllable technological connections. This can be realized by making compound positions with selfcontained tasks, so that they need little support from connected compound positions. Connections are easier to control if they are made buffered instead of rigid (see section 6.3; Galbraith calls this policy the creation of slack resources; however, buffered connections also have disadvantages, not only because they usually involve more operating costs than rigid ones, but also because they can cause difficult control problems as discussed in chapter 9).

Furthermore, Control in the Large has to create conditions for integration by incorporating the coordination structure in the Aufbau, not only with respect to mode-1 coordination (the classical line control structure), but also with respect to the other three coordination modes (as discussed in chapter 12 and 13, there are many possible ways of supplementing the mode-1 coordination). Control in the Large has to select the proper span of the hierachy of mode−1 coordination, the specialization principles to be used at each Aufbau level (see section 13.2), and may use a multidimensional stratification (or matrix structure).

Finally, various integration questions have to be considered when dealing with the Ablauf structure, e.g. the amount of selfcontrol of each control level (see section 14.3) and the degree of connectiveness of the control systems at each level.

16. AN EXAMPLE: THE PROSPECT-BLUEPRINT

16.1 Introduction

As an illustration of some of the concepts developed in the foregoing we will discuss their application in one of the Product Divisions of Philips Industries. This application concerns a project, which was given the name PROSPECT (*PRO*totype *S*ystem for *P*lanning *E*valuation and *C*oupling *T*echniques). The project aimed at developing a *blueprint* for redesign of a specific part of the divisional planning system and building a *prototype* of the computerized information systems to be incorporated in the new planning system.

The project was realized for the Audio/Video Division, which produces and sells consumer electronic equipment in some 70 countries, at that time (1972/73) with a sales volume of well over 10^9 dollar. The Division has some 60 factories, manufacturing both end products and subassemblies. These factories are connected to each other, to the suppliers of parts and components (from inside and outside Philips Industries) and to the sales organizations by complex flows of products: a total of several billion units a year of some twenty thousand different types pass between the various centres. This flow is continually changing in composition and volume owing to fast developments in technology and changes in the market.

PROSPECT deals with the problem of the mutual adaptation of production and sales, a subject discussed in some depth in part III. With respect to this problem the Product Division can be regarded as a network of demand servos, connected by flows of materials, trying to maintain an output equilibrium and resource-equilibria with respect to materials and components.

Compared with the interferences generated by the environment, the purely internally generated interferences are not very serious: the technology of the various separate demand servos is well known from a technical point of view and usually well run from an organizational point of view. In this Product Division, the environmental interferences affect both the demand side and the supply side. Sales are growing fast, but the growth rate is rather erratic; this causes serious interferences. These interferences are partly reduced by the commercial sector with the aid of variations in stocks, sales drives, etc., but there is also a fair amount of transfer of interference to the factories. On the other hand, the supply of electronic components is sometimes insufficient (especially in boom times, of course), causing very expensive production stops in the factories for end products. Furthermore, the Division suffers from the amplification effects discussed in chapters 8 and 9: the variations in aggregate production and supply levels are much higher than one would expect on the basis of the variations in aggregate sales levels.

As regards the interferences generated by variations in demand, the variations in the demand *volume* pose the greatest problems. Variations in the composition or *mix* of demand are usually less serious, as the *mix inertia* of the division (i.e. its resistance to chances in the composition of the output) is rather low. This low mix inertia has been obtained by explicit CL efforts, with respect to both technology and control. Engineering and product design have aimed at the development of only a few 'basic types', many different versions of which can be derived, while care has been taken to ensure that switches in production from one version to another of the same basic type are fairly easy to implement. Furthermore, ordering and scheduling procedures have been given short control dead times in order that variations in the demand mix can be followed smoothly. Finally there is also some 'mix indifference' in the market (especially in the Video-sector), i.e. customers do not really have very strong preferences for one version as compared with another. It is therefore to some extent possible to direct the demand for an unavailable version to an available one e.g. by lowering the price of the latter.

Variations in the demand *volume*, however, are more difficult to follow, owing to the relatively high 'volume inertia' (i.e. resistance to changes in the volume of the output) of the separate demand servos. Furthermore, variations in the demand volume trigger the above-mentioned amplification effects. Thus not only the rather low *local* volume controllability[1] of the separate demand servos, but also the mutual adjustment of their output volume poses serious control problems. It was the desire of various influential members of the Product Division to increase the *integral* volume controllability of the Product Division that initiated PROSPECT.

16.2 The project

Although there was no official vertical Ablauf decomposition in the Product Division, it is possible to distinguish various levels of control. These are shown in Fig. 36. The divisional Aufbau-Ablauf framework is shown in Fig. 39.

---

[1] In agreement of definition 42 of section 7.3 we can define the volume-controllability of a demand servo as unity minus the time average of the relative adaptation costs caused by changes in the demand volume.

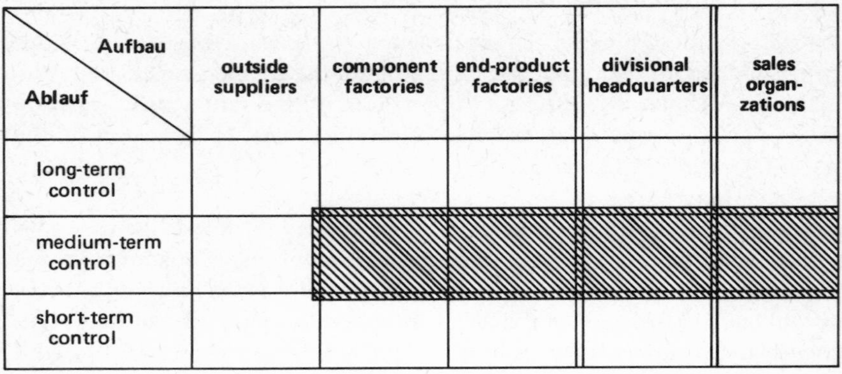

Aufbau / Ablauf	outside suppliers	component factories	end-product factories	divisional headquarters	sales organ-zations
long-term control					
medium-term control		////	////	////	////
short-term control					

Fig. 39. The divisional Aufbau-Ablauf framework.
The framework is shown at the Aufbau level just below that of the division as a whole. For certain design purposes it may be necessary to use lower levels as well (strictly speaking the outside suppliers do not belong in the framework; they are shown, because they play a role in various planning procedures). The shaded area was the field covered by PROSPECT.

In the terms of Fig. 36 it is the task of Medium Term Control (MTC) to provide the adaptation of the divisional activities to changes in the *volume* of demand. At the time the project was initiated (1972) MTC consisted of a set of procedures (formalized and non-formalized) in the different suborganizations such as factories, sales organizations and Divisional Headquarters, which were at best *adjoining*, but not coupled or fused (see section 14.4 for a discussion of these concepts).

The initiators of the project wanted a redesign of the divisional MTC (with new automated information systems) to improve the volume controllability of the Product Division. They felt, however, that this was a very complicated undertaking. New control systems are expensive to develop and to implement (especially if they encompass several suborganizations) and failures are very costly, in terms both of money and disillusionment. They therefore started up PROSPECT to explore the possibilities for improvement before undertaking a large-scale CL effort to improve the divisional MTC.

The objective of PROSPECT was in the first place to develop a *blueprint* for a new MTC, together with the interfaces with other levels of control. MTC was to become an integrated system for the planning of aggregate sales, production and supply (remember that 'integrated' does *not* mean 'fused', i.e. something like a 'total computerized management control system'). In the second place the project was to develop a *prototype* of the automated information systems which were to be incorporated in the new planning system. Blueprint and prototype were to be used as a guide for subsequent large-scale design and implementation of improvements in the divisional MTC.

178

The prototype was to be a small scale version of the real information system for only a small section of the Product Division. Its development had a dual purpose. In the first place it was to be used to test and appraise the design. In the second place it was to be a tool to obtain user participation in the design process. Models, verbal descriptions or flow charts are rather abstract, but a prototype produces information based on the actual situation with respect, for example, to sales, production and stocks, so the users are in a position to compare the possibilities of the new system with those of the existing one and can be expected to participate sooner in discussions on possible improvements.

In the terminology of Langefors (1974) the objectives of the project (including the prototype) were purely *infological*, i.e. the aim was to determine what information the control system should provide in order to satisfy the user's needs and what control procedures should be followed. *Datalogical* problems, i.e. problems concerning how the information systems are to be realised 'physically', were left almost entirely out of consideration (although the possibilities of present-day information-processing technology naturally formed an important element of the background of the project).

The project was to improve the divisional Ablauf structure of control (with respect to MTC). As is often the case with such projects, it had to use the existing Aufbau as a constraint.

PROSPECT was started in May 1972. The project team consisted of 4 men from the corporate automation department (including the author, who was the project manager) and 6 men (on a part-time basis) from various departments in Divisional Headquarters. The design of the blueprint took 4 months, prototype development 8 months and transfer of results, withdrawal of the corporate members of the project team another 4 months. In all some six man-years were spent on the project.

In the course of 1973 the project was rather unexpectedly complicated by a major change in the Aufbau of the Product Division: the latter was split up into an Audio and a Video Division. Although the design was equally valid for the separate Divisions, this interfered heavily with the transfer of the project results to actual CL operations, the more so because most of the supporters of the project in the Divisional Management moved to the management of only one of the two new Divisions. A final complication was that with the change of management the priorities with respect to automation changed too. At present (1978) the results of the project are indeed being used to guide control-system development in one of these Divisions (the one to which the supporters moved), whereas the impact on the other is less clear. Furthermore, the ideas generated by the project are used in various corporate training programmes on planning and automation.

179

16.3 The blueprint

In the present section we will describe the official-routine planning procedures, designed to 'fill' the MTC boxes of Fig. 39 (the non-routine and unofficial parts of MTC, which are to be supplemented by the actors in MTC themselves, will not be discussed). A somewhat more detailed discussion of the design has been given by Van Aken, Van Beek and Polderman (1974); see also Van Aken (1974).

In the PROSPECT-blueprint, MTC is performed at *capacity-group level*. A capacity group is a set of workers and means of production producing a homogeneous group of various products. In a factory for end products this can be an assembly line with workers, producing a certain *basic type* (see section 16.1), in a component factory a number of machines with their operators. A typical factory has some twenty to fifty capacity groups.

The *decision horizon* of the designed MTC is equal to the current year plus the next two years[1]. Planning is performed in a two-monthly planning cycle (in the terms of section 14.2: the *control period* of MTC is two months). During this period all plans within the Division concerning aggregate sales, production and supply are adapted to the most recent developments in sales trends, production and supply possibilities and to interferences such as production stops, overdue product development, or strikes (and once a year a new year is added to the plans; the actual horizon of the plans is never shorter than 30 months).

An automated information system will play an essential function in this planning process. The system will in fact be a system of information systems: local systems in the sales organizations and factories and a central one at Divisional Headquarters. It can be regarded as a *distributed* Management Information System. At a logical level it is designed as a whole, but its physical realization is distributed over the various suborganizations.

The information system has *recording functions* and more explicit *decision-support functions*. The latter are described below; the former provide storage and retrieval of information on e.g. sales, actual production, stocks, production capacity and the current sales, production and supply plans.

The Medium Term Planning cycle is to pass through three stages (see Fig. 40):

---

[1] Commercial planning decisions in this Division are predominantly expressed in terms of sales per calender year per product (group). Sales per month or per quarter mean little to sales managers (in particular because of the strong seasonal variation in sales). Thus a moving two- or three-year horizon, though feasible in the technical sector, was not feasible for an integrated MTC.

180

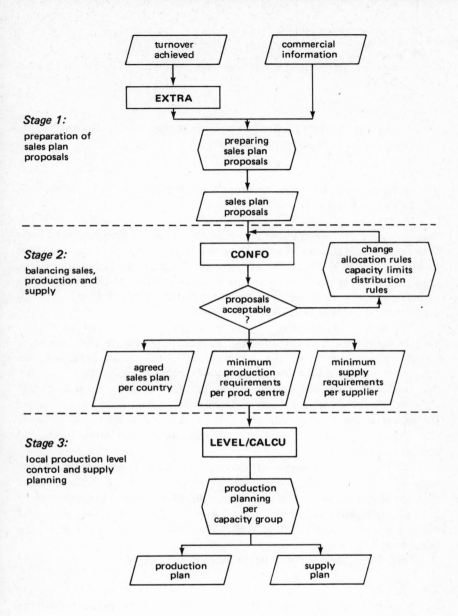

Stage 1:
preparation of
sales plan
proposals

Stage 2:
balancing sales,
production and
supply

Stage 3:
local production level
control and supply
planning

Fig. 40   The PROSPECT planning cycle for divisional Medium Term Control.

⬭ input/output   ▢ automated information processing

⬡ decision procedure.

181

Stage 1:

preparation of proposals for sales plans (supported by the subsystem EXTRA)

Stage 2:

preparation of agreed sales plans and minimum production and supply proposals (supported by the subsystem CONFO)

Stage 3:

preparation of production and supply plans (supported by the subsystems LEVEL and CALCU).

Stages 1 and 2 are carried out at Divisional Headquarters, where the main roles with respect to MTC are played by Divisional Management, the Divisional Sales Department (DSD) and the Divisional Planning Department (DPD). Decision-making is based on consultations between these parties and the sales organizations and factories; it is to be supported by EXTRA and CONFO, subsystems of a MIS at Divisional Headquarters.

The main problems with respect to *integration of control*, i.e. in this context the mutual balancing of sales, production and supply plans, are to be solved during stage 2 of the planning cycle. The major inputs to this integration process are the new sales proposals prepared during stage 1, and the data on production and supply stored in CONFO. Integration is chiefly obtained by the Divisional Planning Department, using mode-2 coordination (i.e. *non-stratified* direct coordination). The various suborganizations thus have the opportunity to defend their interests during the above-mentioned consultations.

The production requirements resulting from stage 2 are transferred to the factories concerned. They prepare their production plans during stage 3, using these requirements as starting point, but still having room to adapt their plans to local contingencies. However, stage 2 is designed in such a way, that these changes are in principle not so drastic that the whole balancing procedure needs repeating.

These three stages will now be discussed in more detail.

Stage 1

The purpose of stage 1 of the MTC planning cycle is to prepare proposals for sales plans for each capacity group of end products for the current year plus the next two years.[1] To this end the current sales plans are compared with

---

[1] Decision-making during this stage is concerned with world sales plans; the allocation of planned sales to the different countries is performed in stage 2.

actual sales and the opinion of DSD with respect to recent market developments (among other things based on consultation with the sales organizations and DPD). If DSD feels that the current sales plans are no longer correct, new *sales-plan proposals* are prepared; these proposals are the input of stage 2.

EXTRA supports decision-making by providing:

- actual sales data for the past year and the current year (the latter figure is obtained by dividing the actual sales in the past months of the current calender year by the average share of those months in the total turnover of a calender year)
- the current agreed sales plans (as determined during the previous planning cycle)
- a sales extrapolation for the current year, using double exponential smoothing with seasonal correction (see e.g. Brown, 1963) and for the next two years by fitting sales time series to growth or life cycle curves (see e.g. Lewandowski, 1974).
- warnings that the difference between current sales plan and extrapolation exceeds a given limit (if this is the case).

Stage 2

The purpose of stage 2 of the MTC planning cycle is to balance sales, production and supply of materials and components.[1] The output of this stage consists of agreed sales plans for each capacity group in each country for the current year plus the next two years and of minimum production and supply proposals for each factory and supplier per capacity group, also for the current year and the next two years. An agreed sales plan is one which has been checked by DSD and DPD for basic feasibility, both from the commercial and the production/supply points of view, and which is authorised by DSD after consultation with the other interested parties.

Decision-making is supported by CONFO. This automated information system performs the following operations:

- the sales-plan proposals (expressed in annual figures) are converted to monthly figures and allocated to the various production centres according to *allocation rules* given by LTC
- the plans are then 'exploded' into product and capacity quantities and shifted in time, level by level, to incorporate technical transfer times between the various production levels, while stocks of finished products and components are subtracted. The results of these operations are monthly minimum production and supply requirements for each capacity group and the minimum capacity needed (per capacity group and per production centre). These calculations use *condensed parts lists* (giving for each basic type the components needed at capacity group level), plus capacity data (required man-hours, machine-hours and space-hours per unit).

---

[1] The planning activities at Divisional Headquarters during stage 2 with respect to the supply from outside the Division pertain only to items, used by several factories and obtained from only one supplier (this is chiefly the case for electronic components). In the terms of section 6.3 these factories are connected in parallel with respect to these items. Because parallel connections can cause competition among the factories concerned in case of shortages, this supply is centrally coordinated by DPD. The planning of the remaining supply (typically some 60 to 70% of the total supply volume) is performed locally during stage 3 of the planning cycle.

- for each level of production and supply, the cumulative proposals are compared with the maximum cumulative production and supply capacities. These *capacity limits* are based on decisions from LTC and are provided by the factories or suppliers concerned. In calculating the feasible production levels CONFO takes into account:
  - i   technical dead times during which it is impossible to change the production level
  - ii   production space (present space and already planned changes)
  - iii machines and equipment capacity (present capacity and already planned changes)
  - iv   work force (present level and possible changes)
  - v   agreed supply levels from suppliers
- *capacity bottlenecks* and finished products affected are determined; these results are printed out on a *'bottleneck list'*
- the shortages due to capacity bottlenecks are distributed over the sales proposals for end products per basic type and subsequently per basic type per country according to *distribution rules* given by DSD. These distribution rules can be based on profit or added value or one can just use a proportional distribution.
- the result of these calculations are provisional agreed sales plans (checked for basic commercial feasibility during stage 1 and for technical feasibility by CONFO) and feasible minimum production and supply requirements. These results are printed out. If the calculations show that the load on a certain factory falls below a given limit, this fact is reported by CONFO.

Bottleneck lists, provisional agreed sales plans and feasible minimum production and supply requirements are used in the subsequent decision-making. Possible ways for dealing with certain bottlenecks are discussed with the parties concerned, and possible solutions of problems using different allocation rules are explored. Bottlenecks expected in the second or third year of the plans may trigger an investigation with respect to new investments in fixed assets. Too small a load on a given factory may induce a change in allocation rules. Finally, the consequences of different distribution rules may be studied, if DSD feels that certain basic types should be pushed more than others. For all these questions CONFO can be used to investigate the effects of changes in capacities, allocation rules, etc. (e.g. the removal of one bottleneck may produce little improvement, if subsequently another bottleneck prevents a higher supply of end products).

After this process the agreed sales plans are passed to the sales organizations; they are also recorded in EXTRA to serve as starting point for the next planning cycle. The minimum production and supply proposals are passed to the production centres and suppliers to serve as a starting point for local production-level control during stage 3.

Stage 3
The purpose of the third stage of the planning cycle is to prepare local production and supply plans. Stage 2 defined in principle a range of possible production plans: on the one hand the minimum production requirements define a minimum, while the capacity and supply limits impose a maximum.

Decision-making is supported by the subsystems LEVEL and CALCU, which are to be incorporated in local management information systems. LEVEL calculates a production-plan proposal based on minimization of the costs of stockholding and of production level changes, according to a relatively simple cost model. It uses a combination of dynamic programming and the version of the linear control rule of Holt et al. (1960) discussed in chapters 8 and 9 (see Van Aken et al., 1974, and in particular Van Beek, 1975). Dynamic programming is used to calculate a production programme for each capacity group, and the linear control rule is then used to smooth the sum of these programmes per capacity group in order to avoid too large variations in the production level of the factory as a whole.[1]

The subsystem CALCU then calculates the outlay of the production programme according to a much more detailed cost model than could be used by the optimalization programme LEVEL. This programme also produces information concerning e.g. stocks, utilization of various means of production (including the possible violation of capacity limits) and in particular work force (work force on payroll, work force expected to be present, work force needed for the production programme, number of new recruits needed, possible reserve workforce due to a temporary low load on the factory, etc.).

Subsequent decision-making by factory management will take the results of the optimalization by LEVEL as a starting point. However, there can be various reasons to deviate from this proposal (because the LEVEL model cannot contain every aspect of the decision). CALCU can then be used to calculate the consequences of alternative production programmes (in terms both of outlay and use of capacity). If for instance the decision-makers want to deviate from the economically optimum production programme, CALCU can be used to calculate the economic consequences. In this way the decision-makers can assess the costs of possible non-economic considerations. We feel that it is essential to supplement an optimalization programme with a facility for calculating the costs of deviations from the 'optimum' decision: an optimalization programme hardly ever contains every aspect of the decision to be made, so that the actual decision taken will often deviate from the one suggested by the optimalization programme.

16.4 Integration concepts in PROSPECT

The basic aim of PROSPECT was to improve the integration of divisional control. It had, however, to use the existing Aufbau of the Division as a

---

[1] Some advantages and disadvantages of the linear control rule are discussed by Silver (1972); in sections 8.2 and 9.2 we show why this rule is well suited for production level control at high levels of aggregation.

constraint, in particular the existing power structure as determined by the mode-1 coordination (the structure of line management). It therefore tried to achieve its aims by creating an Ablauf structure at MTC level consisting of *coupled control systems*. A fused control system was not feasible (nor desirable), because of the many non-programmed decisions (Simon, 1960) in the field of MTC and because of the necessity to make ample use of the selfcontrol of the suborganizations (due to the complexity, uncertainty and high rate of change).

Furthermore, the desired integration of control is in PROSPECT to be obtained mainly at MTC level. At this Ablauf level, the plans of *all* the divisional conversion systems are adjusted to one another (during stage 2 of the planning cycle, with the aid of CONFO). Within the frame work of the MTC plans short-term control can be realized through direct customer-supplier contacts; as long as the MTC plans remain balanced, it is not necessary to investigate the consequences of changing short-term plans in organizations more distant than the adjacent ones.

The integration of the various plans during stage 2 of the PROSPECT planning cycle aims predominantly at maintaining *integral output equilibrium:* the control system is designed to balance demand and supply both for the Division as a whole and for the suborganizations at various levels of production (sales organizations, end-product factories, component factories and suppliers from outside the Division). This balancing is based on feasibility rather than on optimality (in the terms of Simon, 1957, it aims at satisfycing rather than maximizing): we felt that it was still too difficult to use optimalization techniques in a system like CONFO.

In the process of balancing demand and supply for various levels of production, PROSPECT uses the principle of *direct transmission of information on final demand,* advocated in section 9.4 as the basic solution of the amplification problems discussed in chapters 8 and 9. Instead of receiving information on desired supply only from direct customers (containing all the distortion effects discussed in section 9.1), as was the pre-PROSPECT case, all production centres and suppliers receive up-to-date information on final demand during stage 2 of the planning cycle — moreover, converted in terms of their own capacities by CONFO.

The interface between MTC and STC is rather simple: MTC determines the production level for each capacity group, while the distribution of production over the various types is determined by STC on the basis of orders received from the direct customers. If the sum of these orders exceeds the production level as determined by MTC, some orders simply have to be shifted to future periods (any excessive backlogs can, if necessary, be taken into account in the next MTC planning cycle). If orders are insufficient, one can produce some 'evergreens' (again, if this situation persists, the production level can be decreased in the next MTC planning cycle).

The official-routine interface between MTC and LTC is largely incorporated in the CONFO data base: LTC influences MTC through capacity limits and allocation rules. The capacity limits are the results of LTC decisions on investment in fixed assets (and on the capacity of the local labour market). The allocation rules are also LTC decisions, because of the high initial costs of a transfer of production of certain products from one production centre to another.

In PROSPECT, MTC uses a *coordination mix* with much selfcontrol and mode-2 coordination (the latter chiefly by the Divisional Planning Department). Medium-term production and sales plans are not imposed from above, e.g. by Divisional Management, but prepared in consultations between sales organizations, production centres and departments from Divisional Headquarters. By using such a coordination mix MTC can make ample use of the discretion of the various suborganizations in decision-making (although this conjures up naturally various 'political' processes which do not always operate in the best interests of the whole).

Mode-1 coordination by Divisional Management is of course not absent. MTC plans have to follow the guidelines of divisional policy and mode-1 coordination still has to solve the conflicts which remain after the above-mentioned consultations. Mode-1 coordination is in particular necessary to resolve conflicts on distribution issues (because then the interests of the conflicting parties may conflict too much). There are two types of distribution problems (both caused by parallel connections), viz. the distribution of shortages of (electronic) components over the various production centres and the distribution of shortages of end products over the various sales organizations. In both instances, Divisional Management may have to interfere in MTC, in order to prevent the free play of power (and local ingenuity) from producing a suboptimum distribution (as seen from a divisional viewpoint).

PART V

CONCLUSION

17.1 Organization and Control

In the present section we will give a synopsis of this book, in particular of the system of control concepts developed here which can be used in designing organizational control systems.

There are various ways of conceptualizing organizations; we will therefore begin by summarizing our position in this respect with three statements.

The organization is an artefact

An organization is a group of human beings, combining their activities through a relatively stable network of social relations. This network is man-made and can thus be designed and constructed to serve human needs.

An 'organizer' follows a profession and not a science (which does not, of course, exclude the possibility that he can learn a lot from scientists in the field of the 'theory of organizations'[1]). *The essence of any profession is design.* It is the purpose of this book to contribute some ideas to the profession of organization design.

To organize is to control

An organization is an open system, which must be able to secure its resources from its environment. This is often done in exchange for a certain output. Resource acquisition and output disposal must be controlled in order to respond adequately to threats and opportunities.

To organize is to promote certain stable patterns of behaviour of the organization's participants through the creation of a 'control system'. Apart from possible other design criteria this control system must produce an optimum or at least a sufficient *'integral controllability'* for the organization in order to make it a viable one.

Control is a symbiosis of selfcontrol and coordination

The activities of the organization's participants, or groups of participants, are controlled through a combination of selfcontrol by these participants

---

[1] See section 2.3 for the distinction between the theory of organizations and organization theory.

themselves and coordination by some other specific participants. It is impossible to obtain sufficient controllability for the organization without a certain amount of selfcontrol (among other things because of the cognitive limits of coordinators). On the other hand, a certain amount of coordination is needed to 'integrate' the control activities of selfcontrol to arrive at satisfactory overall control; without coordination the organization may fall apart. The symbiosis must thus not deteriorate into parasitism of one of the two partners.

The following synopsis will present the main concepts discussed in this book; the formal definitions of these concepts will be listed in the next section.

Systems

An *element* is the smallest entity in a discussion. An element can have various properties; one type of properties comprises the relations with other elements. A *system* is a set of elements and a set of relations between these elements, the relations having the property that all elements are directly or indirectly related. The relations of the elements with other elements (inside or outside the system) form the *structure* of the system.

A system can be studied by making *subsystems* or *aspect systems*. A subsystem of a system is a subset of its elements with all their properties; an aspect system of a system contains all its elements, but only a subset of their original properties are considered.

A special type of system is a *conversion system,* a system converting physical inputs to physical outputs with respect to quality, quantity, place and/or time. One can regard such a system as a system with metabolism. It is a very general concept; all living beings can be regarded as conversion systems, but so can e.g. transistors, cars and industrial organizations.

A *hierarchic system* is a system with a parts-within-parts structure: it is a system the elements of which are themselves systems, and may in their turn also be hierarchic systems. A *stratified system* is a system the elements of which are ordered, individually or combined to subsets, according to a given priority criterion.

A stratified system is partitioned into subsystems. As every level of a hierarchic system describes the whole system, one can say that these levels are aspect systems (describing the system at different levels of detail).

The classical line organization has two defining characteristics, viz. hierarchy and stratification. An organization can be regarded as a *stratified hierarchic system.* Hierarchy and stratification form two *distinct* issues in organization design.

Organizations

The basic unit of any organization is the *position*, a set of relatively stable role expectations which is to be occupied by a person, which is to carry out a programme and which has a specific place in the organizational communication structure. Positions can be clustered to subdepartments, departments, divisions, etc. Such a group of positions is called a *compound position*. Now an *organization* can be defined as a system of occupied positions with their physical means of operation (note that positions and compound positions are abstract systems, whereas an organization is defined here as a concrete system, with its system of positions as its defining characteristic).

The *structure* of an organization is the set of relations of its occupied (compound) positions with other occupied (compound) positions, inside or outside the organization. These relations can be physical or non-physical. A physical relation refers to exchange of manpower, materials or money. A non-physical relation refers usually to information exchange; it can be an 'information support' relation (such as a research department or efficiency department has with its customers) or a control relation (such as e.g. Divisional Headquarters has with its factories and sales organizations).

One can distinguish two aspect systems of an organization, viz. the *Aufbau* and the *Ablauf structure*. The Aufbau is the system of positions, the Ablauf structure the structure of the organizational processes, i.e. it refers to the relations between the elementary events of these processes.

The *technology* of an organization is the set of physical conversion functions and information-support functions contained in the programmes of its (compound) positions, together with the physical expedients used to perform these functions. The *control system* of an organization is the system of formal and informal rules of behaviour, information systems and physical expedients used by the actors of an organization to control the organization's technology. Both technology and control system have an Aufbau and an Ablauf structure.

Industrial organizations can be described as systems consisting of conversion systems (such as factories) and non-conversion systems (such as research departments and accounting departments). The conversion systems are connected by physical flows; there are various types of such *physical connections:* series and parallel, proportional and non-proportional, rigid and buffered. Because of these connections, the activities in the various conversion systems of an industrial organization are interdependent.

193

Control

Control is defined here as the use of interventions by a controller to promote preferred behaviour of a system-being-controlled. It is a fairly general definition, applicable in many situations.

The definition makes a distinction between a controller and a system-being-controlled. For technical systems a controller is often a distinct *sub*system, for organizations it is always an *aspect* system: every actor contributes at least to the control of the execution of his own programme (however, some control more than others, see e.g. the discussion on coordination below).

The controller promotes certain behaviour. This can mean complete determination of behaviour, but e.g. the control of government actions by an individual voter falls also within the scope of our definition.

The process of control almost always uses the classical feedback loop, which can be divided into three phases: the *sensor phase* (observation of the system-being-controlled and possibly of its environment), the *selector phase* (evaluation of the system's behaviour and selection of a control intervention) and the *effector phase* (application of the intervention).

One usually needs control interventions to start and maintain steady-state operation of the system-being-controlled. However, the essence of control is the promotion of preferred behaviour in a changing environment, thus the promotion of appropriate responses to threats and opportunities. The latter process can be described as one of *reduction of interference*.

To define an interference we must first define the concept of *equilibrium*. According to our definitions a controlled system is in a state of equilibrium, if its controller refrains from a control intervention after the evaluation of this state; the system is in a state of disequilibrium if its controller chooses to apply a control intervention. Now an *interference* is an event causing a disequilibrium in a controlled system and *interference reduction* is the process of restoring the equilibrium of the system (by changing the state of the system-being-controlled or by changing the norms or preferences of the controller).

Changing the state of a system-being-controlled usually involves the consumption of resources, because most concrete systems have *inertia*. A necessary, but not sufficient, condition for the viability of an organization is that it must have sufficient resources at its disposal to reduce interferences. This requirement can be expressed in terms of the *interference reduction capacity* of the organization. The interference reduction capacity of a controlled system is the ratio of the resources available for interference reduction to the resources needed for interference reduction. Thus, if the interference reduction capacity of an organization is smaller than unity, this means that it has insufficient resources to maintain equilibrium.

An organization usually consumes resources not only to reduce interferences, but also to maintain steady-state operation. Thus the total amount of resources spent by an organization can be split into two types of costs: *operating costs,* consumed by operating the organization in a state of equilibrium and *adaptation costs,* consumed in maintaining equilibrium.

The *relative adaptation costs,* i.e. the proportion of adaptation costs in the total costs, can be seen as an indicator for the organization's efforts to maintain equilibrium; we use it, therefore, in our definition of controllability: the *controllability* of a system is equal to unity minus the time average of the relative adaptation costs. The controllability is thus a dimensionless figure between unity and zero: if there are no adaptation costs (no inertia or no interferences), it is maximum (equal to unity) and the harder (or the more expensive) it is for an organization to maintain equilibrium, the lower is its controllability.

Inertia is a 'closed-system property', denoting the resistance of a system to *change*, while controllability is an 'open-system property', denoting the systems capacity to *adapt* to changing circumstances. The controllability of an organization depends on both its own properties and the properties of its environment.

The core of an industrial organization consists of a network of conversion systems, connected by physical flows. The control of these flows is a major issue for such an organization.

The state of the physical part of an industrial organization can be adequately described in terms of levels and flow rates. Now the control of this *physical part* can be described as a process of interference reduction, which in this case is a *process of maintaining the levels and flow rates of physical flows in equilibrium.*

Viable industrial organizations cannot define their equilibria arbitrarily. They should at least maintain an *output equilibrium* and various *resource equilibria.* An industrial organization is in output equilibrium if its material output is on the average equal to the demand for this output; it is in resource equilibrium if the resources acquired by it are on the average at least equal to the resources consumed. As the environment of an organization is usually dynamic, both the above-mentioned equilibria are dynamic too.

The process of maintaining physical equilibria by industrial organizations can often be analysed with the help of the *demand servo* concept. A demand servo is an industrial conversion system designed so that its material output follows the external potential demand for this output. When a demand-servo approach is used, the results of control theory can be applied to derive various demands on the organizational control system such as short control dead times, suppression of disturbances, the proper damping of the response to variations in demand, etc.[1]

The physical connections between the conversion systems of an industrial organization cause interdependences between them. Hence the reduction of an interference by one of them may cause interferences to connected ones. This phenomenon is called *transfer of interference*.

Transfer of interference, however, is not an automatic process but in many cases a matter of choice. A conversion system may be able to choose between *internal* and *external reduction* of an interference. In the first case this reduction does not cause interferences to connected conversion systems, in the second case it does. For instance an interference to a picture-tube factory due to a machine breakdown can be reduced internally by using overtime after the machine has been repaired, or externally by simply cutting the deliveries to its customers (TV factories). Of course, the latter method causes serious interferences to these TV factories.

By using internal reduction of interference, the various units of an industrial network can *absorb* part of their internally or externally generated interferences, so that the smooth and efficient operation of the connected units is not unduly disturbed. On the other hand, full absorption of every interference is neither possible nor desirable, because this would prevent any adaptation to changing circumstances. Thus there exists an *optimum* degree of transfer of interference.

Control in the Large and Control in the Small

The concept of control has been used above with respect to the actual control of the operations of an organization. However, the construction (or modification) of the controller itself or of the system-being-controlled can also be regarded as a mode of control. The latter process is called here *Control in the Large* (CL), whereas the actual control of operations is called *Control in the Small* (CS). Just like CS, CL is also driven by *dissatisfaction* with the existing situation and it is used to attain adaptation to changing circumstances; CS tries to attain adaptation by changing operations, whereas CL tries to do so by changing the organization's technology and/or control system.

---

[1] Part III gives a detailed analysis of some dynamic phenomena in networks of demand servos.

Control in the Small follows in principle the three-phase cycle mentioned above. Decision-making, i.e. the choice of interventions made during the selector phase, forms the core of this cycle. Control-system design is therefore essentially the design of the decision-making system, defining the types of decisions to be made, the conditions for each type and the relations between the various types of decisions.

Because it is impossible to solve the overall control problem of an organization directly, CS is preceded by CL, which structures (or 'organizes') decision-making to make it manageable. To this end the overall decision problem is *decomposed* into subproblems involving the control of technological subsystems or aspect systems. The subproblems are smaller and more homogeneous than the overall problem and therefore easier to solve by CS. However, decomposition conjures up an integration problem. *Integration of control,* i.e. the mutual adaptation of the control interventions which solve control *sub*problems, is one of the major issues in organizational control. The organizational control system should create the conditions for integration; or, in other words: a major objective for control-system design is the optimalization[1] of the 'integral controllability', i.e. the controllability of the organization as a whole.

Selfcontrol and Coordination

The execution of the programmes of (compound) positions is partly controlled by *selfcontrol,* i.e. by the actors assigned to these (compound) positions themselves. Integration of control can also be realized partly through selfcontrol, i.e. the mutual adaptation of control interventions in order to arrive at satisfactory overall behaviour can to some extent be obtained through direct consultations between the actors concerned.

However, selfcontrol is essentially a *local* activity. The possibilities of achieving integration of control through selfcontrol are rather limited, due to a phenomenon which we have called the *'pars-pro-toto dilemma'.* On the one hand it is in the best interests of the organization as a whole that its suborganizations should aim at the protection of their own operations from external interferences (which refers to interferences both from outside the organization and from other suborganizations), i.e. the suborganizations should serve the *'pars'.* On the other hand, their missions are in principle not ends in themselves, but should serve the organization as a whole: the suborganizations should operate *'pro-toto'.* The proper weighing of local interests against overall

---

[1] As a control system involves development and operating costs, one should optimize and not maximize the organizational controllability.

ones is often very difficult, posing a *true* dilemma. The *complexity* of the interactions between the suborganizations and the conflicts between them due to possible diverging interests therefore generally require complementation of selfcontrol by *coordination* to obtain the above-mentioned satisfactory overall behaviour.

Coordination is performed by actors in *coordinating (compound) positions.* A coordinating position is a position which has as a programme the control of the execution of the programmes of other specified (compound) positions. Managing positions naturally belong to this category, but, as we shall see, so do e.g. planning departments, accounting departments and standardization departments.

Coordination is in our conceptual framework the control of people by other people. The 'levers' of coordination are *power* and *influence.* A social system has influence on another if it is able to induce behaviour of the latter which deviates from its behaviour without the influence, but which is still in agreement with the latter's preferences. A social system has power over another if it is able to induce behaviour of the latter which is in conflict with its preferences.

Now we can define two types of coordination, which we will call respectively *stratified coordination* and *non-stratified coordination.* Stratified coordination uses power to control the activities of coordinated groups, whereas non-stratified coordination only uses influence.

We can also make a distinction between *direct* and *indirect* coordination; the first type intervenes directly in the process of local decision-making, whereas the second type modifies it through e.g. general instructions or regulations before local decision-making actually takes place.

These two types can be combined to give *four coordination modes:*
— mode 1, stratified direct coordination is the traditional, powerful and well tested mode of coordination by line management
— mode 2, non-stratified direct coordination, is the coordination by e.g. product managers, liaison officers or planning departments; it is a direct mode, but it uses officially only influence to control the actions of the coordinated actors
— mode 3, stratified indirect coordination, uses regulations, standards, instructions, etc. to modify local selfcontrol; it is a stratified mode, so the instructions are backed up by a coordinator who has the power to impose them
— mode 4, non-stratified indirect coordination, tries to condition local decision-making in such a way that it acts 'automatically' in the best interests of the organization as a whole. Examples are the use of profit

centres (an intra-organizational simulation of Adam Smith's 'invisible hand', which coordinates the actions of independent economic agents in a perfect market) and intra-organizational management training.

The activities of the actors in (compound) positions are controlled by a combination or mix of selfcontrol and one or more of the above-mentioned coordination modes. This combination is called the *coordination mix*. The choice of coordination mix depends on the situation (see section 12.5).

Organizational control systems

The decomposition of the overall control problem by Control in the Large aims at the creation of small and homogeneous control subproblems. This can be attained if decomposition aims at the creation of subproblems which consist of choosing interventions with unity of time, place and action. Unity of place means that the interventions in question deal with activities which have minimum geographical dispersion, unity of action means that these activities have minimum technological diversity; unity of time means that the interventions have as far as possible the same *futurity* (the futurity of an intervention is the time over which it commits organizational resources; this concept is more accurately defined in section 14.2).

Decomposition creating subproblems with unity of place and action is the well known process of departmentalization, the creation of the organizational *Aufbau* (i.e. the system of positions). Decomposition creating subproblems with unity of time (or unity of 'futurity') decomposes the *control Ablauf* and forms various *control levels* (which can be labelled e.g. strategy and tactics or long-term, medium-term and short-term control).

Decomposition and the subsequent definition of the conditions for integration creates the organizational control structure. This structure can be described in terms of an *Aufbau-Ablauf framework* (see Fig. 31, 34 and 39 for examples).

The creation of the control Aufbau often starts with the creation of the mode-1 coordination structure, the structure of line management. In order to reduce the complexity of coordination, this structure is usually a stratified hierarchy. One obtains a reduction of coordination complexity through hierarchy if, at any level of the hierarchy, coordination concentrates on the interactions *among* suborganizations, while leaving the interactions *within* suborganizations veiled under the cover of selfcontrol.

In order to obtain compound positions with homogeneous programmes one can use one or more *specialization principles:* transformation, object, geographical or environment specialization (see section 13.2). Unfortunately, a technology which is homogeneous with respect to one of these principles is often heterogeneous with respect to others. The possible drawbacks of the use of a given principle in a specific situation may be compensated by the use of other principles at different levels of the hierarchy, by the use of a special kind of stratification (matrix organizations), by the complementation of mode-1 coordination with other coordination modes, or by the use of a proper Ablauf structure.

Decomposition of the control Ablauf can be performed horizontally and vertically (if we take the Aufbau-Ablauf framework of e.g. Fig. 34 as reference for determining what is horizontal and what is vertical). We have already mentioned vertical decomposition, which creates various levels of control, each level dealing with interventions of about the same futurity. These levels form a stratified system: decisions taken at higher levels are dominant over decisions taken at lower levels.

Horizontal decomposition of the control Ablauf refers to the extent one can discern the boundaries between compound positions in the control procedures at a given Ablauf level (e.g. to what extent decision-making deals with interventions concerning individual positions, or departments, or divisions, etc.). With respect to this question we have distinguished various *degrees of connectiveness:* disjoint, adjoining, coupled and fused (see section 14.4).

Control-System Design

It is advantageous to use a holistic approach to control-system design. Such an approach has three aspects:
— control-system design should fit the strategic plans of the organization
— the design of a new subsystem or aspect system of the control system should be based on a view of the control system as a whole in order to create the proper interfaces with the rest of the control system
— the design of a new sub- or aspect system should be based on a holistic view of the evolution of the whole organizational control system: large changes in an organizational control system involve great hazards, but if one makes a succession of small changes, each change should be based on a long-term perspective.

Once the function of the system to be designed is specified, the process of design moves between two poles: the *synthesis* of solutions and the subsequent *analysis* of these solutions (see section 15.2). The *representation* of the design plays a key role in these synthesis-analysis iterations. We hope that this work has contributed some concepts, including their functions in organizational control, which can be used for such a representation.

17.2 A System of Control Concepts

We now give a list of formal definitions specifying the system of control concepts developed here. Many of these concepts are well known, some are new or have been given a more suitable definition; concepts in the latter category have been marked with an asterisk. However, the main claim for originality is that they form a *system* (i.e a coherent set) of concepts. The definitions are arranged according to their order of appearance in the text.

Systems

1. An *element* is the smallest entity considered in an argument.
2. A *set* is a collection of elements.
3. A *system* S is a set E of elements with a set R of relations between the elements, R having the property that all elements of E are directly or indirectly related.
4. A *black box* is an entity the behaviour of which is not described in terms of its internal structure, but in terms of input, output, and − if necessary − a postulated internal state.
5. The *environment* of a system S consists of all elements outside S.
6. The *structure* of a system S is the set R of the relations of its elements with other elements. The *internal structure* R_i is the subset of R containing the relations between the elements of S. The *external structure* R_e is the subset of R containing relations of S with elements outside S.
7. A *closed system* is a system for which the set R_e of external relations is empty; an *open system* is a system for which R_e is non-empty.
8. A *subsystem* of a system S is a subset of E (the set of the elements of S) with all the attributes of the elements in question. An *aspect system* of S is the set E with only a subset of the original attributes.
9. The *state* of a system S at a given moment of time is the set of values of the attributes of its elements at that time. An *event* is a change in the state of the system. A *process* is a sequence of related events in the course of time.
10. A *conversion system* is a system converting physical inputs into physical outputs; this conversion may involve changes in quality, quantity, place and/or time.

11. A *nearly decomposable system* is a system which can be partitioned into subsystems with the property that the relations between the elements of each subsystem are stronger than those between elements from different subsystems.

12. A *hierarchic system* is a system the elements of which are themselves systems and may in their turn also be hierarchic systems.

13. The *span* of a level of a hierarchic system is the number of subsystems into which each subsystem is divided at the next level of the hierarchy.

14.* A *stratified system* is a system the elements of which are ordered, individually or combined to subsets, according to a given priority criterion.

15.* A *stratified hierarchic system* is a hierarchic system having at each level one or more subsystems which have priority over the other subsystems at that level.

Organizations

16. A *position* is a set of addressable role expectations with the following three properties:
   (i)   it is to be occupied by a person
   (ii)   it is to carry out a programme
   (iii) it is to have limited communication possibilities with other positions.

17.* A *compound position* is a set of addressable role expectations with the following three properties:
   (i)   it has to be occupied by a number of persons
   (ii)   it is to carry out a programme or a set of programmes
   (iii) it is to have limited communication possibilities with other compound positions

18.* An *organization* is a system of occupied positions with their physical means of operation.

19. The *structure* of an organization is the set of relations between its occupied (compound) positions and other occupied (compound) positions.

20. The *technological structure* of an organization consists of the physical relations and information support relations between its occupied (compound) positions, while the *control structure* consists of the information relations between the occupied (compound) positions which are directly or indirectly used to control the execution of their programmes

21. The *Aufbau* of an organization is its system of positions. The *Ablauf*

structure of an organization is the structure of the technological and control processes in the organization.

Control

22.* *Control* is the use of interventions by a controller to promote preferred behaviour of a system-being-controlled.

23.* *Control in the Large* (CL) is the construction or modification of a system, while *Control in the Small* (CS) is the subsequent control of the operations of that system.

24.* The *control system* of an organization is the system of formal and informal rules of behaviour, information systems and physical expedients used by the actors of an organization to control the technology of that organization.

25. A *coordinating (compound) position* is a (compound) position which has as a programme the control of the execution of programmes of other specified (compound) positions.

26.* *Selfcontrol* is the control of the execution of the programmes of a (compound) position by the actors assigned to that (compound) position themselves. *Coordination* is the control of the execution of the programmes of a (compound) position by actors in coordinating (compound) positions.

27. Social system S_i has *influence* on social system S_j if it has the capacity to induce behaviour of S_j which deviates from its behaviour without intervention from S_i, but which is still in agreement with S_j's preferences.

28. Social system S_i has *power* over social system S_j if it has the capacity to induce behaviour of S_j which is in conflict with its preferences.

29.* The *power ratio* of a system consisting of coordinators and coordinated groups, is the ratio of the power of the coordinators over the coordinated groups to the power of the latter over the coordinators.

Technology

30.* The *technology* of an organization is the set of physical conversion functions and information support functions contained in the programmes of its (compound) positions, together with the physical expedients used to perform these functions.

31. Conversion system S_i has a *series connection* with conversion system S_j if (part of) the physical output of S_i is used as input for S_j. System S_i

has a *parallel connection* with S_j if S_i and S_j draw (part of) their input from the same source or feed (part of) their output to the same drain.

32* Conversion system S_i, supplying conversion system S_j, has a *proportional connection* with S_j if the input from S_i needed by S_j, averaged over a certain period, is proportional to the output of S_j.

33.* Conversion system S_i, supplying conversion system S_j has a *rigid connection* with S_j if the input to S_j has to be continuously proportional to the output of S_i after a *fixed* interval of time. Such a connection is *buffered* if the time interval between the production of the output by S_i and the receipt of the input by S_j can vary.

Control as interference reduction

34. A controlled system is in a state of *equilibrium* if its controller refrains from a control intervention after the evaluation of this state; the system is in a state of *disequilibrium* if its controller chooses to apply a control intervention.

35. An *interference* is an event causing a disequilibrium in a controlled system.

36. A *state interference* is an event causing a disequilibrium in a controlled system without changing the controller criteria. A *norm interference* is an event causing a disequilibrium by changing the controller criteria.

37. *Interference reduction* in a controlled system is the process of restoring the equilibrium of the system.

38.* The *inertia* of a transition between two system states is proportional to the *resources* needed to bring that transition about. This inertia is also proportional to the *time* needed for the transition.

39.* The *interference reduction capacity* of a controlled system is the ratio of the resources available for interference reduction to the resources needed for interference reduction.

40.* *Operating costs* are the resources consumed by operating a system in a state of equilibrium; *adaptation costs* are the resources spent in maintaining equilibrium. The *relative adaptation costs* are the proportion of the adaptation costs in *total costs,* i.e. operating costs plus adaptation costs.
The difference between the resources acquired in a given period and the operating costs in that period is the *operating result* for that period.

41.* The *transition costs* of a system in a given period are the resources consumed by changing the state of the system; the *disequilibrium costs* in a given period are the resources consumed by being in disequilibrium for some time during that period.

204

42.* The *controllability* of a system is equal to unity minus the time average of the relative adaptation costs.

43.* An industrial organization is in *output equilibrium* if its material output is on the average equal to the demand for this output; it is in *resource equilibrium* if the resources acquired by it are on the average at least equal to the resources consumed.

44. An interference is *internally reduced* by a system if this interference reduction only involves adaptation costs for the system in question; in so far as the interference reduction by a system leads to adaptation costs for connected systems, the interference is *externally reduced*. External reduction of interference causes *transfer of interference*.

45. A *servomechanism* is a controlled system designed so that its output will follow a given 'reference signal' (a certain time function or time series) as closely as possible. A *regulator* is a servomechanism with a constant reference signal.

46.* A *demand servo* is an industrial conversion system designed so that its material output follows the external potential demand for this output.

Organizational control systems

47.* An *integral organizational control system* is a control system that enables and stimulates all actors in the organization to promote the minimization of both local and integral adaptation costs.

48. *Decomposition* of the overall control problem by Control in the Large is the partitioning of the problem into subproblems involving the control of technological subsystems or aspect systems.
Integration by Control in the Small is the combination and subsequent mutual adjustment of the partial solutions of control subproblems in order to arrive at a satisfactory solution of the overall control problem.

49.* *Direct coordination* promotes preferred behaviour of coordinated groups by intervening directly in the ongoing process of local selfcontrol; *indirect coordination* promotes preferred behaviour by conditioning local selfcontrol before actual decision-making takes place.

50.* *Stratified coordination* is coordination by coordinators who have official power over the coordinated groups; *non-stratified coordination* is coordination by coordinators who have officially only influence over the coordinated groups.

51. A system is *ultrastable* if it can reach an equilibrium state even after the occurrence of an interference which its normal mode of control cannot reduce.

52.* A system-being-controlled is in *ultimate equilibrium* if its state is in accordance with the preferences of its controller; it is in *provisional equilibrium* if its state is not in accordance with the preferences of its controller, but the latter nevertheless refrains from control interventions.

53. The *futurity* of a control intervention is the expected period of time between the moment it is implemented and the attainment of the ultimate equilibrium state aimed at.

54.* The *control period* of an intervention is the time that has to elapse after it is implemented, before a new or adapted intervention can be implemented.

18.1 Industrial Organizations

One of the basic objectives of this study was to establish fundamental structural elements which all industrial organizations have in common, and to determine the properties of these elements which can be varied during organization design to fit the structural element in question to a particular situation. Examples are *hierarchy, coordination modes* and the *Aufbau-Ablauf framework*. The fitting of a hierarchy concerns e.g. the choice of the span of the various levels and the choice of the boundaries between the subsystems at each level (using one or more of the specialization principles of section 13.2). The fitting of coordination modes concerns e.g. the choice of the coordination mix (see section 12.5), including the choice of the power ratio to be used by mode-1 coordination, and finally the fitting of an Aufbau-Ablauf framework concerns e.g. the choice of the number of control levels in the Ablauf structure, the determination of the interfaces between these levels and of the degree of connectiveness of the various control subsystems at each control level.

However, this study is based on the author's experience within one specific company, viz. Philips Industries. Although this company offers a fairly wide range of technologies and situations (see chapter 3), the one-company background will have introduced some bias into this study. One of the possible sources of bias is the fact that the study has been made in a European organizational climate.[1] Further research could therefore be directed towards questions with respect to the differences, but certainly also the similarities, in the control of industrial networks in different settings, e.g. in an American, Japanese or East-European social environment, or in steel, chemicals or car manufacturing, or in smaller companies or in non-profit industries (like practically every European public utility).

[1] Kassem (1976, p.14) has developed a typology of European and American approaches to organization theory. If one follows his typology, this study has used a European approach: it is more macroscopically (structurally) oriented than microscopically (behaviourally); its focus is on the organization as a whole rather than on needs and attitudes of people; its background consists of case studies, not laboratory experiments; it gives much attention to conflict; it makes ample use of abstract theories, not only practical theories and it is more theory (know-why) than technique (know-how) oriented.

Furthermore, various concepts such as inertia, interference reduction capacity, controllability, operating and adaptation costs, coordination mix and power ratio are introduced only with suggestions for operationalization; actual operationalization has not been carried out. Thus, further research could consist of case studies in which this is done. In our opinion it would particularly be interesting if a link could be made to the field of accounting, where several related concepts are used.

Such case studies could also give some more insight into the relations between specific organizational structures and the organizational situation; this can support organization design through statements like 'if you have this situation, *then* choose that structure' (like the tentative statements in section 12.5 with respect to the relation between the coordination mix and the organizational situation).

As mentioned before, the present study is more macroscopically (structurally) oriented than microscopically (behaviourally). It may therefore be worthwhile to complement the present results with a more systematic treatment of the influences of individual behaviour (aspects such as compliance, motivation, zone of acceptance) on organization and control structures.

18.2 Research Beyond Industrial Organizations

The focus of interest of this study was on the industrial organization. However, several concepts discussed here have deliberately been defined in such a way that their use can be extended to other areas of organized human cooperation. Examples are stratified hierarchies, control, Control in the Large and Control in the Small, compound position and organization, Aufbau-Ablauf framework, interference reduction capacity and controllability, selfcontrol and coordination, coordination modes and coordination mix.

These concepts could thus be used in further research directed towards the development of a conceptual framework for control and organization design at all levels of organized human cooperation, ranging from small one-level units (like a retailer with some assistants) to large multi-level organizations (like industries, universities, government agencies, hospitals and armies), but also including the control of whole national economies[1] or the coordination of sets of sovereign states in e.g. EEC, NATO or UN. Such a framework should provide the means for describing both the similarities and the differences between the various areas of human cooperation.

---

[1] In this case one might want to use the concept of a network of demand servos to describe the industrial sector of the economy, see section 8.4.

This research is proposed not because of the elegance of such a unified conceptual framework, but because of its possible contribution to the solution of some important present-day problems. Several of the problems facing industrial organizations have already been mentioned in section 11.2, but the problems at higher levels of human cooperation, those of the sovereign state and sets of sovereign states, seem to be even more pressing.

At both these levels, the system-being-controlled has become less 'nearly-decomposable' (see section 4.2), i.e. the comparative mutual independence of the subsystems on those levels has disappeared.

At the level of the sovereign state the 'night-watchman state' with nearly independent economic agents has disappeared, because of e.g. the desire of governments to create a more even income-distribution, to control business cycles and to deal with 'externalities' (see Mishan, 1971) in the field of pollution and also because of the emancipation of workers, employees and consumers. At the next level up the (economic) independence of national states is decreased by increased international trade, approaching limitations in the supply of energy and some raw materials (see Meadows, 1972, and Mesarovic and Pestel, 1974) and because of the political emancipation of the developing countries (demanding among other things a 'new economic order').

At the level of the sovereign state some feel that the 'end game of industrialism might well be that of the *entropy-state*'[1] (Henderson, 1976). The stronger interdependences and the externalities may lead to an increased need for coordination (in particular by the government), but one should not allow coordination to stifle selfcontrol. A well-balanced amount of selfcontrol and of small-scale coordination structures seems to be essential to avoid the above-mentioned 'entropy-state' (see among others Macrae, 1976, on this subject and also Schumacher's, 1973, *'Small is Beautiful'*).

At the next level of human cooperation, the problem seems to be rather the other way around. Organizations consisting of sets of sovereign states with a central (coordinating) agency, like the EEC and the UN, have a power ratio (see section 5.4), which is much smaller than unity, so that the coordination capacity of the central agency is low (when the views of the member states conflict – which they generally do). The increased economic interdependence

---

[1]Henderson (1976, p.337): 'Simply put, the entropy-state is a society at the stage when complexity and interdependence have reached such unmodelable, unmanageable proportions, that the transaction costs generated equal or exceed its productive capabilities. In a manner analogous to physical systems, the society winds down of its own weight and the proportion of its gross national product that must be spent in mediating conflicts, controlling crime, footing the bill for all the social costs generated by the 'externalities' of production and consumption, providing ever more comprehensive bureaucratic coordination and generally trying to maintain 'social homeostasis' begins to grow exponentially and possibly hyperexponentially'.

of sovereign states, however, has nevertheless increased the need for coordination, so that a way must be found to provide this.

A unified conceptual framework, providing a basis for the design of various different coordination structures for many forms of human cooperation, might provide some help to solve the above-mentioned problems. At this moment we can only point out that the concepts presented in this book are in principle applicable in other areas; it is up to further research to establish whether such application would be worthwhile.

210

REFERENCES

- Abels, A.G. 'BICEPS, capacity planning by a linear decision rule', paper presented at the first meeting of EWADOM, Eindhoven, 1976.
- Ackoff, R.L. 'Towards a system of Systems-concepts'. *Management Science* 17 (1971) 661–671.
- Ackoff, R.L. and Sasieni, M.W. *Fundamentals of Operations Research* New York: Wiley, 1968.
- Ansoff, H.I. *Corporate Strategy*. New York: Mc Graw Hill, 1965.
- Ansoff, H.I. and Brandenburg, R.G. 'A language for organization design' *Management Science* 17 (1971) B705–B731.
- Anthony, R.N. *Management Accounting, text and cases.* Homewood: Irwin, 1964.
- Anthony, R.N. *Planning and Control Systems: a framework for analysis.* Boston: Harvard University, 1965.
- Argyris, C. *Management and Organizational Development.* New York: Mc Graw Hill, 1971.
- Ashby, W.R. *Design for a Brain.* London: Chapman and Hall, 1952.
- Ashby, W.R. *An Introduction to Cybernetics.* London: Chapman and Hall, 1956.
- Banbury, J. 'Information system design, organizational control and optimality'. *Omega* 3 (1975) 449–460.
- Barnard, Ch.I. *The functions of the executive.* Cambridge (Mass): Harvard University Press, 1938.
- Beer, S. *Brain of the Firm.* London: Allen Lane, the Penguin Press, 1972.
- Bensoussan, A., Hurst, E.G. and Näslund, B. *Management application of modern control theory.* Amsterdam: North Holland Pub. cy., 1974.
- Bennis, W.G. *Organization Development: its nature, origins and prospects.* Reading: Addison-Wesley, 1969.
- Blau, P.M. *Exchange and Power in Social Life.* New York: Wiley, 1964.
- Blumenthal, S.C. *Management Information Systems.* Englewood Cliffs: Prentice Hall, 1969.
- Bonini, Ch.P. 'Simulation of Organizational Behaviour' in Ch.P. Bonini, R.K. Jaedike and H.M. Wagner. *Management Control: New Directions in Basic Research.* New York: Mc Graw Hill, 1964.
- Boulding, K.E. 'General System Theory, the Skeleton of Science'. *Management Science* 2 (1956) 197–208.
- Bouman, P.J. *Anton Philips.* Eindhoven: Centrex, 1956.

- Brown, R.G. *Smoothing, Forecasting and Prediction of Discrete Time Series.* Englewood Cliffs: Prentice Hall, 1963.
- Burns, J.F. *Derivation and simulation of an ordering rule for the multi-echelon supply chain.* Gainesville: University of Florida, department of industrial and systems engineering, technical report no. 45, 1970.
- Casimir, H.B.G. 'Door meten tot weten in de Natuurwetenschap' (knowledge through measurement in the sciences; in Dutch). *Statistica Neerlandica* 16 (1962) 317–320.
- Chandler, A.D. *Strategy and Structure.* Cambridge (Mass): the M.I.T. Press, 1962.
- Checkland, P.B. 'Towards a Systems-based methodology for real-world problem solving'. *International Journal of System Engineering* 3 (1972) 87–116.
- Clark, A.J. 'An informal survey of multi-echelon inventory theory' *Naval Research Logistics Quarterly.* 19 (1972) 621–650.
- Cohen, M.D. and March, J.G. *Leadership and Ambiguity.* New York: Mc Graw Hill, 1974.
- Conant, R.C. and Ashby, W.R. 'Every good regulator of a system must be a model of that system'. *International Journal of System Science* 1 (1970) 89–97.
- Crozier, M. *The bureaucratic phenomenon.* London: Tavistock, 1964.
- Cyert, R.M. and March, J.G. *A behavioural theory of the firm.*Englewood Cliffs: Prentice Hall, 1963.
- Dale, E. 'Functions of the manager of tomorrow'. *Training Directors Journal* 9 (1963) 25–36.
- Dantzig, G.B. *Linear Programming and Extensions.* Princeton: Princeton University Press, 1963.
- Dearden, J. 'MIS is a Mirage'. *Harvard Business Review* (Jan–Feb 1972) 90–99.
- De Leeuw, A.C.J. *Systeemleer en Organisatiekunde* (system theory and organization theory; in Dutch). Leiden: Stenfert Kroese, 1974.
- De Leeuw, C.G. and Grünwald, H. 'Het IPSO-middellange termijn besturingssysteem' (the IPSO-medium term control-system; in Dutch). *Internal Philips Report,* 1971.
- De Sitter, L.U. 'A system theoretical paradigm of social interaction: towards a new approach to qualitative system dynamics'. *Annals of System Research* 3 (1973) 100–140.
- Drucker, P.F. *Management, Tasks, Responsibilities, Practices.* London: Heinemann, 1974a.
- Drucker, P.F. 'New Templates for today's Organizations' *Harvard Business Review* (Jan–Feb 1974b) 45–53.
- Elgerd, O.I. *Control Systems Theory.* New York: Mc Graw Hill, 1967.

212

— Elmaghraby, S.E. *The design of production systems.* New York: Reinhold, 1966.

— Emery, J.C. *Organizational Planning and Control Systems.* London: Mc Millan, 1969.

— *Encyclopaedia Brittannica,* 15th edition. Chicago: 1974.

— Etzioni, A. *A basis for comparative analysis of complex organizations.* New York: The Free Press of Glencoe, 1961.

— Ezekiel, M. 'The Cobweb Theorem'. *Quarterly Journal of Economics* 52 (1938) 255—280.

— Faludi, A. *Planning Theory.* Oxford: Pergamon Press, 1973.

— Fayol,W. *Administration Industrielle et Générale.* Paris: Dunod, 1925.

— Forrester, J.W. *Industrial Dynamics.* New York: Wiley, 1961.

— Forrester, J.W. *Principles of Systems.* Cambridge (Mass): Wright Allen Press, 1968.

— Forrester, J.W. 'Business Structure, Economic Cycles and National Policy'. *Futures* (June 1976) 195—214.

— Freeman, C. 'The Kondratiev long waves, technical change and unemployment'. Mimeographed paper, OECD, March 1977, to be published.

— Galbraith, J.R. *Designing Complex Organizations.* Reading: Addison — Wesley, 1973.

— Galbraith, J.R. 'Organization design: an information processing view'. *Interfaces* 4 (1974—3) 28—36.

— Galbraith, J.R. *Organization Design.* Reading: Addison — Wesley, 1977.

— Georgiou, P. 'The goal-paradigm and notes toward a counter-paradigm'. *Administrative Science Quarterly* 19 (1974) 291—310.

— Gloor, M. 'Developing and managing multinational operation'. CIOS-conference, Munich, 1972.

— Goggin, W.C. 'How the multi-dimensional structure works at Dow Corning'. *Harvard Business Review* (Jan—Feb 1974) 34—65.

— Gorry, G.A. and Morton, M.S. 'A framework for Management Information Systems'. *Sloan Management Review* (Fall 1971) 55—70.

— Gregory, S.A. *The design method,* London: Butterworths, 1966.

— Greiner, L.E. 'Evolution and revolution as organization grow'. *Harvard Business Review* (July—Aug 1972) 37—46.

— Grochla, E. 'Die Gestaltung allgemeingültiger Anwendungsmodelle für die automatische Informationsverarbeitung in Wirtschaft und Verwaltung'. *electronische datenverarbeitung* 21 (1970) 49—55.

— Grünwald, H. 'Entwurf und Analyse eines Management Informations Systems für die Steuerung einer grossen industriellen Organisation'. In *Planungsforschung und Forschungsplanung im öffentlichen und privaten Bereich.* Wien: Springer, 1972.

213

- Grünwald, H. 'Analyse van het KETEN-simulatie model voor drie manieren van informatieverstrekking' (analysis of the chain simulation-model for three types of transmission of information; in Dutch). *Internal Philips Report,* 1973.
- Grünwald, H. and Smit, N.W. 'Dynamisch Plannen' (dynamic planning; in Dutch). *Internal Philips Report,* 1965.
- Gulick, L. and Urwick, L.(ed.) *Papers on the Science of Administration.* New York: Institute of public administration, 1937.
- Henderson, H. 'The coming economic transition'. *Technological Forecasting and Social Change* 8 (1976) 337–351.
- Hickson, D.J. et al. 'A strategic contingencies theory of intra-organizational power'. *Administrative Science Quarterly* **16** (1971) 216–229.
- Hickson, D.J. et al. 'Structural conditions of intra-organizational power'. *Administrative Science Quarterly* 19 (1974) 22–44.
- Hofstede, G. *The game of budget control.* Amsterdam: Van Gorcum, 1967.
- Hofstede, G. *Measuring Hierarchical Power Distance in Thirty-seven countries.* Brussels: European Institute for Advanced Studies in Management, Working paper 76–32, 1976.
- Hofstede, G. 'The poverty of management control philosophy', *Academy of Management Review* (1978) forthcoming.
- Hofstede, G. and Kassem, M.S. (ed.) *European Contributions to Organization Theory.* Amsterdam: Van Gorcum, 1976.
- Holt, C.C., Modigliani, F., Muth, J.F. and Simon, H.A. *Planning Production, Inventories and Workforce.* Englewood Cliffs: Prentice Hall, 1960.
- Hopwood, A.G. 'Accounting and Organizational Behaviour' in Carsberg, B.V. and Hope, A. (ed.) *Current Issues in Accountancy.* London: Philip Allan, 1977.
- Isard, W. 'A neglected cycle: the transport-building cycle'. *The Review of Economic Statistics* 24 (1942) 149–158.
- Jacques, E. *Measurement of Responsibility.* London: Tavistock Publ., 1956.
- Jenkins, G.M. 'The Systems Approach'. *Journal of Systems Engineering.* 1 (1969) 3–49.
- Kalecki, M. 'Trend and business-cycle reconsidered'. *Economic Journal* (June 1968) 263–276.
- Kassem, M.S. 'European versus American Organization Theories' in Hofstede and Kassem (1976).
- Kast, F.E. and Rozenzweig, J.E. (ed.) *Contingency views of organizations and management.* Chicago: Science Research Associates, 1973.

214

- Knight, K. 'Matrix organization: a review'. *Journal of Management Studies*. (May 1976) 112–130.
- Kosiol, E. *Organisation der Unternehmung*. Wiesbaden: Th. Gabler, 1962.
- Kwakernaak, H. and Sivan, R. *Linear Optimal Control Systems*. New York: Wiley, 1972.
- Laaksonen, O. 'The structure and management of Chinese enterprises'. *Finnish Journal of Business Economics*. (1975–2) 3–22.
- Langefors, B. 'Information Systems' *Proceedings IFIP 1974*. Amsterdam: North Holland Pub.cy., 1974.
- Langereis, J.H. 'De conjunctuur cyclus in het economische leven'. (the business cycle in the economy; in Dutch). *De Ingenieur* 87 (1975) 437–441.
- Laszlo, E. 'The meaning and significance of General System Theory' *Behavioural Science* 20 (1975) 9–24.
- Lewandowski, R. *Prognose- und Informationssysteme unde ihre Anwendungen, Band 1*. Berlin: Walter de Gruyter, 1974.
- Liddell Hart, B.H. *Strategy, the indirect approach*. London: Faber and Faber, 1954.
- Luhmann, N. *Functionen und Folgen formaler Organisation*. Berlin: Duncker und Humbolt, 1964.
- Luhmann, N. 'A general theory of organized social systems' in Hofstede and Kassem (1976).
- Lyden, F.J. and Miller, E.G. (ed.) *Planning Programming Budgeting*. Chicago: Markam Pub.cy., 1967.
- Macrae, N. 'The coming entrepreneurial revolution: a survey'. *The Economist*, December 25, 1976, 41–65.
- Magee, J.F. *Production Planning and Inventory Control*. New York: Mc Graw Hill, 1958.
- March, J.G. and Simon, H.A. *Organizations*. New York: Wiley, 1958.
- Mayntz, R. 'Conceptual Models of Organizational Decision-making and their Application to the Policy Process' in Hofstede and Kassem, 1976.
- Mayo, E. *The human problems of an industrial civilization*. New York: Mc Millan, 1933.
- Meadows, D.L. *Dynamics of Commodity Production Cycles*. Cambridge (Mass.): Wright Allen Press, 1970.
- Meadows, D. 'The Limits to Growth'. New York: Universe Books, 1972.
- Mesarovic, M.D., Macko, D. and Takahara, Y. *Theory of hierarchical multilevel systems*. New York: Academic Press, 1970.
- Mesarovic, M.D. and Pestel, E. *Mankind at the turning point: the second report to the Club of Rome*. New York: Dutton and Co., 1974.
- Mesarovic, M.D. and Takahara, Y. *General Systems Theory: Mathematical Foundations*. New York: Academic Press, 1975.

- Miller, E.J. 'The open system approach to organizational analysis with specific reference to the work of A.K. Rice' in Hofstede and Kassem (1976).
- Mishan, E.J. 'The postwar literature on externalities: an interpretative essay'. *Journal of Economic Literature* 1971) 1–28.
- Mulder, M. *Het Spel om Macht.* Meppel: Boom, 1972 (English version 'the daily power-game' to be published).
- Nadler, G. *Work systems design: the ideals concept.* Homewood: Irwin, 1967.
- Parsons, T. *Structure and process in modern societies.* New York: the Free Press of Glencoe, 1960.
- Perrow, Ch. 'A framework for the comparative analysis of organizations'. *American Sociological Review* 32 (1967) 194–208.
- Philips, F.J. *45 jaar met Philips* (45 years with Philips; in Dutch). Rotterdam: Donker, 1976.
- Polderman, G.L. 'Een vergelijklung van jaarcijfers van Philips met enkele andere electrotechnische ondernemingen'. (A comparison of some figures from the Philips annual report with those from some other electrotechnical companies; in Dutch). *Internal Philips Report,* 1971.
- Porkert, M. *The theoretical foundations of Chinese medicine.* (Cambridge (Mass): the M.I.T. press, 1974.
- Post, J.G. 'Timing in de nederlandse conjunctuurpolitiek' (timing of the Dutch policy to control the business cycle; in Dutch). *Economisch Statistische Berichten,* November 14, 1973.
- Pugh, D. 'The Aston-approach to the study of organizations' in Hofstede and Kassem, 1976.
- Rapoport, A. and Horvath, W.J. 'Thoughts on organization theory and a review of two conferences'. *General Systems* 4 (1959) 90–110.
- Roethlisberger, F.J. and Dickson, W.J. *Management and the Worker* Cambridge (Mass): Harvard University Press, 1939.
- Sagasti, F.R. 'A conceptual 'systems' framework for the study of planning theory'. *Technological Forecasting and Social Change* 5 (1973) 379–393.
- Sasaki, N. 'A comparative study of the decision-making process: Japan and the West'. *Sophia Economic Review* 19 (1973) 37–46.
- Sayles, L.R. 'Matrix Management: the structure with a future'. *Organizational Dynamics* (Autumn 1976) 2–17.
- Schneeweiss, A. *Regelungstechnische stochastische Optimierungsverfahren.* Berlin: Springer, 1971.
- Schreiber H. *Die Hunnen.* Düsseldorf: Econ. Verlag, 1976.
- Schumacher, E.F. *Small is Beautiful.* London: Blond and Brigs, 1973.
- Schumpeter, J. *Business Cycles.* New York: Mc Graw Hill, 1967.
- Shapiro, B.P. 'Can Marketing and Manufacturing coexist?' *Harvard Business Review* (Sep–Oct 1977) 104–114.

- Silver, E.A. 'Medium Range Aggregate Production Planning: a State of the Art'. *Production and Inventory Management* (1972) 15–39.
- Silverman, D. *The Theory of Organizations.* London: Heinemann, 1970.
- Simon, H.A. 'On the application of servo-mechanism theory in the study of production control' *Econometrica* 20 (1952) 247–268.
- Simon, H.A. 'Dynamic programming under uncertainty with a quadratic criterion function' *Econometrica* 24 (1956) 74–81.
- Simon, H.A. *Administrative behaviour.* New York: the Free Press of Glencoe, 2nd edition, 1957.
- Simon, H.A. *The New Science of Management Decision* New York: Harper and Row, 1960.
- Simon, H.A. 'The architecture of complexity'. *Proceedings American Philosophical Society* 106 (1962) 467–482.
- Simon, H.A. *The Sciences of the Artificial.* Cambridge (Mass): the M.I.T. Press, 1969.
- Simon, H.A. 'The organizations of complex systems' in H.H. Pattee (ed.): *Hierarchy Theory.* New York: George Braziller, 1973.
- Taylor, F. *Scientific Management.* New York: Harper and Row, 1911.
- Teulings, A. *Philips, geschiedenis en praktijk van een wereldconcern.* (Philips, history and practice of a worldwide company; in Dutch). Amsterdam: Van Gennep, 1976.
- Theil, H. 'A note on certainty equivalence in dynamic programming'. *Econometrica* **25** (1957) 346–349.
- Thompson, J.D. *Organizations in Action.* New York: Mc Graw Hill, 1967.
- Tocher, K.D. 'Control'. *Operational Research Quarterly* 21 (1970) 159–180.
- Urwick, L.F. 'Why the so-called 'classicists' endure'. *International Management Review* 11 (1971) 3–18.
- Van Aken, J.E. 'Electron Spin Resonance in Liquid Sulfur'. *Physica* 39 (1968) 107–108.
- Van Aken, J.E. 'Middellange termijn productie niveauregeling met lineaire besturingsregels' (medium term production-level control with linear control rules; in Dutch). *Internal Philips Report,* 1970.
- Van Aken, J.E. 'Een simulatie model van een keten van productie-voorraad systemen' (a simulation model of a chain of production-inventory systems; in Dutch). *Internal Philips Report, 1971.*
- Van Aken, J.E. 'Enige micro-economische beschouwingen over conjunctuur' (a micro-economic approach to the business-cycle; in Dutch). *Maandblad voor Bedrijfsadministratie en Organisatie* 77 (1973) 88–94.
- Van Aken, J.E. 'Control problems in a network of factories and sales organizations'. Paper presented at IFAC-workshop on Corporate Control Systems, Twente, The Netherlands, 1974.

217

- Van Aken, J.E. et al. 'The company's internal business cycle'. *Internal Philips Report*, 1971.
- Van Aken, J.E. et al. 'Controlling the concern's internal business cycle' *Internal Philips Report*, 1975.
- Van Aken, J.E., Van Beek, P. and Polderman, G.L. 'PROSPECT, a prototype distributed MIS for operational control of a network of factories and sales organizations'. Paper presented at COMPCONTROL 74, Hungary, 1974a.
- Van Aken, J.E., Van Beek, P., Peeters, G. and Polderman, G.L. 'PROSPECT-PRINCIPLES'. *Internal Philips Report*, 1974b.
- Van Beek, P. 'An Application of Dynamic Programming and the HMMS-rule on Two-level Production Control'. *Zeitschrift für Operations Research* 21 (1977) B133–B141.
- Van de Wouw, C.J.M. 'Information System Planning' *Internal Philips Report*, 1977.
- Van der Grinten, P.M.E.M. 'Uncertainty in measurement and control'. *Statistica Neerlandica* 22 (1968) 44–63.
- Van der Laan, S. *De militaire organisatie* (the military organization; in Dutch). Utrecht: Marka-boeken, 1967.
- Van Gunsteren, H. *The quest for control.* New York: Wiley, 1976.
- Van Hees, R.N. and Monhemius, W. *An Introduction to Production and Inventory Control* and *Production and Inventory Control: Theory and Practice.* London: Mc Millan, 1972.
- Verlage, H.C. *Transfer pricing for multinational enterprises.* Rotterdam: Universitaire Pers, 1975.
- Von Bertalanffy, L. 'General Systems Theory: a new approach to the unity of science'. *Human Biology* 23 (1951) 302–312.
- VVKM 229. 'Handleiding betreffende het maatschappelijk verkeer van marine officieren' (manual for the social behaviour of naval officers; in Dutch). The Hague; Department of Defence, 1963.
- Weber, M. *The theory of social and economic organization.* New York: The Free Press of Glencoe, 1947.
- Weinstock, U. *Das Problem der Kondratieff-Zyklen.* Berlin: Duncker und Humbolt, 1964.
- Wiener, N. *Cybernetics, or Control and Communication in the animal and the machine.* New York: Wiley, 1948.
- Woodward, J. *Industrial Organization: Theory and Practice* London: Oxford University Press, 1965.
- Yuchtman, E. and Seashore, S.E. 'A system resource approach to organizational effectiveness'. *American Sociological Review* 32 (1967) 891–903.
- Zald, M.N. (ed.) *Power in Organizations.* Nashville: Van der Bilt University Press, 1970.

NAME INDEX

SUBJECT INDEX

The bold page numbers indicate the page, where a formal definition or a comprehensive description of the concept in question is given.